Disability and Federalism

Disability and Federalism
Comparing Different Approaches to Full Participation

EDITED BY DAVID CAMERON
AND FRASER VALENTINE

Published for the Institute of Intergovernmental Relations
School of Policy Studies, Queen's University
by McGill-Queen's University Press
Montreal & Kingston • London • Ithaca

National Library of Canada Cataloguing in Publication Data

Main entry under title:

Disability and federalism : comparing different approaches to full participation

(Social union series)
Includes bibliographical references.
ISBN 0-88911-867-1 (bound).—ISBN 0-88911-857-4 (pbk)

1. Handicapped—Government policy. I. Cameron, David, 1941- II. Valentine, Fraser, 1970-
III. Queen's University (Kingston, Ont.). Institute of Intergovernmental Relations. IV. Series.

HV1568.D574 2001   362.4'0456   C2001-902225-5

The Institute of Intergovernmental Relations

The Institute is the only organization in Canada whose mandate is solely to promote research and communication on the challenges facing the federal system.

Current research interests include fiscal federalism, the social union, the reform of federal political institutions and the machinery of federal-provincial relations, Canadian federalism and the global economy, and comparative federalism.

The Institute pursues these objectives through research conducted by its own staff and other scholars, through its publication program, and through seminars and conferences.

The Institute links academics and practitioners of federalism in federal and provincial governments and the private sector.

The Institute of Intergovernmental Relations receives ongoing financial support from the J.A. Corry Memorial Endowment Fund, the Royal Bank of Canada Endowment Fund, Power Corporation, the Government of Canada, and the Government of Ontario. We are grateful for this support which enables the Institute to sustain its extensive program of research, publication, and related activities.

L'Institut des relations intergouvernementales

L'Institut est le seul organisme canadien à se consacrer exclusivement à la recherche et aux échanges sur les questions du fédéralisme.

Les priorités de recherche de l'Institut portent présentement sur le fédéralisme fiscal, l'union sociale, la modification éventuelle des institutions politiques fédérales, les nouveaux mécanismes de relations fédérales-provinciales, le fédéralisme canadien au regard de l'économie mondiale et le fédéralisme comparatif.

L'Institut réalise ses objectifs par le biais de recherches effectuées par son personnel et par des universitaires de l'Université Queen's et d'ailleurs, de même que par des conférences et des colloques.

L'Institut sert de lien entre les universitaires, les fonctionnaires fédéraux et provinciaux et le secteur privé.

L'institut des relations intergouvernementales reçoit l'appui financier du J.A. Corry Memorial Endowment Fund, de la Fondation de la Banque Royale du Canada, de Power Corporation, du gouvernement du Canada et du gouvernement de l'Ontario. Nous les remercions de cet appui qui permet à l'Institut de poursuivre son vaste programme de recherche et de publication ainsi que ses activités connexes.

CONTENTS

INTRODUCTION TO SERIES

This is one of six volumes being published by the Institute of Intergovernmental Relations related to the Canadian Social Union. Three of the volumes compare the way in which different federations handle various aspects of social policy. These volumes, including this one edited by David Cameron and Fraser Valentine, should be of interest to those who study comparative federalism and comparative social policy. The other three volumes are based on a series of case studies of how Canadian governments manage intergovernmental relations in particular areas of social programming.

The work for this series began in 1997, well before the 1999 signing of the Social Union Framework Agreement. Even at that time, as a result of the substantial cuts in federal fiscal transfers to the provinces, it seemed that a new set of relationships was going to be required between federal and provincial governments in order to improve both the quality of social policy in Canada and the health of the federation.

In conceiving of the volumes for this series, two considerations were paramount. The first was that there was relatively little empirical literature on the way in which federal and provincial governments relate to one another, and to citizens and interest groups, in designing and delivering social programs. Yet it is at the level of programs and citizens, as much as at the level of political symbolism and high politics, that the social union is in practice defined. To help fill this knowledge gap, we thought it appropriate to design a series of case studies on the governance of Canadian social programs. And to ensure that the results of the case studies could be compared to one another, the Institute developed a research methodology that authors were asked to take into account as they conducted their research. This methodology built on earlier work by Margaret Biggs in analyzing these governance relationships from the perspective of their impact on policy, federalism, and democracy.

The second consideration was that Canadians were insufficiently aware of how other federations handle these same kinds of social program relationships. As a result, we thought it important to recruit authors from different federations who could explain the governance of social policy in their countries. This volume thus compares the way in which five different federations deal with disability policy.

While the research for these volumes was under way, a series of roundtables and workshops (nine in total) was held. Those invited included officials from provincial and federal governments, representatives from stakeholder groups and individuals from the research community as well the case study authors. The purpose of these roundtables and workshops was to review and comment on the Canadian and comparative case studies. I thank the numerous participants in these events for helping the authors and editors with their work.

This series received financial assistance from the federal government and the governments of New Brunswick, Ontario, Saskatchewan, and Alberta. An advisory committee that included officials from these same jurisdictions as well as from academe also assisted in the development of the project. In fact, it was this committee that helped in the selection of the three social sectors that are the subject of this series: disability, labour market, and health.

The 1999 Social Union Framework Agreement is open for review early in 2002. The agreement states that this review process will "ensure significant opportunities for input and feedback from Canadians." It is hoped that this series will constitute a significant input to that process.

Harvey Lazar
General Editor
Social Union Series

PREFACE

This volume is one of a series of studies exploring the ways in which different federations handle social policy. The focus of this comparative volume is on disability policy from the experience of five federations: Australia, Belgium, Canada, Germany, and the United States. Our primary interest in undertaking a comparison was to gain an understanding of the impact of alternate federal regimes on the disability sector, and on persons with disabilities.

Scholars in each of the federations were commissioned to write a paper on the disability policy sector in their country. The contributors were: Linda Hancock, Public Policy and Governance Program, Deakin University, Melbourne (Australia); Johanne Poirier, Centre for Public Law, Université Libre de Bruxelles (Belgium); Sherri Torjman, Caledon Institute of Social Policy, Ottawa (Canada); Ursula Muench, Fakultät fuer Sozialwissenschaften at the Universität der Bundeswehr Muenchen (University of the Federal Armed Forces Munich) (Germany); Stephen L. Percy, Department of Political Science and Center for Urban Initiatives and Research, University of Wisconsin-Milwaukee (United States).

The authors were asked to evaluate the disability policy domain in their respective countries using a common set of criteria which were provided by the Queen's Institute of Intergovernmental Relations. Draft versions of the papers were discussed in a workshop held in Canada. The authors, editors, and federal/provincial government officials gathered at Queen's University in Kingston, Ontario in September 1998. This comparative disability workshop afforded all the participants an opportunity to discuss and debate the issues and questions arising out of each federation. The editors of the volume provided critical feedback to each author, as well as an organizing template aimed at achieving a common set of evaluative principles across the federations. Next, the authors revised their papers based on the information from the workshop. Finally, with the revised papers in hand, the editors completed an evaluative essay comparing the experiences in each of the federations. This volume is the product of that process.

The editors would like to thank each of the authors for their thoughtful analyses of a complex topic. As well, thanks to the various federal and provincial officials who provided useful comments at various points in the preparation of this volume. Finally, we wish to extend a special thanks to Harvey Lazar and his colleagues from the Institute of Intergovernmental Relations, Queen's University. At the Institute of Intergovernmental Relations, both Patti Candido and Mary Kennedy provided administrative support in the preparation of the manuscript and Marilyn Banting, Valerie Jarus, and Mark Howes, of the School of Policy Studies Publications Unit, provided copyediting, desk-top publishing, and design.

David Cameron and Fraser Valentine
July 2001

CONTRIBUTORS

DAVID CAMERON, Department of Political Science, University of Toronto

LINDA HANCOCK, Public Policy and Governance Program, Deakin University, Melbourne, Australia

URSULA MUENCH, Fakultät fuer Sozialwissenschaften at the Universität der Bundeswehr Muenchen

STEPHEN L. PERCY, Department of Political Science and Center for Urban Initiatives and Research, University of Wisconsin-Milwaukee

JOHANNE POIRIER, Centre for Public Law, Université Libre de Bruxelles and University of Cambridge

SHERRI TORJMAN, Caledon Institute of Social Policy, Ottawa

FRASER VALENTINE, Department of Political Science, University of Toronto

1

COMPARING POLICY-MAKING IN FEDERAL SYSTEMS: THE CASE OF DISABILITY POLICY AND PROGRAMS – AN INTRODUCTION

David Cameron and Fraser Valentine

GENERAL FINDINGS

All modern democratic states have fashioned policies and programs in response to the needs of persons with disabilities. They vary, however, from nation to nation. Our interest in this study lies with five federal regimes — Australia, Belgium, Canada, Germany, and the United States — and the approach they have taken to disability.

This volume tries to answer two general questions: (i) In the five countries under review, what impact has federalism had on disability policy and programming? and (ii) Has disablement — including its international, organizational, political, and attitudinal dimensions — affected the operation of federalism in the five countries studied, and, if so, in what ways?

These are not easy questions to answer, for reasons that will be made clear in the course of this introductory chapter. Nevertheless, based on our comparative assessment, we summarize our broad findings below.

With respect to the impact of federalism on disability policy and programming, we uncovered the following three general findings: first, at the level of broad philosophy, the values that underlie policy-making and the general policy orientation to disabled persons at any particular historical moment, neither federalism nor the specific type of federal regime appears to make much difference. The understanding of disablement, and the beliefs about what could and should be done about it, do not vary substantially from one federal regime to another, and, indeed, do not appear to vary widely between many federal and non-federal regimes. It is our impression that there is a broad policy environment which is widely shared among most modern democratic states of all types.

Second, with respect to the formulation of disability policy, however, the federal reality lies at the heart of this process in the countries we examined, and the policy-making function assumes its character from the distinctive federal arrangements that each country displays. The means employed to transform policy goals into political decisions, government programming, and public initiatives are profoundly shaped by the fact that they are occurring within a federation and by the particular kind of federal regime within which they are occurring. Clearly, policy-making in a federation will be quite different from policy making in a unitary state; equally, policy-making in the German federal context, with its concept of "joint tasks" and its strong intrastate institutions, will be quite different from policy-making in Canada, where interstate bargaining between powerful federal and provincial executives composes the heart of the policy nexus. The distinctive institutions and processes which characterize the given federal system define the policy-making system by which community aspirations and objectives in the disability field are mediated.

Third, as for policy outputs in the disability field, we found striking variations among the five federations in program design, in the choice of delivery vehicles, and in administrative organization. While we would not argue that federal differentiation offers the only explanatory factor in understanding these differences, it is clear that the distinctive character of the federal regime makes a significant difference. This will become clear as we examine and compare each of the five federations.

What of our second question, which asks about the impact of disablement on the five federations under review? We have found that the existence of disablement and the public response to it has had very little impact on the nature and functioning of the five federations under study. Examining the disability policy field in comparative terms has uncovered a partial explanation for this pattern.

While most individuals will experience some form of disablement during their lifetime (especially as one ages), there is a common perception that disability does not affect everyone in society. Disability is often understood as a phenomenon which affects only a minority of a nation's population. Matters of health and illness, by contrast, are perceived as universal phenomena; they are viewed as affecting everyone in a society. We have found that these perceived and structural realities shape the two policy fields. It seems clear that health care, being of central and universal public concern, has a palpable impact on federalism, certainly in the Canadian case, and vice versa. Disability, on the other hand, being viewed to some extent as a "niche concern," yields a much more limited, lower profile policy discourse, which drastically reduces its capacity to affect the federal system in the countries we examined. Thus, the story of our country studies is primarily an account of the impact of the federal regime on the disabled policy field. We will return to this point later on in our discussion.

Let us conclude this section on the general findings arising out of the five country studies with the following five observations.

First, disability, in the five federations, does not present itself as a relatively coherent policy field, like health or the labour market. Instead, it is understood as an array of more or less distinct social phenomena and issues that call for a variety of responses from government. The result is that the coherence of public debate and the coherence of policy responses which one finds in some other fields are not evident in the area of disability.

Second, while some of the five federations have a fuller response to disability than others, the policy field in all of them is fragmented and uncoordinated. Third, in all of the federations examined, the state presents itself to the disabled citizen as a complex set of institutions: the opposite of user-friendly. So complicated are these institutions, in fact, that citizens require third-party organizations to successfully navigate both the rules and the infrastructure of the system. Fourth, despite good intentions, the policy confusion and policy fragmentation raises fundamental questions concerning the equity and effectiveness of disability policy in each federation.

Finally, the political culture and institutional structure of the federation condition the role of disability organizations in advocating on behalf of persons with disabilities. In Australia, Canada, and the United States, "rights frameworks" have spawned a network of disability rights organizations which play an important role in influencing disability policies and programs. Belgium and Germany, on the other hand, do not have politically salient disability movements. The social federal state model, coupled with the growth of a mature welfare state, have truncated the development of disability organizations run by persons with disabilities themselves. Instead, self-help and service organizations have prominence; their role is to assist individuals to navigate the complexity of services and supports.

As we said at the outset, the impact of the disability policy field on the nature and functioning of the federal regimes in Australia, Belgium, Canada, Germany, and the United States appears to have been minimal. On the other hand, the federal systems in the five countries have affected the disability policy field in many different ways — not at the level of basic philosophy and general policy orientation — but at the level of policy design and program implementation. The chapters that follow explain how and why this is so. They offer a detailed examination of the nexus between federalism and disability policy in Australia, Belgium, Canada, Germany, and the United States.

DISABILITY: A PROFILE

Evolution of Disability Thinking

What does it mean to be disabled, or to have a disability? For over a century, any debate in response to such a question would necessarily be framed within the discourse of biomedical science. Disability was about functional limitation which sometimes, through medical intervention, could be ameliorated to attain a level of so-called "normal" functioning. Today, however, questions about the proper understanding of disablement may provoke a different analysis: one that actively examines the social, political, and legal constructions that attempt to give meaning to the experience of disablement.

The evolution of disability thinking has a long, complicated, and overlapping history. Thus, it is useful to divide the general history of disability across western industrial nations into three basic periods: (i) institutionalization (1600s–1900s); (ii) medicalization (1900s–1970s); and (iii) post-medicalization (1970s–present), see Table 1.[1] Prior to the early 1900s, people with some forms of disability — deaf, blind or so-called insane individuals, for instance — were put in institutions provided by religious orders, charities, the community, or the state. The goal was education or training, as well as protection and hiding the "seriously" disabled away from so-called "normal" people.[2]

The second period, medicalization, took a foothold during World War I. It was during this period that a new relationship emerged among the state, the increasingly powerful medical profession, and persons with disabilities. The state required healthy men to fight the war and doctors seized the opportunity to increase their authority by assuming the responsibility for telling the state who were "fit." Across all nations, the war significantly increased the number of persons with disabilities, and, because their disabilities had resulted from the performance of their citizenship duties, the state assumed some responsibility for their welfare.[3] The medical profession, however, now also played a role in "certifying" that their condition warranted support; in addition, it was assigned responsibility for their ongoing care. Many advanced industrial democracies, including all of the nations in this study, fostered the development of disability-specific, medically oriented non-governmental organizations.[4] As Stephen Percy notes in his chapter, for instance, veterans founded, but did not control, several such organizations in the United States, and Canada had organizations paralleling the American experience.

TABLE 1
Historical Periods in the Evolution of Disability Thinking

1600–1900s	*Institutionalization*

- Medical profession had little influence
- Institutionalization in public and charity asylums, hospitals
- Focus was on education, employment activities, protection for "incurables"
- There were no disability organizations

1900–1970s	*Medicalization*

- Disability developed as a clinical concept and formal administrative category — search for a "cure"
- Persons with disabilities were deemed "passive" and "sick"
- War issues propelled the development of disability rehabilitation organizations
- Disability organizations *for* persons with disabilities emerged
- Single disability organizations prevailed

1970–present	*Post-Medicalization*

- Persons with disabilities rejected the medicalization and rehabilitation of their bodies
- Organizations of persons with disabilities advocating on their own behalf and organized autonomously emerged
- Increasing international profile, and emergence of symbolic role among international organizations, especially the United Nations
- Persons with disabilities challenged medicalized definitions to which they were assigned, asserting instead their identities as full citizens with social, political, and civil rights
- Mature welfare state providing a range of programs and services
- Neo-liberal reaction to welfare state and resulting contraction

Note: There is overlap between these periods.

These developments meant that the lives of persons with disabilities were increasingly medicalized and a large cadre of rehabilitation professionals emerged in many nations. Their focus was on rehabilitating or "curing" persons with disabilities who were viewed as "sick." While successful rehabilitation of disabled individuals lessened the state's obligations, it also increased the authority and control of medical professionals over the lives of persons with disabilities. In her study on the evolution of Disabled Persons' International (DPI) — the only international disability organization controlled by and for persons with disabilities — Diane Driedger concludes that the medicalization period along with the development of rehabilitation professionals "led to many more rehabilitated people, but it also medicalized *all* aspects of life for disabled people by classifying them as sick."[5] This labelling of persons with disabilities as "sick" carried with it other attributions including "passive" and "dependent." In short, medicalization began to undercut the social adulthood of those with disabilities since they were increasingly considered to have diminished capacity to make their own decisions, including medical decisions.

Advancements in medicine also *created* more people with disabilities. New medical knowledge and technological innovations meant people who previously died (e.g., from polio, spinal cord injuries, accidents) now lived longer. Moreover, life expectancy increased significantly, resulting in many more individuals experiencing disablement in old age. In 1998, the World Health Organization (WHO) estimated that while the world's population grows at an annual rate of 1.7 percent, the population over 65 years of age increased by 2.5 percent per year. In the developing world 7.5 percent of the population is elderly, compared to 18.3 percent in the developed world. By 2025, the WHO estimates that the elderly populations will be 11.9 percent and 23.6 percent.[6] Declines in maternal deaths during childbirth meant that women lived longer and, therefore, became disabled more often. Finally, better neonatal knowledge and techniques saved babies who would otherwise have died, increased the number of individuals who lived out their lives with disabilities.

While the medical profession during this period controlled both the meaning of disability and the lives of persons with disabilities, many organizations *for* persons with disabilities emerged, which primarily devoted their efforts to the further medicalization of these individuals. This was usually done by raising money for research toward a single kind of disability type. Thus, persons with disabilities were defined primarily by the medical category of their disability and whatever demands were made on the state or society were made *on their behalf* by parents, medical professionals, researchers or, most recently in North America, televized charity telethons. It became clear, there-fore, that although the commitment to rehabilitation increased the mobility of persons with physical disabilities, it also reinforced "dependency" assumptions about persons with disabilities. Further, the rehabilitation and reintegration processes marked by this period were often not extended to all kinds of disabilities, in particular persons with cognitive disabilities, nor did these processes focus on the economic needs or political concerns of persons with disabilities.

In the third period, post-medicalization (1970–present), movements *of* persons with disabilities advocating *on their own behalf* and organized autonomously in *cross-disability* groups emerged in many industrialized nations.[7] Through these organizations, many persons with disabilities challenged the medicalized definitions to which they were assigned, asserting instead their identities as full citizens with social, political, and civil rights. This period is marked by the claim among persons with disabilities to be treated as social adults entitled to personal autonomy, self-determination, sexuality, and other rights and freedoms enjoyed by other citizens. Some persons with disabilities developed a collective identity, which transcended both their disability "type," and the image assigned to them as "sick," passive, asexual, and apolitical.

The emergence of disability organizations run by and for persons with disabilities in many advanced industrial countries post-1970 has resulted in, among other things, the introduction of an entirely new set of ideas into disability thinking and the disability policy domain. Even a seemingly simple question such as "What is disability?" sparks controversy as the disability rights movement struggles to reject both purely medical definitions and the stigmas and stereotypes which preceded and accompanied them.

The rise of disabled persons' movements, particularly in the United States, Canada, the United Kingdom, Australia, and New Zealand pushed persons with disabilities, researchers, policymakers, and medical professionals to view disability increasingly as a socially created category, a product of a series of complex political, economic and social relationships. While it is not clear that this "push from the grass roots" has shifted official discourse about disability significantly, our understanding of disablement has broadened in recent years because of the self-assertion of movements of persons with disabilities. Disablement remains constructed as a formal administrative category, a legal category, a multi-million dollar business activity, a research area, and a set of medical conditions, but there is a growing awareness that disablement means much more.

During this period, persons with disabilities have challenged the widely-held view of the identity and role of persons with disabilities as passive, sick, asexual, and apolitical in three ways: (i) by asserting their right to organize autonomously; (ii) by asserting their right to equal treatment as social adults with full citizenship and all the rights citizenship confers; and (iii) by arguing that disability is *socially constructed* and often reflects the fears, biases, and aversions of so-called normal individuals more than the lived experiences of persons with disabilities. Movements of persons with disabilities who have organized on their own behalf have pushed researchers and medical professionals to understand that disability is neither wholly an "attribute" of an individual nor an objective "fact." Instead, it is a socially created web of relationships, influences and forces.[8] Sandra Carpenter, a Canadian disability researcher and activist, has referred to the multi-faceted nature of disablement as the "undefinable nature of the disability collective" involving "a slippery hodgepodge of conditions, diseases, genetic disorders and malformations" which are "all validated ... by disabled individuals themselves, the cultures they come from and the times they live in."[9] Persons with disabilities are *not* a monolithic group. Instead, they are heterogeneous in terms of race, class, sex/gender, language, ethnicity, sexual orientation, and geographic location/climate.

The new ideas associated with the post-medicalization period, and the contested terrains upon which they are premised necessarily raise fundamental questions of identity concerning disability. Our study reveals that there is no conventional understanding of disablement across the federations. Instead, there is a high degree of variation concerning disability definitions, that is, what it means to have a disability. In each of our cases, albeit to varying degrees, we found that the definitional debate and lack of coherence in the disability domain shape the policies and programs that affect the daily life of persons with disabilities. The international community, especially through the United Nations, has attempted to influence domestic disability policy and programs through a series of symbolic gestures, as well as the development of standardized disability classifications. This has not, however, been a simple task.

International Trends and Influences

In each of the federations, activities at the international level, especially from the United Nations, have influenced domestic disability policy-making and political discourse. The United Nations first concerned itself concretely with disablement in 1971 when it affirmed the Declaration on the Rights of Mentally Retarded Persons and in 1975 with the Declaration on the Rights of Disabled Persons. These international declarations were to give concrete expression to the principles set out in the 1948 Universal Declaration of Human Rights (see Table 2). The rights contained within these early declarations are simply the right to respect for the human dignity of persons with disabilities; the right to civil and political rights; economic and social security; the right to live with family and the right of access to education.

UN declarations have served primarily to provide a philosophical and moral foundation for national governments to protect persons with disabilities in human rights laws and other forms of legislation.[10] Nevertheless, our study confirms that the pronouncements, declarations, and conventions of the UN expanded notions of individual and collective citizens' rights and contributed to the pace and direction of domestic public policy in all of the countries in our study.

TABLE 2

Initiatives Undertaken by the United Nations Concerning Persons with Disabilities

Date	Initiative
1948	Universal Declaration of Human Rights
1971	Declaration of the Rights of Mentally Retarded Persons
1975	Declaration of the Rights of Disabled Persons
1981	International Year of Disabled Persons (IYDP)
1982	Adoption of the World Program of Action on Disabled Persons
1983–92	Declaration of the "Decade of Disabled Persons"
1990	Publication of the Disability Statistics Compendium
1993	Declaration of the International Day of Disabled Persons (3 December)
1993	Adoption of the Standard Rules on the Equalization of Opportunities for Persons with Disabilities
1994	Appointment of the Special Rapporteur on Disability of the Commission for Social Development
1994	Salamanca Statement on Principles, Policy and Practice in Special Needs Education
1995	Establishment of the Statistics Division of the United Nations Secretariat for the UN Disability Statistics Database

Note: Data complied by the authors.

In the 1980s, the UN began to play a more active role in promoting the citizenship rights of persons with disabilities. Perhaps the most important was the United Nations International Year of Disabled Persons (IYDP)[11] in 1981 and the World Program of Action (WPA) concerning Disabled Persons which was associated with the United Nations Decade of Disabled Persons (UNDDP), 1983–92. The IYDP defined its goal as nothing less than "full participation and equality" of persons with disabilities and the elimination of the barriers they face. The UN's establishment of a trust fund with $1 million to pay for projects concerning disability issues in various member countries, albeit limited, represented the first time the international community took concrete action on disability issues. Governments of some countries responded with domestic initiatives. In Canada, for instance, the government established a Special Parliamentary Committee to investigate the obstacles faced by persons with disabilities in Canadian society.[12]

While the IYDP, the WPA, and the UNDDP are all important international influences on domestic disability policy and programs, many of the projects undertaken by member countries were severely curtailed because of lack of funds from the United Nations. Cherie Lewis argues that the "low level funding [from the UN] reflects a basic conflict within the United Nations ... about the status of the disabled."[13] Nevertheless, the UN declarations also "put disability into a global context and posed the question of how [disablement] may be understood in a multicultural world."[14] Disablement discourse was widened to include discussions on disability from a cross-cultural perspective, in particular, the difference of meanings and experiences of disability in affluent and poor countries.[15]

An important outcome from the international sphere was the recognition among domestic policymakers of the rehabilitation needs and citizenship rights of people with disabilities, as well as the impact of disability on national indicators of health, education, and economic prosperity. Consequently, policymakers began to request information in these areas. A commonly asked question, for instance, is simply: How many people with disabilities are there in the population? The answer, however, is anything but clear. The WHO, for instance, estimates that persons with disabilities (including physical, mental, deaf and blind) comprise between 7 and 10 percent of the population in any country.[16] Questions, however, must be raised about the reliability of this figure. In fact, the United Nations acknowledges that the body of statistical data currently available is "somewhat limited for the purposes of comparative analysis."[17] The reason, in part, is because there is no common understanding or agreement on the meaning of "disablement." Thus, disability is confounded by divergent use of terminology among governments, professionals, legislators, and persons with disabilities and their organizations. In addition, there exists no intergovernmental data collection system that systemically requests countries to submit national disability statistics from censuses, surveys, and registration systems for use at the international level.[18]

The lack of reliable comparative data on the incidence and prevalence of disability has not gone unnoticed by the WHO and the UN. Beginning in the mid-1970s, the international community began calling for the production of comparative and standardized statistical information on disability and disablement. Most of the work at the international level has focused on achieving standardization through the development of guidelines and technical manuals from which domestic governments could implement statistical collection techniques. Obstacles at the domestic level — the variability of screening rates, the nature of the questions asked, and the manner in which questions are interpreted by domestic governments — have made achieving a level of international standardization difficult.

In 1975, the WHO developed a new conceptual framework within which to understand disablement in the age of the contemporary welfare state. Published in 1980 by the WHO, the *International Classification of Impairment, Disabilities and Handicaps: A Manual for Classification Relating to the Consequences of Diseases* (ICIDH) was produced to act as a guideline for domestic disability policy-making. In fact, many industrialized states have adopted the ICIDH classifications and incorporated them into some of their policies and programs.[19] Our study confirms, however, that rather than clarifying the muddied waters surrounding the conceptual aspects of disablement and introducing a level of standardization across disability policies and programs, the ICIDH classifications have been heavily contested by persons with disabilities and their organizations because the classification makes some debatable theoretical and methodological assumptions. Although the definitions acknowledge wider social, political, and economic factors affecting persons with disabilities, they remain grounded first in the physical bio-medical condition of the individual, and not a broader array of variables such as the environment in which we live and work. As well, it is argued that the methodology used by the WHO revolves around the false neutrality of objective scientific investigation.[20] This contested ground has called into question the relevance and applicability of the ICIDH classifications.

Despite these challenges, the UN has taken concrete action toward the collection of statistical data on disability. Building on the momentum gained through the IYDP and the WPA, in 1988, the UN produced the United Nations Disability Statistics Data Base (DISTAT).[21] Given that there was a complete dearth of comparative disability data, DISTAT was created to collect, consolidate, standardize and integrate national disability data from countries around the world. This process brought together data from national censuses, surveys, and administrative reporting systems on selected issues of disablement. The result was the *Disability Statistics Compendium* (1990) in which a series of tables presented the first set of internationally standardized data of disabled statistics.[22] Although an important contribution to our understanding of disablement across nations, like the ICIDH classifications, the reliability of the data presented in *Disability Statistics Compendium* has been called into question. In fact, the authors themselves concede that because data collection techniques vary from country to country, and the understanding of disablement is variable across nations, the "data quality is highly variable."[23]

Under pressure from persons with disabilities and their organizations, the WHO has undertaken a global initiative to revise the ICIDH. Attempts have been made to broaden meaningfully the classification beyond simply human functioning of the body, to include the individual at the social level taking into account the social and environmental context in which people live. Human functioning and disablement, it is argued, can only be understood against the background of existing social and physical factors. Thus, the revised ICIDH-2 includes a classification of contextual factors (environmental and personal) which affect the experience of disablement for an individual. Although the UN Disability Statistic Division is expected to release updated comparative data on the prevalence of disability around the world, this data is not premised on the updated ICIDH-2 classifications. Thus, the data's variability persists resulting in an inability to answer even the most basic question: How many people with disabilities are there in the population?

THE FIVE FEDERATIONS UNDER REVIEW

All of the five federations under study are modern democratic states with advanced market economies and high standards of living. All are free societies, active internationally; their governments see themselves as being members of an increasingly integrated international community whose emergent norms and standards merit acknowledgement. All have experienced in their own way the great, shifting patterns of ideas and practices that have swept through the postwar western world: Keynesian economics and the construction of the welfare state; the rise of neo-liberal thinking; the emergence of the objective of fiscal restraint and the often fruitless effort to contain and reduce the social obligations of the state; the recent establishment of fiscal health and economic prosperity; and socio-demographic trends, in particular an aging population.[24] All have been affected by the shifts in conceptions of citizenship and representation that have been the result. It is evident that this offers a substantial common foundation upon which to rest our comparative review.

Yet the countries and their federal systems differ significantly from one another, and in ways that make comparative investigation profitable. Two of the federations — Belgium and Germany — display the continental European social model. One, the United States, is highly distinctive in the level and the character of its social policies and programs. Two, Australia and Canada, appear to occupy middle ground between Europe and the United States, with welfare state structures that are more fully developed than those of the United States, but sharply less developed than those evident in our two European federations.

Canada and Australia are endowed with Westminster-style parliamentary systems, which concentrate political power in the executives at both the subnational and national level. The United States, Germany, and Belgium have developed, in comparison to Australia and Canada, effective arrangements to provide for regional participation in central decision-making in the federation.

Three of the countries under review — Canada, Australia, and the United States — are "new societies," which carry the memory of looking back at their origins in Europe; they have Aboriginal populations and a lengthy experience with immigration which have been crucial to their self-definition and demographic character. Each, unlike Belgium and Germany, covers a vast continental land mass. The United States is the only remaining global super power and in population by far the largest of the federations studied. Germany's Nazi experience earlier in the twentieth century is, inevitably, an unforgettable backdrop when discussing disability policy in that country. Its recent reunification, requiring the integration of two profoundly different social and economic orders poses a challenge unknown in the recent experience of the other federations.

Belgium and Canada are, unlike the others, countries defined by deep cultural and linguistic cleavages. Germany, despite its east-west socio-economic divisions, is highly integrated linguistically and culturally. Three of the countries — Belgium, Canada, and Australia — are monarchies, the latter two revealing their colonial roots.

We believe that these variations in society, culture, demographic patterns, and historical experience both help to explain the nature of federalism in each case and offer sufficient biodiversity to make different social policy and programming likely. How all of this plays out in the field of disability is the subject of this volume. We will turn now to a brief account of the leading characteristics of the federal systems in each of the five countries insofar as they appear to relate to the matter of disability.[25]

Australia

Australia established its federal system in 1901, bringing together — like Canada — a number of self-governing British colonies. Comprised of six states, a capital region and a Northern Territory, Australia has a population of about 18 million people. Like Canada, it has vast virtually unpopulated regions, and a citizenry concentrated in large urban centres. Despite its predominantly British origins, Australia has, in recent decades, experienced increasing levels of non-European immigration.

Again, similarly to Canada, Australia combines federalism with parliamentary government at both state and Commonwealth levels. The Australian federation, despite its states-oriented origins, has become over the years more centralized, particularly with respect to fiscal arrangements. It has fashioned stronger intergovernmental institutions than Canada has, and has an elected Senate which, however, acts more like a "party house" than a house of effective regional representation.

Belgium

Belgium is quite different from the other federal countries in this comparative study as it has just recently established for itself an explicitly federal constitution, and is thus the youngest federation in our review. Belgium came into being as a unitary constitutional monarchy in 1830. In recent decades, it has been transformed into a federal state by a series of constitutional changes in 1970, 1980, 1988, and 1993 which have dramatically decentralized policy-making and public administration in the country.

Belgium, despite being a small and compact country, has created for itself a federal system of impressive complexity, and this shapes disability programming, as it does other areas of public policy. The federation is composed of six constituent units. Three are *Regions* defined territorially: the Flemish, Walloon, and Brussels Regions. The Councils of the Regions are generally responsible for economic issues in the territory. Then there are three *Communities*, which overlap the three Regions. The Dutch-speaking, French-speaking, and

German-speaking Communities also have councils that are responsible primarily for cultural and educational matters. Just to make things more interesting, the Flemish Region and Community have effectively amalgamated their operations, and function more or less as a single entity, while the French-speaking parts of the federation have not. While policy incoherence and program complexity are features of all of the countries we examined, the institutional engineering in which the Belgians have engaged in the last three decades has produced a system unrivalled in its opacity for the citizen. This is only increased by the fact that the basic structures of Belgian constitutional life have been in a recurrent state of transformation in the last 30 years, thereby producing real uncertainty and confusion as programs, resources, and civil servants are shifted from one jurisdiction to another.

Belgium is a binational polity. Driven by the desire for greater autonomy of the larger Flemish/Dutch-speaking part of the country, which constitutes 58 percent of the population of just over 10 million, the "federalizing process" has created to a striking degree a federation of watertight compartments:

- little or no information sharing, joint planning or policy coordination;
- limited systems of interregional redistribution and no formal, publicly acknowledged equalization program (this is in part a consequence of having a centralized tax system, and an integrated national public social security system); and
- territorial unilingualism.

Ironically, therefore, though the Belgian federation is the most recent arrival among the cases we have studied, it is also the system that practises classical federalism to the greatest extent.

Canada

Canada is the product of the 1867 union of four British colonies in what was known at that time as British North America: Nova Scotia, New Brunswick, Quebec, and Ontario. Six other provinces joined the Canadian Confederation over time: Manitoba (1870); British Columbia (1871); Prince Edward Island (1873); Saskatchewan and Alberta (1905); and Newfoundland (1949). In addition, there are three northern territories: Yukon; the Northwest Territories, and, since 1999, Nunavut Territory.

Canada was the first country to establish itself as a parliamentary federation; that is to say, as a *federal system* in which the central and regional governments are both constituted according to the principles of *British parliamentary democracy*. This combination has produced strong executive-led government in Ottawa and in the provincial capitals, and that, combined with a weak upper house (Senate), has led to executive domination of relations between and among the federal partners.

Canada was designed in 1867 as a centralized federation, with the key powers of the day vested in Ottawa, and a strong, paternalistic oversight role assigned to Ottawa vis-à-vis the provinces. Despite this beginning, Canada has become in its first 129 years highly decentralized. This is for several reasons: (i) judicial interpretation of the division of powers broadly favoured provincial governments over the federal government; (ii) provincial areas of responsibility, such as health, welfare, and education, which were of little governmental consequence in the nineteenth century, mushroomed in the twentieth, greatly enhancing the role of provinces; and (iii) postwar Quebec nationalism helped to force a process of decentralization, which several other provinces began to advocate, and from which they benefited.

The result is that Canada as a multinational state has powerful and sophisticated governments in Ottawa as well as in the provinces, engaged in nation-building and province-building. This creates both interdependence and competition resulting in elaborate forms of intergovernmental coordination and at times bitter intergovernmental conflict among various jurisdictions (federal, provincial/territorial, and Aboriginal).

In addition, Canada is a multinational state. The polity's historical development has involved three distinct people (or nations): Anglophone, francophone, and Aboriginal.[26] Many of Canada's defining moments in its political history have centred on attempts to renegotiate the terms of the federation among anglophone, francophone, and Aboriginal peoples. Canada's French-speaking population, composed of just under one-quarter of the Canadian population, is largely located in the province of Quebec, although significant francophone populations exist outside the province's borders, chiefly in Ontario and New Brunswick. Quebec is home to a vigorous nationalist movement which has sponsored two referendums in the province on sovereignty. the 1995 referendum brought the country to the verge of collapse. Canada's English-speaking population, totalling more than three-quarters of the population, is chiefly located outside Quebec, although a substantial English-language minority community remains within Quebec. Aboriginal peoples are descended from the nations and peoples who were living in North America when settlers from Europe (and elsewhere) arrived more than 400 years ago. The total population of Aboriginal people in Canada is estimated to be between 720,000 and 1,000,000 people.[27] In the last several decades, the expression of Aboriginal people's right of self-determination has formed an important part of Canadian political discourse.

Germany

Germany's "interlocking federalism" is the polar opposite of the classical federalism or the federalism of watertight compartments which we observed in the Belgium case. It features:

- a distribution of powers giving the central government responsibility for the formation and passage of legislation in most fields and the Länder or states responsibility for nearly all aspects of legislative implementation;
- a highly integrated system of taxation;
- a sophisticated mechanism of fiscal equalization, both horizontally and vertically;
- a federal upper house (the Bundesrat), composed of Länder government representatives, with the power to veto federal legislation affecting the states; and
- a linguistically homogeneous society.

Established on the ruins of the Third Reich in 1949, West Germany became the Federal Republic of Germany with 11 Länder. Reunification in 1990 extended the borders of the Federal Republic eastward, added five new Länder for a total of 16, and expanded the population to more than 80 million people.

The German federal system is marked by intense, continuous intergovernmentalism at all stages of the policy cycle. The federal government has a decisive role in shaping social policy, although it must secure the support of the Länder through the upper house. A premium has been placed on intergovernmental compromise, but at the expense of legislative accountability and transparency.

As in the case of Belgium, a central animating principle of the federation, accepted by all participants, has been the concept of "uniformity of living conditions" or social equity. This has been understood to mean not just equity among citizens, but horizontal and vertical equity among the constituent units of the federation. Thus, the relative role and capacity of the federal government vis-à-vis the Länder is a matter of concern, but so is the relative position of the Länder vis-à-vis one another. The principle of equity has been expressed in many of the programs of the German federation. The fiscal and economic weakness of the five new Länder of the former East Germany has put a serious strain on this principle, and has encouraged some of the stronger subnational jurisdictions to assert their need for greater autonomy and their belief in greater self-reliance.

There are two other levels of government acting in the social policy field which are worth mentioning. Although the responsibility of the Länder governments, the municipalities play an important, if not powerful, role in this sphere. Also, the European Community has assumed an increasingly significant place in the social-policy life of member states.

United States

The United States is the first, and most enduring, modern federation in the world. Originally comprised of 13 states, the United States has evolved into a federation of 50 states plus two federacies, three associated states, three local home-rule territories, three unincorporated territories, and over 130 Native American domestically dependent nations. It has a population of just over 280 million.

The United States is a diverse society, with large Black and Hispanic minorities. In addition, there is significant regional variation in political culture across the federation, with state and local governments playing important roles in the life of the country.

The American federal institutions are based on the principle of separation of powers between the executive and legislative branches. The institutions of the presidency and Congress provide for a complex web of checks and balances. Congress includes a Senate in which the states are equally represented with members elected directly (since 1912).

The fundamental structure of American federalism is the product of the US Constitution, enacted in 1789. In its original conception, the United States was a strong example of classical federalism. The Constitution grants the government a series of enumerated governing functions, but given the strong distrust of central authority in American political culture, the states have substantial governing rights as well. In particular, the tenth amendment to the Constitution, known as the Reserve Clause, holds that all powers not specifically delegated to the national government are reserved to the states.

In the twentieth century, however, a series of constitutional interpretations has resulted in an increase in the relative power of the national government.

The exercise of this power has directly affected the development of disability policy, including civil rights protections. In particular, the fourteenth amendment (and its equal protection clause) has extended the constitutional rights and responsibilities of the national government to the actions of state governments. Thus, the United States "nationalized" civil rights protections to cover not only the national government, but to include state and local governments, as well as certain areas of private industry. The national government's spending power has also been a central feature of the American political system, and has had a profound impact on the development of state and local social policy frameworks, especially in the disability policy domain.

DISABILITY IN THE FIVE FEDERATIONS: AT THE NEXUS OF FEDERALISM AND SOCIAL POLICY

Introduction

We turn now to an examination of the point of intersection between federalism and disability policy. Figure 1 gives a crude picture of the policy nexus in Australia, Belgium, Canada, Germany, and the United States. Despite its gross over-simplification, the figure distills some of our most general findings and will, we hope, make more readily intelligible the discussion that follows.

FIGURE 1
Federalism–Disability Policy Nexus

Disability \ Federalism	Federalism Less Salient	Federalism More Salient
Less Policy Comprehensiveness	Australia	Canada
More Policy Comprehensiveness	Germany United States	Belgium

What we have tried to do, at the most general level, is display the five countries according to their position with respect to our central analytical categories, namely, disability and federalism. The classification criterion for the federalism dimension is the degree to which the institutions and processes of federalism are more or less salient in the general political life of the country as compared to other institutions and processes, such as the party system, the legislative system, the political versus the judicial process, the specific constitutional foundations, and so forth. We contend that federalism is less salient in Australia, Germany, and the United States, and, relatively speaking, more salient in Belgium and Canada. We justify this contention below.

The classification criterion we have selected for the disability dimension is the degree of policy comprehensiveness, that is to say, the degree to which a coherent and coordinated range of services and supports addressing the needs of persons with disabilities is established in the given country. Assessing this is not a simple task, given the complexity of the policy environment in the five federations and the different ways in which the policies are embedded in the social and cultural life of the given countries. Nevertheless, it is our opinion, based on the country chapters contained in this volume, that Belgium, Germany, and the United States have developed a more comprehensive array of policies and programs to respond to disability than have Canada and Australia. Belgium, Germany, and the United States each works in its own distinctive way, but our sense is that, in aggregate, they have moved further down the policy track than either of the other two.

That this must be a tentative judgement, rather than a categorical conclusion, is evident from the following observation. While the articulation of legislation, policy, and programs specifically directed at disability is more advanced in the United States than in Canada, a disabled person — faced with the abstract choice of whether, as a person with a disability he or she would rather live in the United States or in Canada — might, in fact, rationally choose Canada. This is only paradoxical on its face, because persons with a disability have needs that extend beyond their disability, and such a person might quite reasonably prefer to inhabit a country with a more fully developed range of social supports which provide broader protection to the individual in the various circumstances in life that he or she might confront. A disabled American without health care might look with envy at a disabled Canadian with public health care and personal supports, even though the response to disability in Canada is probably thinner than it is in the United States.

Let us turn now to a more detailed review of what emerges from the five country studies.

The Development of Disability Policy

Our comparison reveals that the development of disability policy is influenced by both the diverse political cultures and institutional complexities in each of the federations. In each federation, however, the disability policy domain has also been shaped by negative and patronizing stereotypes, as well as the stigma associated with what it means to have a disability, that is, to be "not quite" human.[28] Although international organizations, such as the UN, as well as persons with disabilities, have challenged these stigmatizing attitudes, the impact of stigma on the development of disability policy has been pronounced and difficult to overcome.

In Australia, Canada, and the United States, the development of the disability policy domain can be clearly traced back to the history of negative attitudes — fear, pity, stigma — attached to persons with disabilities. As both Stephen Percy and Sherri Torjman suggest respectively, in the United States and Canada most of the policies and programs in place to support the particular needs of persons with disabilities were established in an incremental fashion. Often these policies were simply add-ons to programs that did not have issues of disability as a central focus when they were conceived. The assumption was that persons with disabilities would not be part of the mainstream of society, nor the mainstream of institutions. Consequently, the structures established, the education system and the labour force, for instance, were not designed to be inclusive of those with disabilities.

Since the 1970s, however, persons with disabilities have been demanding their rightful place in the mainstream of society. Canada, in 1982, included disability as a protected ground in its *Charter of Rights and Freedoms.* Germany and South Africa have also added disability as a constitutionally protected ground: Germany in 1994 and South Africa in 1996.

In each of these three countries, the emergence of disability rights movements has pushed their respective governments to respond to the demands of persons with disabilities by broadening our understanding of what constitutes disability policy. Our comparison confirms that overcoming the historical impediments of the policy domain, especially by accommodating the demands of persons with disabilities, has been difficult and the response by governments uneven. Nevertheless, across these three federations, the field has broadened (albeit unevenly) from custodial care, to workers compensation, to vocational rehabilitation, to income support, to rights-based frameworks.

The disability policy domain has developed somewhat differently in Belgium and Germany. This is explained, in part, because disability policy is an assumed component of a mature welfare state.

Like Belgium, Germany's political culture has more directly influenced the development of disability policy. The German system of interlocking federalism, its embedded commitment to a social federal state, and the concept of uniformity of living conditions (or social equity) has directly affected the development of disability policy. As Ursula Muench notes, the commitment to a social federal state is the foundation upon which a sophisticated and comprehensive welfare state has been constructed. Although significant gaps exist in supports and services aimed at persons with disabilities, the concept of uniformity of living conditions has been understood to mean not just equity among citizens, but also horizontal and vertical equity among the constituent units of the federation. Clearly, this approach is different from that of the Anglo-American nations.

Belgium, however, is a recently federated nation. Thus, it is quite distinct from the other federal countries under review. The basic character of disability policy and service in Belgium was established, first, by the unitary state in the 1960s and 1970s. With Belgium's transformation into a federation, disability policy is now being implemented nationally, as well as in each of the federated entities. As a long-standing, mature European welfare state, Belgium has developed a sophisticated range of high-end social programs and social supports. Nevertheless, disability policy has never figured prominently in jurisdictional or policy debates, but instead is driven primarily by the forces of language and culture.

Definitions of Disability

As we discussed above, definitions of disability for the purpose of policies and programs is a highly politicized and contested terrain. While the international community, through the UN and the WHO, has attempted to introduce a level of standardization to disability definitions through the development of the ICIDH, the effort to achieve commonly accepted definitions remains complex and potentially divisive. Indeed, our comparison confirms a high level of variation in disability definitions both within a single nation, as well as across nations. This variety of definitional forms leads to confusion in the policy domain, and for the disabled citizen, results in an uneven level of supports and services.

Among the federations studied, Belgium is the only country that applies a single, broad, and uniform definition of disability. This definition, in turn, serves as the foundation for the development and implementation of disability policy. It is important to note that, while Belgium applies a uniform disability definition across each of the three orders of the federation, this uniformity emerged, not because of a focused commitment among the federated entities on disability policy-making. Instead, the common definition grew out of the country's experience as a unitary state. Thus, as Johanne Poirier notes, the federal government and the federated entities could choose, if they wished, to independently modify the definitional criteria. To date, however, this has not occurred, so a common disability definition prevails.

In Australia, Canada, Germany, and the United States, no coherent, authoritative understanding of the meaning of disability has been constructed to serve as the foundation for policy and programming in the field. The influence of the socio-political model of disability on the evolution of disability thinking in Australia, Canada, and the United States has created a tension in the field. In Canada, the disability community frames its issues as nothing short of complete inclusion with "full citizenship" as the ultimate goal. As Torjman notes, however, the prominence of classical federalism in this policy area has meant that varying definitions of disability are applied across the federation, as well as across the disability policy domain. Consequently, individual program definitions vary, especially with respect to what is meant by severe and long-term impairment. Furthermore, the retrenchment of the state in the 1990s has resulted in a tendency to limit the ambit of disability definitions to primarily bio-medical attributes. This narrowing has resulted in a restriction of program eligibility and therefore a reduction in public expenditures.

Like the Canadian experience and reflecting the development of the disability policy domain, the definitions of disability in the United States are ill-conceived, complex, and fragmented. Definitions of what constitutes a disability vary from program to program — which, as Percy notes, means that an individual could be considered "disabled enough" to receive income support, but not "disabled enough" to access support for education. With the passage of the *Americans with Disabilities Act* (ADA) in 1990, however, some level of uniformity has been achieved across the federation. The authority of the federal government over the state and local levels of government has resulted in increased standardization in disability policy, especially in the areas of public transportation and public accommodations. Nevertheless, some of the ground gained through the passage of the ADA has been lost because the US courts, especially the Supreme Court, have been narrowly interpreting the meaning of disablement, especially as it applies to employment-related matters. The result has been a further narrowing of disability definitions.

Germany is typical of the other federations studied: disability definitions vary across the federation. In addition, there remains a certain stigma in German culture associated with those forms of public support for disability that are based on need, and are a part of the welfare system, as opposed to those that are founded more on compensation for workplace injury. Ursula Muench notes that the central government has adopted legislation that speaks of disability as "the consequences of an impairment of functions that is not just of a temporary nature and which is based on an irregular physical, mental or psychological state. An irregular state is a state that is different from the state typical for a certain age." Thus, a person is considered "severely disabled" if he or she is more than 49 percent disabled. Nevertheless, the German commitment to subsidiarity means that the Länder government, or subnational governments, tend to fashion definitions of disability which are more concretely related to the human-life circumstances of the people concerned and are frequently more appropriate when it comes to doing justice to the situation in which disabled persons live.

Australia, like Canada, Germany, and the United States, has a history of applying a variety of definitional forms in the disability field both across the federation and across the disability policy domain. Linda Hancock points out, however, that in 1991, the Commonwealth and states/territorial governments initiated a process aimed at creating a "national, whole-of-system, whole-of-government approach for disability service." The strategy sought to rationalize the roles and responsibilities for the delivery of disability services, and in so doing, achieve a level of equity, service quality and intergovernmental cooperation while, at the same time, fostering local flexibility, responsiveness, and innovation. Despite these efforts at achieving coherence, disability definitions remain variegated across the federation, and confusing for the individual citizen with a disability attempting to obtain services and supports in a consistent manner.

The Institutional Landscape: Disability Policy and Program Support

When one examines the nexus between the intergovernmental regime and disability policy and programming in the five federations, it is possible to see the countries falling generally into two categories. In the first category there is

Belgium and Germany, two advanced European social-welfare states which, despite their quite different experiences with, and approaches to, federalism, have nevertheless fashioned a set of arrangements in response to disability which bear some relation to one another. Both are on the high end in their overall provision of support to persons with disabilities, although neither has fashioned a very coherent set of policies and programs; both use para-public, quasi-insurance funds to do the lion's share of program delivery. Thus, they are quite different from Australia and Canada, which rely far more on public resources to deliver programs to persons with disabilities. Unique among the five federations is the United States, which primarily relies on personal investment of private insurance plans for program delivery. While the United States has public programs targeted primarily for low-income populations, these programs are not robust.

The phenomenon of a decentralized federation emerging out of a mature welfare state has created an unusual situation so far as Belgium's disability policy and programs are concerned. Disability policy was not by any means a key element in the discussions about transferring jurisdiction. Yet the bulk of responsibilities in this field were transferred relatively early in the reform process, chiefly, it would seem, because it was uncontentious and relatively easy to do. Jurisdiction over disability, as a matter affecting individuals, was shifted to the three cultural Communities in 1980, although it took more than a decade for the full concrete transfer to be realized in practice. It occurred as a consequence of the restructuring of the state to respond to tensions between the two main linguistic groups. Disability policy played no part in these tensions.

Despite this, the social safety net has not become frayed in Belgium as it has in many other advanced industrial societies, nor does there appear to be any taste for a shrinkage of the state or for the canons of the new public management. The three Communities, now responsible for most aspects of disability policy, have, by and large, maintained the generous programs they have inherited, and have done so in much the same form, which means that, despite the watertight compartments into which the Belgian state is substantially divided, there continues to be a relatively high level of rather similar disability services and programs.[29] This appears to be a case of continued policy convergence maintained, not by design and coordination, but by inheritance. Path dependency means, in this case, that Belgium has separate but parallel disability regimes as a result of the residual momentum of the country's earlier, unitary political experience. One would expect to see growing policy divergence over time as the federated units begin to gather their own momentum and begin to follow distinctive paths.

Para-governmental, quasi-autonomous funds have been a key policy instrument for the delivery of services to disabled persons, as they have been in Germany. The 1960s, under the unitary Belgian system, saw the most important developments in the field: the creation in 1963 of a national rehabilitation fund for persons with disabilities; the creation in 1967 of a fund responsible for the medical, residential, and pedagogical care of persons with disabilities; the passage in 1969 of a comprehensive *Income-Support Act* for disabled persons. The rehabilitation fund was financed by an extra premium on certain kinds of insurance policies; since the insurance business was in a period of expansion at that time, the resulting increases in revenues permitted the expansion of services to the disabled. The federated entities have continued to use the fund model as the policy instrument in acquitting their responsibilities in this field; each has established a para-governmental fund responsible for the implementation of most of its disability policies.

With federal devolution, starting in the 1980s, the policy picture has become very complex. The federal government, which retains responsibility for social security, continues to provide income-replacement and integration allowances for the disabled. In addition, aspects of its responsibilities in other social security programs, in employment policies, in the taxation and justice systems, in transportation and in public utilities regulation address the needs of disabled citizens. The communities have the broadest mandate, given that they are responsible for disabled persons in relation to education and training, residential and home care, a range of financial supports and subsidies, and counselling. The regions, with their responsibilities for social housing and public transit, have a role to play as well.

Rather like Belgium, Germany displays a notion of social solidarity expressed in a corporatist model in which the major organized groups or social partners in society assume substantial responsibility for the management of the social affairs of the country and for working out arrangements among themselves. Embedded in Germany's Basic Law is the declaration that the Federal Republic is a social federal state. This is the foundation upon which a sophisticated and comprehensive welfare state has been constructed. A self-governing process carried out by employer and employee organizations manages significant dimensions of the German social security system. The broad policy framework within which these relationships are conducted is set by the state, but it is as important, in attempting to understand the German system, to analyze the organizational and group structure of social security as it is to study the intergovernmental regime itself.

For purposes of presentation, one might look at the disability field from two perspectives: first, the vertical allocation of authority in the federation (as between the federal and Länder governments); second, the horizontal allocation of authority among the various social-security organizations.

Vertically, the allocation of responsibility for disability follows the general pattern set for the German welfare state. The relevant laws are federal, having been passed by both houses of parliament — e.g., the Social Code, the *Rehabilitation Adjustment Act*, the *Employment Promotion Act*, the *Federal War Victims Relief Act*, *Severely Disabled Persons Act*, and the *Federal Social Welfare Act*. The task of the Länder mainly consists of the implementation and enforcement of federal legislation; to this end, they pass the necessary regulations, allocate the necessary resources and supervise the operation of the system. The Länder are responsible for providing the necessary resources themselves, either through taxation or through the allocation of the resources they receive from the horizontal and vertical fiscal equalization system; direct federal transfers are rarely used. In addition, there is a compensatory levy or tax imposed on firms and government agencies that do not employ their ratio of severely disabled people; this revenue is shared between the federal and Länder governments.

The actual services themselves, however, are generally offered by social-security organizations, charitable organizations, and self-help organizations (in this case, associations for disabled people). This is consistent with the principle of subsidiarity, which plays a very important role in German social policy; government authorities are only to take action when non-governmental organizations are not capable of doing so. In addition to these programs, which are mandated by federal law and to which citizens have a legal claim, the Länder offer in varying degree what are called "voluntary subsidies." These benefits arise out of administrative regulations or guidelines, not directly out of legislation, which means that they can be allocated more flexibly and that they can be more readily curtailed when financial resources are short. These voluntary subsidies to disabled persons or to non-governmental organizations assisting persons with disabilities are the main reason why in Germany disability programming varies significantly from Land to Land, even though the central legal provisions in the field are federal in nature and of universal application.

As for the horizontal allocation of responsibility, the main work of the German system of disability programming is carried out by social-security organizations, charitable organizations, and self-help organizations. The most important of these are the social-security organizations, which are corporations under public law, subject to government supervision, but which manage their affairs themselves. Employer/employee boards are responsible for management. These are large-scale insurance funds in which the benefits are linked to the contributions made. Their mandates differ, focusing, for example, on workers' compensation, on pension insurance and on rehabilitation, but each has a responsibility for a dimension of the disability landscape. As major investment vehicles, their regulation and location matter greatly to regional economic development in Germany. The charitable organizations, composed of volunteers as well as professional staff, play a significant role in the field of disability, generally filling in the gaps left by public policy. There are five leading associations of private welfare work, three of which have a religious orientation. Self-help groups have become increasingly important in recent years, partly because of the sense many members of the disability community have that government and welfare institutions are sometimes patronage ridden and restrictive in their approach. These groups are designed to defend the interests of their members. Despite their role as government critics, they could not exist without government support, which is mainly provided by the Länder and the municipalities. Party politics plays an important role here, with Länder and municipalities governed by the Christian Democrats tending to give priority to the promotion of the disabled and Länder and municipalities ruled by the Social Democrats and the Greens tending to give priority to other social minorities.

In principle, the range of services and support for the disabled in Germany is very broad. The needs not covered by the social security funds are covered by welfare. In practice, however, this comprehensive coverage is limited in several ways. First, German disability programs are highly complex and in a number of cases are inconsistent with one another. Citizens often have great difficulty in understanding what they are entitled to, and obtaining it. Sometimes they are not informed about which services and support they are actually entitled to. Second, there are frequent disputes between organizations and agencies about administrative and financial responsibility. Third, welfare, as the fall-back option for those not having access to social security through the funds, is still stigmatized to a degree. Psychologically, for persons with disabilities there is an important difference between receiving welfare or social-security benefits; people are often reluctant to apply for the former, and do not do so at all, or only at a very late stage. Thus, Germany has a generous but highly complex system which makes it very difficult to tackle the problems of disabled people directly and coherently. Its difficulties in this respect are shared with the other countries we studied.

In the United States, as in Australia and Canada, disability supports and services have been developed in the twentieth century, and have evolved primarily as add-ons to existing programs. Like Germany, the disability field in the United States is fragmented both vertically and horizontally. At the national level, disability policy in the United States can be divided into four sections: workers' compensation, vocational rehabilitation, income support/ replacement, and civil rights protections.

Contemporary vocational rehabilitation policy in the United States traces its origins to 1918, but the program received permanent status at the federal level in the *Social Security Act* of 1935. Throughout the twentieth century, although legislative changes have expanded the program's scope, it is primarily a service-oriented program and focuses on assisting persons with disabilities to enter or re-enter the workforce. The rationale rests on the notion of investing in human capital which will reduce dependence on social-support spending and will increase payroll tax collections. Since its inception, the program has been operated through a 50/50 cost-shared arrangement between the national government and the states. The national government sets the basic program parameters, while the states operate the programs and provide the direct services. While the cost-shared arrangement has been an enduring feature of the program, significant policy differences between the national government and the states have emerged, particularly concerning inadequate levels of federal funding.

Similar intergovernmental skirmishes are evident in the federal income support programs: Supplemental Security Income (SSI) and Social Security Disability Insurance (SSDI). Established in 1935, the *Social Security Act* was a national program providing states with funds to assist individuals through the most severe economic depression to date. Fearing the costs associated with the provision of disability benefits, however, the legislation did not establish a program of disability insurance. It was not until 1956, after pressure from the states, and through intergovernmental partnerships, that a system of disability benefits, SSDI, was established. The entitlement-based nature of the program meant that once judged eligible, an individual's participation in the program was automatic. In addition, spending caps were not established for entitlement programs such as SSDI. Thus, government spending was determined by program participation, and not through a legislative budget process. In the 1970s, the national government began to retreat from entitlement-based social programs, fearful of their fiscal drag. By the 1980s, SSDI was significantly constrained by the Reagan administration and many individuals lost their disability benefits. Thus, unlike Canada, Belgium, and Germany, the United States does not have a system of universal health care or personal supports. Instead, a series of fragmented, under-funded programs and income-replacement schemes have been created to support individuals with disabilities.

The United States does, however, have a strong tradition of civil rights legal protections for persons with disabilities. These protections have evolved from a series of federal statutes, including: the *Americans with Disabilities Act*; the *Fair Housing Act*; the *Air Carrier Access Act*; the *National Voter Registration Act*; the *Individuals with Disabilities Education Act*; the R*ehabilitation Act*; and the *Architectural Barriers Act*. These federal statutes have established a comparatively forceful set of physical accommodations for persons with physical disabilities in public and private buildings, public transportation systems, interstate bussing, and air travel. The ability of the national government to legislate and enforce compliance in the state, local, and private spheres has ensured an enviable level of physical accessibility. Indeed, the federal government is recognized as the key player in bringing both the public and private sectors into line on eliminating disability discrimination across a variety of sectors.

As Percy notes, the *Americans with Disabilities Act* nationalized disability policy in the United States. Through the power of the federal government, this statute set a minimum benchmark to which all 50 states, and private industry must adhere. The idea of enforceable national standards has been a rallying cry for many persons with disabilities in other nations, especially Canada and Australia. The institutional environment in these countries, however, makes designing policy similar to the scope of the ADA very difficult.

The judicial branch of the American political system is an important and central actor in the disability policy domain. The American tradition of creating legislation that empowers individuals to litigate when their rights are transgressed by government or private action is at the core of disability civil rights policy. The ADA, which most observers identify as the single most important federal statute for Americans with disabilities, is premised on the central position of the court system in American life.

While the Canadian welfare state rests somewhere between the European federations and the American system, Canada does not have a comprehensive and integrated system to meet the needs of persons with disabilities. There is no national disability policy. Instead, disability policy is mediated through a complex federal reality where jurisdictional division, duplication and overlap, and policy fragmentation are common.

In recent years, the Canadian federation has further decentralized — the provinces have assumed greater flexibility and control over health, postsecondary education, social assistance, and labour market training. Each of these policy areas directly affects the lives of Canadians with disabilities. The Canadian disability movement has raised public concerns about further decentralization because it views this move as a threat to national standards. As Torjman notes, since the enactment of the *Charter of Rights and Freedoms* (1982), disability policy has been viewed through a so-called "citizenship lens," not simply from the perspective of a particular policy area, such as health or education. Thus, at a symbolic level the federal government's role, at least outside Quebec, is seen as central in all disability policy discussions. In many respects, the federal government is viewed as a leader in protecting the citizenship rights of Canadians with disabilities.

At the same time, however, the federal government has sought to appease provincial concerns in the area of social policy by adopting a more decentralized, yet collaborative approach known as the Social Union Framework Agreement (1999). As Torjman notes, while we do not yet know the full impact of the Social Union Agreement, this new collaborative approach could positively benefit disability-related policy areas, such as attendant care. In addition, it could establish some principles aimed at national coordination in these areas. There is evidence of other collaborative measures in the area of disability policy, at least in principles and vision. In terms of concrete policy changes, however, very little progress can be measured. This has left the many persons with disabilities uneasy and fearful of potential changes.

Torjman focuses on three policy and program areas affecting Canadians with disabilities: *personal supports* which "enable persons with disabilities to live independently in the community"; *employment programs* comprised of vocational rehabilitation and training supports; and finally, *income programs* which provide financial assistance to workers on both a permanent and temporary basis. Other important policy areas include: human rights, transportation, and communication. This basket of programs is summarized in Table 3.

It is important to note that, while under stress, the Canadian system of universal health care has had a significant and positive effect on the lives of persons with disabilities. In many ways, access to health care has created a system of quasi-national standards. These standards, however, are quite unlike the standards created through the *Americans with Disabilities Act* (1990). Unlike the ADA, which established a set of enforceable national standards, the *Canada Health Act* (1984) has five, broadly conceived criteria affirming the

TABLE 3
Policies and Programs Affecting Canadians with Disabilities

	Disability Supports	*Employment*	*Income*
Federal	• Tax credits • Aboriginal peoples and Inuit on reserve	• Vocational rehabilitation programs • Aboriginal programs	• Employment Insurance • Canada Pension Plan Disability Benefit
Provincial	• Health and social services • Technical aids and equipment • Tax credits • Welfare special needs provisions	• Labour market training	• Targeted programs • Social insurance • Workers' Compensation • Employment Insurance • Canada/Quebec Pension Plan Disability Benefit • Welfare
Private			• Private insurance

federal government's commitment to a universal, accessible, comprehensive, portable, and public administered health insurance system. These quasi-national standards provide the conditions and the criteria that provincial health insurance plans must meet to receive federal fiscal transfers. The legislation does not, therefore, regulate health care in the provinces. Moreover, these standards do not apply to disability-related supports and services such as attendant care, transportation, and labour market training. Thus, as Torjman argues, the delivery of disability supports varies widely throughout the country. Moreover, the trend toward increased devolution means that local and third sector (both non-profit and profit) organizations have an increased role in the delivery of supports and services.

In addition, as noted above, many of the supports and services created for persons with disabilities were initially conceived on the assumption that persons with disabilities were separate from the mainstream of society. The constitutional protection of physical and mental disability in section 15 of the

Charter of Rights and Freedoms, however, has made it very difficult for policymakers to ignore disability issues. But, rather than engage in major restructuring, Canadian policymakers have established a set of parallel services and programs, which were initially set up as charity, but have since primarily moved to the quasi-public realm and are mostly paid for by the state. Torjman notes that these complexities have created "barriers" for Canadians with disabilities in gaining access to supports, education or training, and jobs.

For Aboriginal peoples with disabilities, Torjman continues, these barriers are compounded by jurisdictional disputes depending on whether or not an individual is considered *status* or *non-status* according to federal law. The federal government assumes responsibility for Aboriginal peoples considered to be status Indians living on-reserve, or Inuit, while provincial governments are mandated to provide services to non-status Indians and Métis. Moreover, Aboriginal peoples often encounter issues of geographic isolation and lack of community supports and services in remote areas of the country.

In Australia, disability policy is a complex and challenging area. By its very nature, Hancock notes in this volume that disability policy in Australia is, "intersectoral, involving all levels of government, both for-profit and not-for-profit non-government sectors; making demands on a range of program areas: in particular, income security, housing, health, community services, workers' compensation, aged care, child care, transport and labour market programs." Key intergovernmental institutions, such as the Special Premiers' Conferences and the Council of Australian Governments (COAG), have played a significant role in pushing a national agenda on disability forward. Active intergovernmentalism is made necessary in part by the fact of extensive constitutional concurrency in jurisdiction and in part by the fiscal might of the central government. Yet, attempts to achieve a nationally integrated system in the disability policy field have been constrained by inertia, funding difficulties, uneven commitment by the states on social spending, duplication and overlap of effort in the policy domain, and cost-shifting between levels of government.

As Hancock points out, there have been some major shifts in disability policy and practice in Australia, as in the United States and Canada, in the last two decades. They include: a shift from residential institutional care to care in the community; a growing focus on integrating people with disabilities into community services, employment and recreation; a move in employment for people with disabilities from sheltered workshops and Activity Therapy Centres to work in the community at standard rates of pay and conditions; increased efforts by governments to rationalize roles and responsibilities in the disabilities policy and services area; and more emphasis on the part of governments at all levels to reduce their role in direct service provision and to become funders and/or purchasers rather than providers, of services, in line with government-wide microeconomic reforms and national competition policy.

The key Australian intergovernmental institutions — the Special Premiers' Conferences and the Council of Australian Governments — played a pivotal role in securing agreement between the Commonwealth and states/territories on a major national reform agenda for Disability Policy and Services Delivery. In 1991, leaders and representatives agreed to proceed with rationalization of roles and responsibilities of disability services; they signed the *Commonwealth/State Disability Agreement* which was the first national framework for disability services. It allocated responsibility to the Commonwealth for employment services and to the states for accommodation and support services. The *Commonwealth Disability Services Act* was passed, providing for Commonwealth funding to the states to cover services transfer and growth of services costs, and laying out the division of responsibilities. Complementary state legislation followed.

These reforms occurred while Australian governments were in the midst of vigorous efforts to reduce government spending and enhance Australia's international competitiveness, leading many to view with a degree of scepticism the alleged success of the current reform agenda in disability. Those with severe or multiple disabilities have often been moved out into the community without sufficient resourcing or provision of appropriate supports; with the result that, for women carers in particular, quality of life has deteriorated. Those with similar disabilities may be treated very differently under state and Commonwealth compensation schemes and those marginalized by structural changes such as labour market changes limiting employment opportunities, may be pressured to bear individual responsibility for their misfortunes.

Australia, then, burdened with a system of disability policy and programs which has been historically fragmented, has made real efforts in the last decade to create an integrated national approach to disability, using the central instruments of Australian executive federalism. Unfortunately, as Hancock notes, this thrust has occurred in the midst of neo-liberal restraint exercises and efforts to cut back on the roles and responsibilities of Australian governments, limiting, in the opinion of many, the practical effects of this laudable reform effort.

Role of Disability Organizations/Movement

Our comparison reveals that disability organizations play an important role in each of the five federations. The purpose and scope of these organizations, however, can be divided into two groups. First, in Australia, Canada, and the United States, "rights frameworks" have spawned a network of disability organizations considered to be a part of the disability rights movement. These organizations form a society-based political movement, and since the 1970s have pushed forward the disability domain by attempting to influence the direction of policies and programs. In Belgium and Germany, however, disability organizations do not appear to be politically salient, that is, associations that form an organized movement vis-à-vis the state. This is explained, in part, because the "social federal state" model coupled with the development of a mature welfare state has truncated the growth of disability rights organizations which focus on advancing individual civil and political rights. Instead, self-help and service organizations have prominence in the federations whose role is largely defined by assisting individuals navigate the complexity of services and supports.

In Canada, the federal government has played a central role in supporting the development of the Canadian disability rights movement. Since the late-1970s, the federal government has provided core funding to a broad spectrum of disability organizations. These organizations have, in turn, attempted to influence the direction of disability policy at the federal level. The movement has had some success in influencing the "ideas" associated with disability policy development. In particular, governments have adopted new policy frameworks, which, like the United States, begin to embrace the socio-political model of disability. The concerted effort by the federal, as well as most provincial governments to reduce the so-called fiscal burden, however, has muted policy innovation in this area.

The influence of the disability movement on the inclusion of "physical and mental disability" in section 15 of the *Charter of Rights and Freedoms* (1982) cannot be underestimated. As Torjman notes, the impact of including disability in the Charter has ensured that disablement and persons with disabilities are recognized politically. As well, the role of the courts as a means to end disability discrimination has taken on a prominence not known in the pre-Charter era. There is evidence that this shift has affected both the way the disability movement is organized, as well as its activities.

Torjman notes that in the contemporary period, the Canadian disability community is focused on the impact of new intergovernmental regimes on disability programs and policies. The movement continues to advocate for a strong federal presence in the disability policy domain to ensure national standards. Canadians with disabilities are, as Torjman observes, "fearful that the federal government will abandon its leadership role in the name of constitutional conciliation and will be less prepared to take action that protects citizens' rights or introduce programs that will provide direct assistance to any given population."

Similar to Canada, Americans with disabilities view the federal government as providing an important leadership role in advancing and protecting individual rights. Thus, the US disability rights movement, while fragmented, is a significant national political force. Although a series of federal statutes paved the way for the legal precedents found in the ADA, it was the disability rights movement that created the political force necessary to ensure its passage. A broad coalition of disability organizations, as well as the labour and women's movement were important actors in pressuring Congress and the White House for its passage.

At the national, state, and local levels, the movement is recognized politically. It plays an important role in monitoring and enforcing the implementation of the ADA. Moreover, the legal wing of the disability movement is an active participant in presenting the US Supreme Court with briefs on important, precedent-setting cases. As more and more cases are litigated concerning disability issues in employment, transportation, and public accommodation, this is becoming a central function of the American disability rights movement.

The picture in Germany is very different from that which prevails in North America. In North America, one has the sense of the disability community confronting the state — federal, state, and municipal governments — in an effort to have their needs addressed. In Germany, the state is the regulator and ultimate back stop, but the bulk of the management and administration of the system of support is done by intermediary institutions: large-scale insurance funds, charitable organizations, and to some extent self-help groups. Thus, disability groups seem, to a greater extent than in Canada and the United States, to be part of the system rather than a force outside the system applying pressure on it. In addition, the link between self-help groups and political parties appears to be much closer than is the case in North America.

Disability does not have a high political profile in Belgium. There is, however, a fairly thick web of organizations that defend the interests of people with disabilities. Interestingly, given the cultural and linguistic divisions in the country, the National Council for Persons with Disabilities operates at the federal level and is composed of a large number of groups acting on behalf of persons with disabilities, both Dutch- and French-speaking. To be a member of the National Council, associations must be national in scope; this means that, for example, the National Association for Mentally Handicapped Persons, while a member of the Council, nevertheless has a Dutch-speaking as well as a francophone section, the latter subdividing again into a Walloon and a Brussels section. All of this may mean that there is a degree of conciliation at the national level between associations representing people with similar needs, irrespective of their linguistic membership.

Similar types of consultative groups exist for the Walloon Region and for French-speaking Brussels. In Flanders, the pattern is slightly different, since these sorts of associations actually sit on the board of the para-governmental fund.

It is important to note, as well, that in the broader environment, the "social partners" in Belgium negotiate major labour policies. The rate of unionization is very high, and unions and employers' representatives will agree on policies such as the minimum wage, labour standards, and so on. Surprisingly, these social partners still operate on a national or federal basis, although language-based subdivisions exist.

CONCLUSION

The chapters following examine five federations which are in some ways quite different from one another and in other ways rather similar. But what is striking in the findings of these studies is not the difference that the specific form of federalism makes in the policy field of disablement, but the degree to which all five countries are shaped by much the same pressures and evolving attitudes, and the degree to which they seek to respond to this shifting environment with the development of policy frameworks that have a good deal in common. Even their failures are shared to a large degree; all the federations are plagued by policy and program fragmentation and complexity, a lack of transparency, and an inability to achieve the full and comprehensive integration of disabled persons into the life of the community as a whole. Much work remains to be done in all cases. Our speculation, and until further comparative work is done it must remain simply that, is that the factors that account for these parallel experiences at the level of philosophy, values, and priorities transcend the federal form, and are endemic to modern democratic states of whatever description.[30]

If there is a good deal of commonality in broad philosophy, there is, as we have found, considerable diversity in the formulation of policy with respect to disabled people, and considerable diversity as well in the programs, administrative organizations, and delivery vehicles each federation fashions to implement its policies. Insurance funds are major delivery vehicles in Germany and Belgium; the claiming of citizen rights before the courts is a distinctive practice in American federalism; federal-provincial and Commonwealth-state agreements are privileged instruments for the implementation of disability policy in Canada and Australia.

The result for citizens with disabilities in each of the five federations studied is a web of confusing and conflicting supports, services, and — in Australia, Canada, and the United States — "rights frameworks" which requires the assistance of third-party organizations to successfully navigate both the rules and the infrastructure of the system. Despite the good intentions of federal and state policymakers, this tangled thicket of programs and services inhibits each state's capacity to meet the goals of social justice, effectiveness, and inclusion to which it aspires.

APPENDIX: CENTRAL ANALYTIC ELEMENTS ARISING OUT OF EACH FEDERATION

	Australia	Belgium	Canada	Germany	United States
Development of Disability Policy	• History of stigma and fear toward persons with disabilities • Developed as "add-ons" to programs that did not have disability as a central focus when they were developed	• Basic character and level of service established by unitary state in 1960s and 1970s – now being implemented nationally and in the federated entities	• History of stigma and fear toward persons with disabilities • Developed as "add-ons" to programs that did not have disability as a central focus when they were developed	• Developed as a dimension of Germany's conceptions of a "social federal state" and "uniformity of living conditions" • Fragmented program delivery	• Historically negative attitudes – fear, pity, stigma – toward persons with disabilities • Developed as "add-ons" to programs that did not have disability as a central focus when they were developed
Definitions of Disability	• Disability is ill-defined across the policy domain – although recent attempts to achieve coherence • Tension between the "medical model" and "socio-political model" of disability in policies/ programs	• Single, broad and uniform definition of disability continues – namely, limited possibility of social or professional integration due to reduced physical activity to 30 percent and mental activity to 20 percent	• Disability is ill-defined across the policy domain – individual program definitions vary, especially to define what is meant by severe and long-term impairment • Tension between "medical model" and "socio-political model" of disability in policies/programs • Governments have narrowed disability definitions to restrict program eligibility	• No coherent, authoritative understanding of disability has been developed to serve as the foundation for German disability policy • Certain stigma associated with those forms of public support for disability which are based on need, as opposed to compensation (such as workplace injury)	• Disability is ill-defined across policy areas – but, the ADA has introduced some uniformity across the federation • Tension between "medical model" and "socio-political model" of disability • Governments have narrowed disability definitions to restrict program eligibility
Impact of Federalism on Disability Policy	• Classical and collaborative federalism • Central government dominates disability policy domain via taxation and agenda-setting function • Recent attempts at intergovernmentalism	• Recently federated • Classical federalism – not flexible • Decisions affecting the policy domain driven by language and culture, not policy • Federalism led to fragmentation, but not a diminution of disability policy	• Classical or collaborative federalism • No national policy or policy development • Provincial governments responsible for most policies affecting Canadians with disabilities • Some cost-sharing, but decreased since 1995 • Federal spending power has a role, but decreased post-CHST, Social Union	• Interlocking federalism • Division of powers is exclusive – federal government responsible for legislation, state responsible for implementation • Strong interstate cooperation	• Cooperative federalism – led to creation of more programs • National policy for development/programs with state delivery • Federal spending power is significant in program development at state/local level • Some state innovation in disability policy

...continued

APPENDIX (continued)

	Australia	Belgium	Canada	Germany	United States
Institutional Complexities	• Attempts to achieve policy co-ordination – integrate disability programs/supports – employment, accommodations, disability services	• Little jurisdictional coordination • Occurs at the level of political parties, and minimally at the level of non-governmental associations	• Weak policy coordination • Increasing intergovernmental collaboration • Judicial branch has increasing role (post-Charter)	• No policy coordination or national consistency between federal/state level • Corporatist relationships in social policy sector, yet fragmented between insurance, charitable and self-help groups	• Weak policy coordination, yet greater national consistency because of ADA, federal spending power • Judicial branch plays a significant role in policy • No regulatory framework
Nature/Depth of Services/ Supports	• Historically fragmented system, but since 1991 federation has attempted to create a national, systemic government approach to disability • Policy domain is weakening because of fiscal restraint	• Fragmented system – services attached to language and culture • Robust level of services/supports	• Fragmented system – across policy domain and geographic regions • Universal health-care benefits policy domain • Quebec has most integrated system of delivery • Local government and third sector playing an increasing role in service-delivery, including First Nations communities	• Premised on "solidarity" model of uniformity, but disability domain is fragmented across policy domain and geographic regions • Subsidiary is central – insurance funds play a crucial role • Local government and charitable sector play a role in service delivery	• Fragmented system – across policy domain and geographic regions – but ADA covers broad mandate: employment, transportation, accommodation in public and private • Nonprofit sector plays a role in service delivery, but private sector has a dominant role
Role of Disability Organizations	• Politically salient at federal, state level • Emerging rights-based role	• Not politically salient • Primarily assist individuals in system navigation • Active at federal, as well as at sub-national levels	• Politically salient at federal level, less so at provincial/local level (except in Quebec) • Expanding rights-based role post-Charter • Strong centrist orientation • Focus is on citizenship principles • Government commitment to consult with organizations but few concrete outcomes in the 1990s (except in tax measures)	• Not politically salient – primarily self-help organizations • Not group-state relations, but complex array of intermediate institutions • Role of political parties is central • Uniformity of living conditions model animates the field, so disability organizations assist in system navigation	• Politically salient at federal, state and local levels • Entrenched rights-based role • Focus is on civil rights protections • Key strategy is judicial activism • Government consultation is weak

NOTES

[1]It is important to note that there is overlap between these periods. They are meant to serve as an organizing principle, and therefore serve only as a rough guide. See Fraser Valentine and Jill Vickers, "Released from the Yoke of Paternalism and Charity: Citizenship and the Rights of Canadians with Disabilities," *International Journal of Canadian Studies*, 14 (Fall 1996):155-77.

[2]For a discussion on the implementation of this approach to disability in Canada, see Richard B. Splane, *Social Welfare in Ontario 1791-1893* (Toronto: University of Toronto Press, 1965).

[3]While the impact of the war on disability policy and programs as they relate to men have been well explored, the effect of this period on women has received less attention.

[4]For a useful overview of the development of these organizations, see Richard Scotch, *From Good Will to Civil Rights: Transforming Federal Disability Policy* (Philadelphia: Temple University Press, 1984); and Diane Driedger, *The Last Civil Rights Movement: Disabled Peoples' International* (New York: St. Martin's Press, 1989).

[5]Driedger, *The Last Civil Rights Movement*, p. 14.

6 World Health Organization. "The Scope of the Challenge." *Ageing & Health Division* (Geneva: World Health Organization, 1998). See WHO Website: <http://www.who.int/ageing/scope.html>.

[7]A cross-disability framework recognizes that people with different disabilities have different needs and therefore ensures that programs and resources are accessible to persons with varied types of disabilities. This notion represents a departure from traditional approaches to disability in which the needs of a specific disability type (i.e., individuals with physical disabilities) were met while other types of disability were ignored.

[8]An emerging analytic framework known as the "social model of disability" informs this conception of disablement. There is little published material on the social model because it is an emerging and, therefore, contested concept developed by disabled researchers and their allies. Given that this mode of analysis is still under development there is some disagreement about what it entails. Nevertheless, it is possible to identify a number of core elements upon which there is broad consensus. The social model shifts the analytic focus from the individual person with a disability to the *interaction* between individuals and the environment. At its core, the social model is a rejection of the so-called "medical model" which has been identified as the central understanding from which most public policy has been developed in industrial welfare states. The medical model holds that individual pathology and functional limitation are the key elements of disablement and these factors can be overcome (or at least stabilized) through medical intervention. For more information, see Fraser Valentine, "Challenging Orthodoxies: New Perspectives in Disability," *Proceedings of the Research in Disability and Public Policy Summer Institute Roeher Institute* (Toronto: Roeher Institute, 1998).

[9]Sandra Carpenter, "Disability: Towards the Transparent," *FUSE*, 14, 3 (1991):25.

[10]Evelyn Kallen, *Label Me Human: Minority Rights of Stigmatized Canadians* (Toronto: University of Toronto Press, 1989).

[11]Canada seconded the resolution at the United Nations General Assembly to designate 1981 as the International Year of Disabled Persons.

[12]In anticipation of the International Year of Disabled Persons, the Canadian government established the Special Committee on the Disabled and the Handicapped in May 1980. Its first report was followed by a series of reports throughout the 1980s and 1990s on the status of disabled citizens in Canadian society. As Valentine and Vickers note, the parliamentary committee structure has served as an important cornerstone for the advancement of disability initiatives within the federal government. See Valentine and Vickers, "Released from the Yoke of Paternalism and Charity." For more information on the first report by the special committee, see Canada. Secretary of State. *Obstacles* (Ottawa: Minister of Supply and Services, 1981).

[13]Cherie S. Lewis, "International Aspects of the Disability Issue," in *The Disabled, the Media and the Informational Age*, ed. Jack A. Nelson (Westport, CT: Greenwood Press, 1994), p. 191.

[14]Susan Reynolds Whyte and Benedicte Ingstad, "Disability and Culture: An Overview," in *Disability and Culture*, ed. Benedicte Ingstad and Susan Reynolds Whyte (Berkeley: University of California Press, 1995), p. 3.

[15]For a rich discussion on the meanings and experiences of disablement in both the first and the third worlds, see Ingstad and Reynolds Whyte, *Disability and Culture*.

[16]See WHO Director General, *Disability Prevention and Rehabilitation*, No. A45/6. (Geneva: WHO, April 1992).

[17]United Nations, *Disabled Persons*, Bulletin No. 3 (New York: Division for Social Policy and Development, 1997), p. 4.

[18]United Nations, *Disability Statistics Compendium*, Statistics on Special Population Groups, Series Y, No. 4. (New York: Department of International Economic and Social Affairs Statistical Office, 1990), p. 13.

[19]The WHO definitions have provided the foundation upon which many national statistical studies have been undertaken. In Britain, see J. Martin, H. Meltzer and D. Elliot, *OPCS Surveys of Disability in Great Britain: Report 1 — The Prevalence of Disability Among Adults* (London: HMSO, 1988); in the United States, see US Census Bureau, *Status of Persons with a Disability* (Washington: US Census Bureau, 1991-92); in Australia, see Australian Institute of Health and Welfare, *Australia's Welfare 1999* (Canberra: Australian Government Publishing Service, 1999); in Canada, see Statistics Canada, *The Health and Activity Limitation Survey (HALS) — Highlights* (Ottawa: Statistics Canada, 1991).

[20]See Michael Oliver, "Defining Impairment and Disability: Issues at Stake," in *Exploring the Divide: Illness and Disability*, ed. Colin Barnes and Gary Mercer (Leeds: The Disability Press, 1996).

[21]For a more detailed discussion of DISTAT, see *United Nations Disability Statistics Data Base, 1975-1986: Technical Manual*, Statistical Papers, Series Y, No. 3. (New York: United Nations Publication, 1990).

[22]See *United Nations Disability Statistics Compendium*, Statistics on Special Population Groups. Statistical Papers, Series Y, No. 4 (New York: United Nations Publication, 1990).

[23]Ibid., p. 70.

[24]It is important to note that neo-liberal ideology has not been embraced to the same extent as the other nations in this study. Coalition governments, which at the federal level in Belgium have included the Socialist party for over 20 years, have maintained a largely "social state." Thus, there has not been a significant withdrawal of the state from the social policy realm, nor is there significant evidence of a new neo-liberal discourse. The only geographic area where there is some evidence of an emerging neo-liberal ideology in Belgium is in Flanders.

[25]In preparing these summaries, we found Ron Watts, *Comparing Federal Systems*, 2d ed. (Kingston and Montreal: School of Policy Studies, Queen's Universeity and McGill-Queen's University Press, 1999) a useful resource.

[26]We are not using the term 'Aboriginal' to refer to a single, homogenous category of individuals. Instead, this term covers three broad categories of Aboriginals: Indian, Inuit, and Métis. The term Indian has been created and elaborated through legal frameworks, and does not clearly recognize the variety of distinct Aboriginal nations with their own histories and communities.

[27]See Royal Commission on Aboriginal Peoples (RCAP), *Report*, Vol 1. (Ottawa: Government of Canada, 1996), pp. 11-15.

[28]It is important to note that in situating Germany in this context, we have not sought to overlook or gloss over the treatment of persons with disabilities during the Nazi regime. Physically and mentally disabled persons were the first victims of systematic extermination by the Nazis. A secret program of killing, authorized by Hitler and code-named "Operation T4" functioned from October 1939 to August 1941. Conceived as a biological "cleansing" of the German gene pool, Operation T4 caused the death of more than 70,000 persons in German hospitals and asylums. The secrecy surrounding this program of medical killing broke down in 1941, when a handful of church leaders, local magistrates and ordinary German citizens protested. Fearing widespread dissatisfaction, Hitler halted Operation T4 on 24August 1941. But the halt order was a public relations ploy, and the program continued under a new name.

[29]In 1993, however, the French community in turn transferred some of its constitutional powers in the field to the Walloon region and to the Commission communautaire française, chiefly because of financial exigencies.

[30]It is interesting to note, for example, that a government report about disability from the United Kingdom, which has a unitary system, points to many of the features with which we have become familiar in this study — resource constraints, demographic change, the rising cost of new technologies, the need to improve service coordination, and the importance of improving the social integration of disabled people. World Health

Organization, *Is the Law Fair to the Disabled?* WHO Regional Publications, European Series No. 29. (Copenhagen: World Health Organization, 1998), pp. 341-42.

2

AUSTRALIAN INTERGOVERNMENTAL RELATIONS AND DISABILITY POLICY

Linda Hancock

In Australian disability policy, the 1980s and 1990s saw a raft of reforms aimed at a national approach. This focused on better coordination between tiers of government dealing with disability, along with better coordination between various government departments at Commonwealth, state, and local government levels and the non-governmental sector. Disability is variously defined, but generally refers to a range of physical, intellectual or social conditions, that may be encompassed by World Health Organization (WHO) definitions of disability, impairment or handicap.[1] In terms of policy provisions and service needs, this includes a diverse range of people, including the infirm aged, those incapacitated for work because of injury or illness, and those unable to work or in need of services, due to various forms of incapacity. Reforms during the 1990s brought a more coordinated approach to disability services and active labour market policies for those previously deemed incapacitated for work; along with supports for independent living for the infirm aged and disabled, and their carers.

In intergovernmental terms disability policy is a complex and challenging area. By its very nature, it is intersectoral, involving all levels of government, both for-profit and not-for-profit non-governmental sectors; making demands on a range of program areas: in particular, income security, housing, health, community services, workers' compensation, aged care, child care, transport, and labour market programs.

Recent reforms to disability policy occurred in a broader policy context of deinstitutionalization and community integration of aged care and the care of those with mental illnesses and intellectual and physical disabilities. Over the last 30 years, large psychiatric institutions were scaled down and active labour market programs, supported by networks of community care services, have sought to provide a better alternative to sheltered workshops. From the 1970s, and the Henderson Poverty Inquiry, there has been recognition of the particular barriers facing disabled people in terms of access to basic material and cultural resources and social participation. Closely identified with "disability poverty" is employment exclusion and exploitation, income deprivation, social service inadequacy and physical inaccessibility. Sheltered workshops have been criticized on the grounds of their isolation from mainstream society, below minimum wage, associated poverty, and demeaning lifestyles.[2] With such shifts in government policy and more vocal and articulate peak bodies representing people with disabilities, recent policies have also sought to better accommodate the needs of carers.

Key issues for disability policy include on the one hand, growth in social security expenditure (a focus of Commonwealth government concerns about the increasing number of Australians receiving government income support, in particular, Disability Support Pensions) and on the other, high levels of unmet need for welfare services.[3]

In terms of intergovernmental relations between Australia's national Commonwealth government and the eight states and territories[4] that make up the federation, constitutionally, most powers are held concurrently by the Commonwealth and the states; although Commonwealth dominance over income taxation results in extreme vertical fiscal imbalance. The Commonwealth's monopoly over taxation has been a central feature of Australian federalism. Relevant to disability policy, the Commonwealth government has exclusive responsibility for social security matters, including pensions/benefits and labour market programs. Hence, responsibility for issues of income security, including Sickness Benefits, Disability Support Pensions[5] (formerly Invalid Pensions), Carers' Pensions and Unemployment Benefit, and active labour market policies, resides at the national level. States are responsible for worker accident compensation-related costs and play a significant role in service delivery, which may be funded from a mixture of their own, Commonwealth government, and community sector organization sources. Services are delivered by a mix of state government, private non-profit and more recently, the for-profit sector and administered by state and local governments. Table 1 presents a breakdown of broad service categories and sector roles in disability funding and service provision. Marking a significant reorganization of

TABLE 1
Formal Services in Australia Relevant to People with a Disability: Broad Service Categories by Sector Roles in Provision and Funding

	Commonwealth Role	State/Territory Role	Local Government Role	Non-Governmental Role
Income Support	Income security programs of DSS, DVA and DHFS* Concessions, fringe benefits	Injury compensation schemes and related services Concessions, fringe benefits	Rate concessions	Emergency relief (non-specific) Disability insurance Superannuation
Disability Support Services	Employment and other services under CSDA, including funding to states and territories HACC services Residential aged care facilities-funding Commonwealth Rehabilitation Service Australian Housing Service	Accommodation and other support services under CSDA HACC services Residential aged care facilities-funding and provision Various equipment schemes	HACC services	CSDA services and HACC services Other support services, including information and advocacy Residential aged care facilities-funding and provision
Relevant Generic Services	Employment programs, including disability-specific Public housing and crisis accommodation including disability-specific Child care services, including disability-specific funding Health services-funding Other, such as sport, library and information	Education-special and integrated Transport, including disability-specific Child care services, including disability-specific funding Health services-funding and provision Other, such as sport, library and information	Physical Access Parking Child care services-provision and coordination Other, such as sport, library	Emergency relief (non-specific) Child care services provision

Note: No distinction is made between for-profit and not-for-profit sectors.
*DSS (Department of Social Security); DVA (Department of Veterans' Affairs); DHFS (Department of Human and Family Services).
Source: Adapted from AIHW, *Australia's Welfare 1995* (Canberra: Government Publishing Service, 1995), p. 259; *Australia's Welfare 1991* (Canberra: Government Publishing Service, 1999), Appendix Tables, p. 361.

Commonwealth involvement, from the early 1990s the Commonwealth government has played a role in funding rather than directly providing services for people with disabilities.

Intergovernmental coordination through intergovernmental mechanisms such as Special Premiers' Conferences and the Council of Australian Governments (COAG) has been central to driving a national agenda on disability and is one of the success stories of the mechanics of 1990s intergovernmental reforms. However, attempts to divide up responsibilities for different aspects of disability policy/service delivery and capacity to deal with the sheer scale of demand, have met with mixed success. Shared Commonwealth/state responsibilities for major programs such as Home and Community Services (HACC) under the *Commonwealth-State Disability Agreement*, still highlight those perennial intergovernmental issues of cost-shifting, duplication, and lack of coordination. Transposed upon these is the emphasis on microeconomic reforms (such as privatization and contracting-out of services and output-based funding models at all three levels of government: Commonwealth, state, and local), thus raising further issues of access, affordability, service consistency, and quality.

Areas of concurrent Commonwealth/state responsibility are especially controversial, as Commonwealth government monopoly over income taxation and the wide interpretation of excise duties have left the states with a narrow revenue base and a dependence on Commonwealth transfers to the states for these and other state-level expenditures. A continuing theme in this chapter is the effectiveness of federalism in terms of bringing together a national agenda on disability policy.

To further explore these issues, section two examines the constitutional and practical division of Commonwealth/state responsibilities for disability-related expenditure and the intricacies of funding transfers, given Australia's extreme vertical fiscal imbalance. Compared with federal jurisdictions such as Canada, the states in Australia have very limited opportunities to raise taxation revenue. This section examines the impact of microeconomic and managerialist reforms and the role of some of the institutions driving national reform agendas (in particular, COAG). The next section profiles the nature and composition of disability in Australia, along with income security and service responses.

The fourth section examines intergovernmental dimensions of disability policy and the complicated area of welfare service delivery for people with a disability. In the late 1980s and early 1990s, faced with a choice between a block-grant model with total devolution to the states (favoured by the states) and a functional split with shared responsibilities, Australian governments opted for the latter.[6] The 1991 *Commonwealth-State Disability Agreement* (CSDA) was a watershed in intergovernmental relations on disability. It made the Commonwealth responsible for employment services, along with policy development and income support (Disability Support Pension and Sickness Allowance); state/ territory governments are responsible for accommodation and related services; with learning, advocacy, and research designated as joint responsibilities and retention of Workers' Compensation as a state responsibility. This section teases out some of the workings of this split, with a focus on labour market programs for disabled, unemployed workers as an area of Commonwealth responsibility; Workers' Compensation as an area of state responsibility; and services provided under the CSDA, in particular Home and Community Care as a major joint Commonwealth/state program. Examination of the changes in jobs placement services for unemployed people with disabilities (a Commonwealth responsibility) brings out the impact of a change of national government, budget cuts to labour market programs and the shift in the sector mix of service providers with the outsourcing of labour market programs. The examination of the CSDA and Home and Community Care program brings out some of the strengths and weaknesses of intergovernmentalism; not the least of which is fragmentation and overlap of services, which in turn raise issues of equity and program quality and effectiveness in relation to achievement of national goals. Unmet need is a major issue, with an aging population and rising demands for community services as well as uneven state and Commonwealth responses.

The final section assesses Australian disability policy and programs from an intergovernmental perspective. Some final comments are made on likely future outcomes for disability policy, especially in the light of a Commonwealth Welfare Review and federal tax reforms that have far-reaching implications for intergovernmental financial relations.

AUSTRALIAN FEDERALISM

Constitutional Provisions

Australian federalism and the principle of power-sharing between federal and state governments is written into the Australian Constitution of 1901, and federalism is based on a constitutional division of powers between two spheres of government: the Commonwealth and state/territory governments. A third sphere, local government, is set up under state constitutions and laws but has no formal recognition in the Australian Constitution.[7] Described by Emy and Hughes as "a perennial source of tension and debate in Australian politics," federation, they say, was a "pragmatic compromise between the need to cede just enough power to the centre to create a viable Commonwealth government, while leaving the States with sufficient responsibilities for them to agree to join the new union."[8] The founders of Australian federalism intended it would preserve a regional form of government in which states are free to pursue their own policies and the Commonwealth acts "where national interest requires national uniformity."[9] Commenting on Australian federalism, Galligan argues that rather than separate and distinct governments with separate jurisdictions and policy responsibilities, the "basic principle of design is concurrency, with the Commonwealth and the States having, for the most part, shared roles and responsibilities in major policy and fiscal areas," with overlap and duplication "grounded in the underlying Constitutional system."[10] "By world standards, Australian federalism exhibits a very high degree of concurrence."[11]

Thus, given that very few powers are held exclusively by the Commonwealth government,[12] Australian federalism does not reflect a simple hierarchical model. The relationship is in the main, concurrent with only some separate and exclusive areas of jurisdiction. Regarding these areas of Commonwealth jurisdiction, of relevance to disability policy, the Commonwealth has power over social-security matters: disability (formerly invalid) pensions and age pensions (section 51(xxiii)) and over-provision of maternity allowances, widows' pensions, child endowment, unemployment, benefits to students and family allowances (section 51(xxiiiA)).

For historical reasons, the Commonwealth government has control over income taxation, the major source in Australia of government revenue. Although the Commonwealth's taxation power is a concurrent power under section 51 (ii) of the Constitution, the Commonwealth took over the levying of personal income tax during World War II, and a uniform tax scheme came into effect in 1942. After 1946 the Commonwealth decided to continue uniform taxation with tax reimbursement grants to the states; a practice that continues to the present day.

Regarding concurrent areas, section 51 of the Constitution of Australia lists 40 subjects or heads of power on which the Commonwealth Parliament may pass legislation, but in which it exercises power concurrently with the states. However, Commonwealth law prevails in instances of conflict. Concurrency brings its own challenges. As Painter observes, "there are no constitutionalised mechanisms for pooling governments' law-making or executive authority to deal with these shared functions. Practical exigencies in fulfilling constitutionally sanctioned functions bring governments together, but at the same time the Constitution sets them apart as distinct political entities. This is one reason for the rich complexity of administrative and political machinery of intergovernmental relations."[13]

Financial: Commonwealth Transfers to the States

Of the five provisions in the Constitution that were set up at the time of federation to deal with the consequences for states of uniform Commonwealth duties, only one, section 96, is still operative and all Commonwealth/state transfers are made under section 96. This section permits the Commonwealth to give grants to the states on such terms and conditions as it sees fit. However, states refute the suggestion that "Commonwealth transfers to the states represent largesse on the part of the Commonwealth" and favour the interpretation (under section 94) that states are entitled to the constitutionally determined surplus.[14]

A combination of Commonwealth monopoly over income taxation and the historically wide interpretation of "excise duties" in section 90 of the Constitution,[15] has left the states with a narrow revenue base.[16] The Commonwealth's postwar monopoly of income taxation and recent High Court decisions preventing the states from imposing certain taxes on goods have contributed to Australia having a large vertical fiscal imbalance.[17] Hence, funding transfers from the Commonwealth to the states are a central focus of much intergovernmental activity, conflict and cooperation within Australian federalism. Vertical fiscal imbalance impacts at the policy level. As the Federal-State Relations Committee of the Parliament of Victoria noted "the States' role in shaping policy as equal participants in the federation is undermined by the Commonwealth's fiscal dominance."[18]

Commonwealth-State Transfers

Although disability and carer pensions and employment training and placement services for people with a disability are a Commonwealth responsibility, disability services (accommodation, information services, independent living training, respite care and home and community care programs) are funded by a mix of Commonwealth and state sources; with service delivery overseen by state and local government authorities. Arrangements exist within the federal system for collection of revenue, transfer of funds between governments, and public spending — principally as grants. Australia has been characterized by "the largest degree of vertical fiscal imbalance between its tiers of government of any federal nation."[19] Income tax is by far the most important source of Commonwealth revenue. The federal government raises about 73 percent of combined Commonwealth-state general government revenue but its outlays for its own expenditure were only 58 percent of total general government outlays.[20] After the Commonwealth spends on its own needs, funds are transferred to state and local governments through grants. The states rely substantially on Commonwealth grants (for about 46 percent of their revenue) and raise their own revenue, principally through property, gambling, and business taxes, since they are not permitted to levy income tax or more recently, excise duties (taxes on the manufacture, distribution and sale of goods).

Payments from the Commonwealth to the states and territories are made principally[21] as either General Revenue Assistance,[22] or Special Purpose Payments (SPPs). These payments are the predominant mechanism for overcoming both vertical fiscal imbalance and the horizontal fiscal imbalance which results from variations in revenue-raising capacities of different states and differences in the costs of providing goods and services across the country. Grants made under General Revenue Assistance are unconditional, constitute 51 percent of total net Commonwealth transfers to the states (1999–2000) and comprise mainly Financial Assistance Grants (FAGs).[23] Specific Purpose Payments, discussed in more detail below, are subject to conditions that reflect Commonwealth policy objectives or national policy objectives agreed between the Commonwealth and the states. SPPs, of which there are over 120, must be spent by the states according to agreed upon conditions. These comprised 49 percent of total net Commonwealth transfers to the states in 1999–2000.[24] Because of the open-ended nature of some of its programs, especially in the social policy area, the Commonwealth has increased its own outlays at a greater rate than its assistance to the states, and gross assistance to the states has declined overall from 34 percent of Commonwealth outlays in 1976–77 to 27 percent in 1997–98.[25] The declining Commonwealth funding base is a source of persistent complaint from states.

SPPs come in two forms. Payments from the Commonwealth "through" the states (about one-quarter of SPPs or 12 percent of total Commonwealth payments to the states) are payments not spent by them, but passed on to other bodies such as higher education, university research, non-governmental schools and local government. In such cases, the states act as agents for the Commonwealth, regarding what are essentially Commonwealth government programs, which for constitutional reasons, the Commonwealth must fund via the states. In contrast, payments "to" the states (about three-quarters of SPPs or 37 percent of total Commonwealth payments to the states) fund programs administered at the state level. These include hospitals, education, aged and disability services, housing, roads, and legal aid.[26]

Most SPPs are tied grants which are subject to conditions that reflect Commonwealth policy objectives or national policy objectives agreed by the Commonwealth and the states; although as discussed later, some of the mechanisms for states to account back to the Commonwealth for their spending appear to be weak. Although the conditions differ between programs, the provision of grants to the states in the form of SPPs is seen as a means for the Commonwealth to pursue its policy objectives in areas where the states are the primary service providers.

As noted earlier, section 96 gives the Commonwealth powers to make grants to the states on its own terms and conditions. Nevertheless, this is a controversial aspect of Commonwealth power from the states' point of view. Conditions attached to SPPs can limit the ability of state governments to set their own spending priorities. Furthermore, the ability of states to switch tied grants to other purposes is limited because a substantial proportion of SPP funding is for programs in which the Commonwealth exerts either direct control or imposes substantial conditions.

Reflecting the role of the two main political parties that dominate Australian politics, Specific Purpose Payment assistance has varied over time, with Labor governments generally favouring tied grants (which give more national control by requiring states to comply with conditions) and the Liberals/National Party Coalitions reducing them.[27] Moves were made in the COAG in 1995 and 1996 to untie funds and to broadband previously separately funded programs into one payment (as prevails, for example, in public health program funding) obliging the states so meet Commonwealth objectives or outcomes, but giving them greater discretion over the means to do so.

In recent years, states have put pressure on the Commonwealth to reduce the proportion of tied grants, in order to enable states to better determine their own spending priorities. Painter sees this as states reinforcing their own vision of "competitive arm's-length federalism."[28] However, at the 1999 Premiers' Conference, the Commonwealth indicated that it had no intention of further reducing aggregate SPPs as part of the reform agenda outlined under the 1999 Intergovernmental Agreement on the Reform of Commonwealth-State Financial Relations.

INSTITUTIONAL ARRANGEMENTS: NEW FEDERALISM AND THE COUNCIL OF AUSTRALIAN GOVERNMENTS

In terms of institutional mechanisms that mediate federalism, the Constitution established two powerful federal institutions: the Inter-State Commission (inoperative for most of federation) and the Senate or Upper House of the Commonwealth Parliament.[29] Since neither has provided a forum for mediating between Commonwealth and state governments[30] other more influential intergovernmental institutions are discussed below. Historically, Premiers' Conferences have been the main vehicle for determining the amount and distribution of General Revenue Assistance to the states. Premiers' Conferences have frequently highlighted states' claims about the negative impact of vertical fiscal imbalance and the need for more funds to flow in untied form to the states. Other mechanisms for intergovernmental cooperation include Commonwealth-State Ministerial Councils, Special Premiers' Conferences (up to 1992), The Council of Australian Governments (from 1992), the Loans Council and the Treaties Council, along with conferences on specific policy areas, officials' committees, and bilateral communications between Commonwealth, state, and local government agencies. The Leader's Forum, established in 1994, has been an important adjunct to states/territories' involvements in COAG, and allows state leaders to develop a cooperative approach in their dealings with the Commonwealth.

Council of Australian Governments

However, by far the most important driving force for national and intergovernmental reform has been COAG; and its precursor, the Special Premiers' Conferences. COAG emerged out of the joint review of Commonwealth-state financial arrangements conducted by the Special Premiers' Conference in 1991, under Prime Minister Hawke's New Federalism policy.[31] It was established in 1992 as an ongoing council and comprises the prime minister, the premiers and chief ministers, and the president of the local government association. It needs to be understood as a reflection of the basic concurrent nature of Australian federalism and signalling "cooperative federalism in Australia."[32]

New Federalism and the continuing role of COAG have constituted a major means of dealing with coordination of intergovernmental arrangements through establishing national priorities and developing new ways of administering overlapping roles and responsibilities. During the 1990s, New Federalism set an agreed framework for improving Australian federalism and prompted a review of the distribution of taxation powers to reduce vertical fiscal imbalance in order to provide a clearer definition of roles and responsibilities of governments in program and service delivery. It entailed a commitment to downscale the then current trend to increased reliance on tied grants (SPPs), with a view to increasing national efficiency and international competitiveness and moving toward a single national economy.

COAG has played a central role in bringing about state/Commonwealth agreement on National Competition Policy,[33] which in turn has profoundly shaped intergovernmental arrangements across a range of areas. It has thus been an important catalyst for states' economic reforms and for accelerating intergovernmental agreement on a range of topics. The 1990s national reform agenda involved structural reform of public monopolies, competitive neutrality between public and private sectors and oversight of prices charged by utilities with monopoly power; and greater use of contracting-out and compulsory competitive tendering for government-funded services. The intention was to subject a range of sectors to international and domestic competition. This national agenda has important implications for federalism. State governments were given some discretion as to how they might implement the plan and various state governments took a practical approach to implementation to minimize adverse community impacts and to implement sectoral reforms of perceived net benefit to business and the community. Nevertheless, National Competition Policy is clearly aimed at an integrated national economic policy and more consistent business regulation nationally. Critics warned of the tensions between its agenda, harmonization, uniformity and decreased regulation, along with pressures for local diversity, and increased regulation.[34] States still compete for foreign corporate investment as well as areas such as taxes on "high roller" gambling which is seen as undercutting cooperative federalism.

Building on the Hilmer report in April 1995, the Commonwealth, state, and territory governments endorsed three intergovernmental agreements relating to National Competition Policy. States and territories agreed with its principles, subject to the proviso that recommendations apply to all Commonwealth and state government-owned enterprises and that states and territories share in the benefits of reform and privatization of state trading enterprises

and have the capacity to authorize exemptions from the *Trade Practices Act*.[35]
These committed the governments to implement significant reforms, aimed at
breaking down barriers to competition within and between public and private
sectors, starting with electricity, gas, and road transport.

COAG has dealt with a wide range of issues including microeconomic
reforms, social policy, environmental issues, intergovernmental administrative
issues, and regulatory reform issues. Its effectiveness in implementing intergovernmental reform on an unprecedented scale is attributed to the commitment
of Labor prime ministers (Hawke and Keating) and senior ministers within
these governments, to the reform agenda and the strategic placement of COAG's
Secretariat within the Office of Prime Minister and Cabinet.[36]

Painter points out that although the Commonwealth could go some way
on economic reform, constitutional limits mean that states control large sections of essential industry and infrastructure (such as housing, services,
transport, and energy) and are thus an integral partner in implementing national reforms. States often "possess both the jurisdictional competence and
the administrative capabilities" to implement national agendas.[37] From a states'
perspective, COAG is seen as a potential "circuit breaker" on Commonwealth
centralization of government processes and an ongoing forum separate from
traditional Premiers' Conferences. However, the Commonwealth was often seen
as setting the agenda: given "its dominant fiscal position and its advantage in
occupying the high ground of 'the national interest.'"[38]

COAG's success might be perceived as uneven, emphasizing
microeconomic reform, but having less success in negotiations on reforming
community services, child care, public housing, the environment, and Native
Title, and a lack of commitment to addressing the fundamental reform issue of
Commonwealth-state financial arrangements.[39] Although it is a significant
milestone in intergovernmental relations, taking a "whole-of-government" perspective on issues of national importance in recent years, it has been seen as a
Labor invention and has met less often since the election of the Howard government. Nevertheless, COAG reforms in program areas have emphasized the shift
to output-based funding systems and broadbanded funding of related programs.
This has given the states greater freedom in how they deploy funds, but has
tightened up constraints in terms of states having to demonstrate maintenance
of their own contributions. As Duckett observes, under federalism, responsibility is not shared in a coherent or consistent manner and comprehensive
national policies are difficult to achieve. The Commonwealth government, however, has played a central role in policy setting.

Post 1996: The National Commission of Audit

Given its centrality to the national reform of intergovernmental relations under the Howard government, elected in 1996, the National Commission of Audit merits brief examination. The report of the Commission expressed its concerns about the involvement of multiple levels of government, calling for a critical review of these arrangements.[40] The report was critical of government management and reinforced the need for greater productivity, accountability, efficiency, and "value for money." This coincided with the Howard government's commitment to small government and neo-liberal governance, realized in its downsizing of the Commonwealth Public Service from 350,400 to 244,200 people between 1996 and 1999 (a negative growth of –30.3 percent compared to cuts of –7.9 percent under Labor's last four years of government from 1992 to 1996).[41] The National Commission of Audit acknowledged that it may be impractical to cede responsibility entirely to one level of government. It argued that in such cases the Commonwealth could be required to set and monitor national standards with the states delivering the program services in line with these required standards. The Commission observed, however, that even with clear purchaser-provider delineation, it would be difficult to avoid pressures for state involvement in standard-setting or requests for additional funding and it would also be difficult to avoid Commonwealth involvement in program delivery as a way of verifying costs. The Commission concluded that there is no easy solution to this problem, but argued that where practicable, it is best to avoid multiple levels of government involvement. It therefore pressed for a review of all programs involving multiple levels of government.

The Commission identified cost-shifting as a major problem and argued that the allocation of related programs over different levels of government is a design defect that facilitates cost-shifting and even promotes incentives to engage in such practices. Accordingly, it put forth some program design principles to reduce cost-shifting.[42] It also laid down principles to apply to Commonwealth-state funding arrangements:

- for programs entirely the responsibility of the states, funding should be in the form of GPPs, allowing the states allocative discretion between specific programs;
- for programs where there is joint Commonwealth-state responsibility, funding should go to pools that extend to all related programs, rather than being earmarked to specific programs. Again this allows the states some allocative discretion within funding pools.[43]

- where Specific Purpose Payments are considered necessary, the Commonwealth should focus on specifying policy objectives and establishing improved accountability frameworks and give the states greater freedom in deciding program delivery. This would facilitate a reduction in the number of SPPs by grouping together or "broadbanding" SPPs which are directed at broad outcomes for particular groups. This would reduce administrative duplication, overlap, and inefficiency.

The National Commission of Audit was thus sympathetic to states' claims about the costs of duplication and the desirability of clear allocation of responsibilities; opting for an arm's-length role for the Commonwealth of setting national frameworks rather than delivering services itself. It took the strong view that the Commonwealth should not be involved in service delivery and thus set the scene for the radical outsourcing of government services.

As shown below, considerable effort to refine intergovernmental relations on disability policy has followed from the 1990s onwards.

DISABILITY: A COUNTRY PROFILE

Australians with a disability constitute a significant proportion of the Australian population and are a diverse group with regard to disability and need for, and use of, services.[44] Disability groupings (categorized on the basis of underlying impairment, disabling condition or cause, drawing on WHO categorizations) are used in Australia to differentiate activity restrictions and needs; with the main categories being: psychiatric, intellectual and other mental, sensory and physical.[45] Physical disabilities dominate, comprising 14.4 percent of all Australians; followed by sensory disabilities (2.1 percent), disabling conditions affecting intellectual abilities (1.4 percent), and psychiatric disabilities (1.4 percent).[46]

In 1998, 3,610,300 people (out of a national population of approximately 18.6 million) reported a disability; with 53.8 percent male and 46.2 percent female and 66 percent aged less than 65.[47] At this general level, more than half reported they did not need assistance, many were in the labour force and most of those needing assistance received it from their families. Rates of profound and severe activity restriction were lowest for those aged 15 to 34 and increased from 35 onwards, with higher rates of profound restriction for those over 70.

Between 1993 and 1998, the proportion of the total population reporting profound or severe core activity restriction had increased from 2.1 to 3.4

percent. Although this may partially reflect increased identification of people with disability, other explanations focus on population growth, the aging of the population, more people with disabilities (e.g., disabilities acquired through accidents) the shift toward community-based services rather than institutional care for older people and young people with a disability, pressure from early discharge in the acute care (hospital) sector and some changes in definitions used by the Australian Bureau of Statistics.[48] Rates of disability among indigenous Aboriginal and Torres Strait Islander peoples are higher (about double) those for the population generally and these groups have lower life expectancy than other Australians. However, rates of severe or profound disability are lower than expected for people from non-English-speaking backgrounds — especially the more recently arrived. This factor is related to immigration screening.[49]

Over the last two decades, the labour force participation of people reporting a disability has improved, although it remains lower than for the non-disabled population.[50] Women with disabilities earn less than their male counterparts, are less likely to be employed and have less access to labour market programs.[51]

The consideration of disability takes place within the context of population change, changes in aged care residential policy, increasing size of the potential target group, the aging of the target group, and the increasing number of Australians with disabilities living in community settings.[52] With aged care, these concerns are magnified in light of population projections of absolute and relative growth of those aged over 65, from 10.5 percent of the population in 1991 to 22 percent in 2041. Various surveys over time put the age standardized prevalence rate of "profound or severe" disability (used to establish dependency among the elderly) at 17 to 18 percent averaged over the 65 plus age groups. However, inferences that those over 65 represent a drain on the public purse require closer scrutiny. The more crucial variable is the proportion aged 80 or over, who are at greater risk of more costly illness and infirmity. The number of Australians aged over 80 will more than double in the decade from 1986 to 2006; with their proportion of the population increasing from 2 to 4 percent.[53] The other salient point is that gender combined with age, is an important determinant of the likely need and use of formal and informal care. Older women are more likely to enter residential care than older men — a probability of 0.76 for women and 0.48 for men aged over 80.[54] This reflects the fact that older men are more likely than women to have a spouse who will care for them at home. At the same time, increased participation of women in the workforce has diminished the family's capacity to provide high levels of unpaid care. Family fragmentation, geographic separation, and increasing female participation in paid work contribute to this diminished capacity and to increased demands on government for provision of support services.

Carer-focused policy is becoming more prominent as the contribution of the unpaid caring of family and community is realized. The 1998 Australian Bureau of Statistics survey of Disability, Agency and Carers recorded 435,527 people were primary carers for a person with disabilities, requiring assistance on a continuing basis. The majority were women (71 percent) and about one in five was aged over 65. Just over half those cared for were over 65 — indicating that disability and caring needs are not just concentrated among the aged.[55]

In terms of income support for people with disabilities, concerns about increasing numbers receiving Invalid Pensions led to its replacement by the Disability Support Pension in 1991, which supported 577,000 Australians in June 1999 (about 15 percent of the 3.7 million people reporting a disability). Rather than 85 percent permanent incapacity for work requirement for the Invalid Pension, the Disability Support Pension requires a minimum 20-percent impairment and an inability to work for at least 30 hours a week at full wages for at least the next two years. This is referred to as the "continuing ability to work" test. This means that significant numbers who fulfil the impairment criteria do not receive the pension as they have a significant capacity for work. However, the steady increase in pension recipients post-1991 indicates the role of broader factors: in particular, the impact of structural changes to the labour market marginalizing unskilled, semi-skilled, and older workers. At the same time, the increased employment participation of women has decreased the family's capacity to provide unpaid care. Even given an aging population, many see labour market factors as the main driver of the increasing proportion of people on income support due to disability. Prominent among new claimants for Disability Support Pensions are males aged 55 to 64, with musculo-skeletal impairments resulting from prolonged years of manual labour. At the point of writing, compared with unemployment benefits, Disability Support Pension payments give higher remuneration (as they are indexed to average weekly earnings rather than the consumer price index), they are subject to an income rather than the stricter asset test, they are subject to a taper to the assets test (rather than a straight cut-off), benefit from a Pensioner Concession Card, are not deemed to be taxable income (other income support payments are taxable), and avoid the activity or work tests applied to the unemployment New Start Allowance.

The Commonwealth Welfare Review expressed concern about rising expenditure on disability-related income security.[56] Although evincing agreement with broad principles, critics drew attention to high levels of unmet need for services, the inadequacy of current levels of income security in Disability Support Payments, the tightly targeted social-security system, high unemployment, and high levels of employer discrimination against people with disabilities in Australia.[57]

In terms of services provided for people with disabilities, those provided under the CSDA comprise: accommodation support (41 percent of service-providing organizations); community support (23 percent); community access (14 percent); employment support (14 percent) and respite (8 percent) (Table 2). The data on recipients of services show 30 percent receiving accommodation services; 20 percent receiving community support services; 20 percent receiving community access services; 26 percent receiving employment services and 4 percent receiving respite (Table 3). Table 4 shows the age distribution of recipients of CSDA services; reinforcing the point that services are provided across the age range. This flags a continuing concern in disability

TABLE 2

Commonwealth-State Disability Agreement-Funded Services: Service Type by Auspicing Organization, 1998

	Government				Non-Government			
	Common-wealth	State/ Territory	Local	Total	NGCSO*	Other	Total	TOTAL
Accommodation Support	–	944	29	973	949	603	1552	2,525 (41%)
Community Support	–	356	34	390	682	304	986	1,376 (23%)
Community Access	–	60	16	76	511	289	800	876 (14%)
Respite	–	138	13	151	205	119	324	475 (8%)
Employment Support	6	4	5	15	847	9	856	871 (14%)
TOTAL	6 (0.01%)	1,513 (24%)	98 (2%)	1,617	3,209 (52%)	1,348 (22%)	4,557	6,174 (100%)

Note: *NGCSO (Non-Governmental Community Sector Organization).

Source: AIHW, *Australia's Welfare 1999* (Canberra: Government Publishing Service, 1999), Appendix Tables, pp. 362-63.

policy debates that the focus on serving the increasing numbers of aged will further marginalize younger people with disabilities. However, it should be noted that given well-documented unmet need for services, these figures are indicative of services and service recipients rather than reflecting needs of the wider population of those with disabilities.

TABLE 3
Recipients of Commonwealth-State Disability Agreement: Type of Service, 1998

Accommodation Services	21,124	(30%)
Community Support	13,668	(20%)
Community Access	13,663	(20%)
Respite	2,564	(4%)
Employment Support	18,146	(26%)
Total	69,198	(100%)

Source: AIHW, *Australia's Welfare 1999* (Canberra: Government Publishing Service, 1999), Appendix Tables, pp. 363-64.

TABLE 4
Recipients of Commonwealth-State Disability Agreement: Age of Service Recipient, 1998

Age of Recipient	Number	%
0–9	5,438	7.8
10–19	7,130	10.3
20–29	16,085	23.2
30–39	16,617	24.0
40–49	12,248	17.7
50–59	6,375	9.2
60–69	2,230	3.3
70 or over	2,149	3.1
Not stated	926	1.4
Total	69,198	100.0

Source: AIHW, *Australia's Welfare 1999* (Canberra: Government Publishing Service, 1999), Appendix Tables, p. 364.

TABLE 5

Commonwealth Funding for Disability at State and Commonwealth Levels

A. *Specific Purpose Grants to States/Territories 1998–99*	
Health	
• HACC* (Home and Community Care)	$147,529
• Aged Care Assessment	$ 27,787
Social Security and Welfare	
• HACC* (Home and Community Care)	$349,407
• Disability services	$338,064
(financed under the Commonwealth Disability Program)	
• Supported Accommodation Assistance	$128,958
B. *Disability Program*	
(Commonwealth Department of Health and Family Services[1])	
Comprises:	
• Employment Assistance	$367,085
(an exclusive Commonwealth responsibility)	
• Transfer Payments under CSDA	$338,504
(Commonwealth-State Disability Agreement)	
• Access and Participation	$ 18,161
• Hearing services	$100,835
Total	$824,585

Notes: *HACC funding is used to fund home help, personal care, delivered meals, centre meals, home nursing, paramedical, centre day care, home maintenance/modification, home respite care and carer support.

    [1]The Disability Program Division of the Commonwealth Department of Health and Family Services (Canberra) promotes participation and choice in work and community life for people with disabilities. It administers funds to the states/territories under the Commonwealth-State Disability Agreement, to assist in promotion of accommodation and other support services; it provides funding to organizations under the *Disability Services Act 1986* to provide employment support, advocacy, and related services; and funding for research and development programs. It includes the Office of Disability, which advises the minister on objectives, priorities and strategic directions of the National Disability System including national directions, Commonwealth-state relations (including the Commonwealth-State Disability Agreement); forward planning and gaps in service provision and the strategic Management Branch, and the Office of Hearing Service, which manages the Commonwealth Hearing Services Program.

Source: Author's compilation based on T. Costello, *Budget Strategy and Outlook 1997–98*, Budget Paper Nos. 1 and 3. (Canberra: Australian Government Publishing Service, 1998); Department of Finance and Administration, Portfolio Budget Statements 1998–99: Health and Family Services Portfolio, Budget Related Papers No. 1.8. (Canberra: Department of Finance and Administration, 1998), p. 199.

INTERGOVERNMENTAL RELATIONS IN DISABILITY POLICY: AUSTRALIA

People with disabilities are supported by significant informal care and assistance from family and friends. Formal (government-funded) services mainly encompass income support (disability-specific income support), labour market programs, and job placement services for those with a disability, disability support services and relevant generic services (targeted to those with a disability).

Policy and practice in the disabilities field in Australia reflect a commitment to enhancing and protecting the lives of people with disabilities; to ensuring their respect as citizens; to maintaining their independent lifestyles in community settings; and to achieving a reasonable quality of life — through the provision of disability-specific services and modifications to mainstream services in order to increase accessibility. These accompanied concerns about the needs of carers and the role of government in providing support for the primary carers of people with disabilities. However, policy implementation is extremely complex in the area of disability, with continuing high levels of unmet need.[58]

The Formation of a National Agenda on Disability

A national approach to disability policy and service delivery was high on the agenda at the Special Premiers' Conference in 1991, and was the culmination of events outlined in the brief chronology below. The aim of this strategy was a national, whole-of-system, whole-of-government approach for a disability service system that promotes equity, service quality and cooperation and, at the same time, fosters local flexibility, responsiveness, and innovation. The major policy instruments in the development and refinement of intergovernmental relations in the disability area are summarized in Table 6. The initial 1991 CSDA aimed to establish a framework for rationalizing the administration of state and Commonwealth disability services and to develop a national, integrated system of services that was accessible, appropriate, and met individual needs. This agreement was renewed in late 1998 lasting through to 2002.

TABLE 6
Significant Events in National Australian Disability Policy

1985	*New Directions* report of the Handicapped Persons Review. Home and Community Care Program; establishment of the Office of Disability.
1986	*Commonwealth Disability Services Act* 1986 (came into effect June 1987). This Act set out seven Principles and 14 objectives which form the basis of current disability policy.
1988	Commonwealth Department of Community Services and Health published service type descriptions for each of the nine classes of eligible services approved under the Act (including supported employment and competitive employment training and placement services).
	Social Security Review Issues Paper No. 5, *Towards Enabling Policies: Income Support for People with Disabilities.*
	Minister for Social Security, Brian Howe established the Disability Task Force – an interdepartmental committee (role expanded in 1992).
1991	Commonwealth-State Disability Agreement (CSDA): funding and administration of employment, accommodation, and disability support services. The first national framework for disability services allocating responsibility to the Commonwealth for employment services and to the states for accommodation and support services.
	Disability Reform Package (reforming income support payments for people with disabilities to encourage labour force integration).
1991–93	States and territories implement *Disability Services Acts*; Commonwealth anti-discrimination legislation; Commonwealth and state Strategic Disability Plans.
1992	*Disability Discrimination Act* makes discrimination on the grounds of disability unlawful in certain areas of life, such as employment and protects those with a disability and their associates from unfair or unfavourable treatment based on their disability. It applies to all Commonwealth laws and programs.
1993	Disability Services Standards agreed among Australian governments.
1994	Commonwealth Disability Strategy (A ten-year framework for Commonwealth departments and agencies to ensure that programs, services, and facilities are accessible to people with a disability and to enhance access for people with disabilities to mainstream services).
1995	First progress report: Commonwealth Disability Strategy.
	Main report of the Evaluation and the Disabilities Reform Package (Disability Task Force). Endorsed at a joint meeting of the Australian Health Ministers' Conference and the Council of Social Welfare Ministers.

... continued

TABLE 6
(continued)

1996	Election of the Howard coalition, which suspends the implementation of the report of the Strategies Review of the Disability Services Program including implementation of performance-based funding.
	National Disability Advisory Council (replacing the Australian Disability Consultative Council: developing standards under the *Disability Discrimination Act* in five key areas: building codes, employment, public transport, information, and communication.
	National Carer Action Plan: establishment of a regional carer respite service infrastructure.
	Review of the CSDA.[59] Including the Demand Study providing national figures on unmet need for disability services in areas of accommodation support, respite care, post-school options and day activities.
1997	All Commonwealth departments, agencies, and authorities are required to have developed a Disability Action Plan under the *Disability Discrimination Act*.
	Disability Quality Assurance Working Party.
	Federal Review of the Disability Advocacy program.
	National disability advisory council established to advise on disability-related issues and to act as a liaison point between consumers, the industry, and government.
	Carer Pension changed to Carer Payment: increased flexibility for carers in receipt of pension to allow them to undertake some unpaid voluntary work.
	Second Progress Report: Commonwealth Disability Strategy.
1998	Formation of the Commonwealth Department of Family and Community Services bringing together income support and a range of community services (including specialist disability employment services) into a single department. Revision of Impairment Tables (first introduced in 1991) and introduction of Work Ability Tables to assist in the assessment of "continuing ability to work."
	From **May 1998**, Centrelink became responsible for eligibility assessment and for referring job-seekers with disabilities to the New Job Network or to specialist disability employment services.
	From **July 1998**, Carer Payment extended to people providing constant care and attention to children less than 16 years old, using Child Disability Assessment Table.

... continued

TABLE 6
(continued)

1998–99   Commonwealth-State Disability Agreement extended to June 2002. In addition
to outlining respective roles and responsibilities, the agreement provides a
national framework to underpin provision of specialist disability services,
acknowledges unmet needs for specialist disability services, specifies the criteria
for allocating new funds for population growth and unmet demand based on
population data adjusted for age, sex, severity of disability, and Aboriginality.[60]

1999 (July)   Carer Allowance combines Child Disability Allowance and Domiciliary
Nursing Care Benefit (means-tested supplements for people with significant
caring responsibilities).

2000   Report of the Disability Industry Reference Group; Report of the Commonwealth Welfare Review.

Funding and Administration

Services for people with disabilities are funded by the following means.
(i) Grants from the Commonwealth. Current Commonwealth-state expenditure
on disability includes SPPs to states/territories. This includes the HACC
program (with 60/40 Commonwealth/state funding) and payment for aged care
assessment. (ii) Expenditures by the Commonwealth via the Department of
Health and Family Services, under the Disability Program. These include expenditures on employment assistance (an exclusive Commonwealth
responsibility), transfer payments under the CSDA;[61] access and participation
programs and hearing services.[62]

In addition, other Commonwealth expenditure of a significant nature
includes payments of income support in the form of Disability Support Pensions and other payments. (iv) Commonwealth government Specific Purpose
Payments direct to local government authorities. (In 1998-99 approximately
$150,000 was paid by the Commonwealth to provide services for people with
disabilities.[63] (v) Expenditures by state and territory governments; in particular, Injury Compensation Schemes, accommodation and other support, and
Home and Community Care services; and (vi) Expenditures by local government and the non-governmental sector (as outlined in Table 1). Funding of
various services for people with a disability is complex and relies on a mixed

economy of care between all three tiers of government, the not-for-profit and the for-profit non-governmental sectors and the community or individual families.

Broadly speaking, the distribution of government funding and service provision for welfare services across various tiers of government and the non-governmental sector is shown in Table 7. About two-thirds of welfare services are funded and/or provided by governments (roughly one-third for each of Commonwealth and state governments) and one-third by the non-governmental sector (including non-governmental community service organizations and households). Across the broad range of welfare expenditure (including family and welfare services, welfare services for the aged, welfare services for people with a disability and other welfare services), from 1992–93 to 1997–98, just under one-third (30.2 percent) of recurrent expenditure on welfare services

TABLE 7

Funding and Provision of Welfare Services by Sector, 1994–95 to 1997–98 (percent)

	Government Sector				Non-Government Sector		
	Common-wealth	State/Territory	Local	Total	NGCSO*	House-holds	Total
Funding							
1994–95	34.0	29.0	1.2	64.2	11.7	24.2	35.9
1995–96	33.8	28.6	1.7	64.2	11.5	24.3	35.8
1996–97	34.0	29.0	1.2	64.2	11.7	24.2	35.9
1997–98	31.0	31.3 ˙	2.0	64.2	11.3	24.5	35.8
Four-Year Average	33.2	29.5	1.5	64.2	11.5	24.3	35.8
Provision							
1994–95	4.9	28.7	7.4	41.1	56.1	2.8	58.9
1995–96	3.6	27.3	7.8	38.8	58.7	2.5	61.2
1996–97	4.9	28.7	7.4	41.1	56.1	2.8	58.9
1997–98	3.9	27.2	7.2	38.2	59.4	2.4	61.8
Four-Year Average	4.4	28.0	7.5	39.8	57.6	2.6	60.2

Note: *NGCSO (Non-Governmental Community Sector Organization).

Source: AIHW, *Australia's Welfare 1999* (Canberra: Government Publishing Service, 1999), p. 16.

TABLE 8

Shifts in Commonwealth and State/Territory Recurrent Expenditure on
Welfare Services for People with a Disability, 1992–93 to 1997–98
(Constant 1996–97 prices, $000s)

	Recipients of Commonwealth Transfer Payments						
	Common-wealth	State/Territory	Local	NGCSO*	Total Common-wealth net of Outlays	State Expenditure	Total Common-wealth/State/Territory Outlays
1992–93	257,586	173,203	4,859	150,000	585,648	870,036	1,455,684
1993–94	161,336	314,135	3,914	147,574	626,959	966,777	1,592,736
1994–95	173,079	352,891	2,938	197,232	726,141	918,936	1,645,077
1995–96	153,522	375,025	3,170	210,619	742,335	902,178	1,644,512
1996–97	143,390	364,567	1,796	218,286	728,039	1,009,381	1,737,421
1997–98	133,143	386,560	1,950	235,830	757,483	1,073,360	1,830,843
(Shown as a % of Commonwealth Total Outlays)	(18%)	(51%)	(0.25 %)	(31%)	(100%)		

Note: *NGCSO (Non-Governmental Community Sector Organization).

Source: AIHW, *Australia's Welfare 1999* (Canberra: Government Publishing Service, 1999), p. 20.

was directed to services for people with a disability.[64] Table 8 shows trends in recurrent government expenditure. Reflecting the withdrawal of the Commonwealth from direct service provision following implementation of the 1991 CSDA, the table shows the decline in Commonwealth direct outlays and the concomitant increase in state and non-governmental sector transfer payments, as disability services are increasingly provided by these two sectors. As can be seen from Table 8, Commonwealth direct outlays on its own disability services have declined from 43 percent in 1992–93 to 18 percent in 1997–98 and state/territory transfer payments from Commonwealth sources have increased from 29 percent in 1992–93 to 51 percent in 1997–98. Over the same period, the balance between Commonwealth outlays (40 percent) and state expenditures net of Commonwealth transfers (59 percent) have remained the same. However, such broad figures on national averages do not have the capacity to reflect differences between the states in their commitments to welfare-related or disability service provision; and states differ on spending patterns on disability and on the proportion of expenditure allocated to disability-related services.

The CSDA

Most prominent among the milestones in National Disability Policy were the 1991 CSDA, its review in 1996, and the most recent 1998-99 CSDA which extends to 2002.[65] The CSDA sought to address the overlap and confusion in funding arrangements for disability services by making the Commonwealth responsible for employment services along with policy development and income support (Disability Support Pension); designating state/territory governments responsible for accommodation and related services, and with learning, advocacy, and research designated as joint responsibilities. States remained responsible for worker injury compensation.

The CSDA sought to provide a framework for rationalizing the administration of disability services by the Commonwealth and the states and to develop an integrated, national service system. It sought to address identified problems including inadequate data for planning and monitoring purposes; funding inequities between the states/territories, regions and individual clients; services that were unaccountable for their outcomes; overlap and confusion between funding from both levels of governments for the same service; lack of clarity for consumers regarding specific government responsibility for services; designation of services and responsibilities according to disability type rather than need; and duplication of effort between different levels of government.[66] The national framework outlined in the agreement was translated into a series of bilateral schedules for transfer of funds and services between the Commonwealth and state/territory governments.

In the following excerpt from Yeatman's comprehensive and insightful final report of the review of CSDA, she summarizes major achievements of the CSDA, the problems and the issues arising from the review.

The CSDA brought with it a number of important reforms and achievements:

- a real increase in the funding provided for disability services nationally;

- parallel legislation in each State and Territory to the *Disability Services Act 1986* (Commonwealth);

- greater clarity about the responsibilities of different levels of government;

- greater expertise and focus by governments;
- capacity for joint governmental approaches to policy, planning and funding; and
- a movement to outcomes approaches.

A number of new problems have emerged since the first Agreement. These include:

- gaps between employment and accommodation service systems;
- a lack of development of service types such as non-employment services and advocacy;
- access inequities across jurisdictions; and
- less cooperation and strategic planning between governments, especially in ways to meet the growing demand for support.

The main issues which commanded broad assent in community forums and submissions following the *Interim Report* were:

- concern about the extent of unmet need for services and supports for people with disabilities;
- the need for a new and stronger Agreement which builds on the work of the first Agreement, and provides a national framework for a more comprehensive, equitable and better coordinated service system;
- nationally consistent objectives, eligibility and assessment approaches for disability services across Australia with local flexibility, and individualised funding wherever possible;
- governments should be more accountable to stakeholders for how they are managing the disability service system;
- equipment and disability-related therapy, the needs of carers and children, should be covered under a new Agreement;
- concern about the lack of meaningful non-vocational activity services available to people with disabilities; and
- the need for better linkages between employment and other support services.[67]

A number of the review's findings merit particular attention in the light of Commonwealth-state relations. The review was critical of "a tight rationing culture" which has prevented strategic thinking and proposed that a broad mission for the disability services system should be "to identify and implement various forms of government-funded activity necessary to support people with disabilities and their primary carers without which neither of these groups would be able to maintain a reasonable quality of life or have access to the opportunities and environments available to other Australians."[68]

As outlined in the review, the broad aims of the CSDA were (i) to establish a framework for the rationalization of administration of disability services by the Commonwealth and the states, and (ii) to develop national systems of integrated services to ensure access for people with disabilities to appropriate services which meet their individual needs.[69] However, the review is critical that the focus has been almost entirely on the former; with significant progress in funding and administration (including needs-based planning, performance-based funding, brokerage and case management, institutional reform, service upgrading and quality standards). It was critical of the lack of national systematic development of these initiatives, inequities, inconsistencies, and duplication of effort along with implementation problems. The latter included different base calculations for various states, lack of overall plan monitoring and evaluation of implementation, inadequate funding for service upgrading and meeting unmet needs, lack of planning of joint initiatives among governments and differing interpretations of the agreement and its objectives. It also drew attention to the lack of publicly available information on expenditure and performance under the CSDA.

In all, the review reinforced the need for a national approach to disability services that fosters flexibility and individualization of service response. However, it was critical of the CSDA as a multilateral agreement: observing a predominance of a bilateral approach, with vertical line-type relationships between governments, and between governments and providers rather than horizontal cooperation or a true networking of systems and organizations. This was reflected in gaps in intersectoral linkages, lack of broad service objectives, inconsistent definitions of eligibility, lack of integrated data collection, and planning and standards development.[70]

The review argued that to deepen multilateral features of the system, a jointly owned, national management capacity is needed to set policy directions and it is important to monitor implementation and information and policy development. This approach builds on good state/local initiatives which require Commonwealth flexibility in negotiating program changes. This would involve a better understanding by each jurisdiction of each other's strengths, experiences and resources; a partnership between both levels of government with all jurisdictions willing to negotiate a workable management strategy;

and a national approach with networked delivery through public, community and private service arrangements, emphasizing "accountable, contestable and cost-effective outcomes." The review goes on to state that "the complexity of this service area is probably unique. What other service area demands the same capacity to work across a relatively large number of distinct program areas as well as many provider organisations of different sizes and types?"[71]

The CSDA funded 6,174 services nationally in 1998: with 41 percent accommodation support services, 22 percent community support services, 14 percent employment support services, 14 percent community access services, and 8 percent respite services for carers of people with a disability."[72]

Given the breadth of disability policy and service provision, the next section focuses on three brief case studies: employment assistance, Workers' Compensation, and Home and Community Care. The issues involved with a Commonwealth funded and delivered program, an area of state jurisdiction, and a joint Commonwealth-state funded program will be discussed.

Case Study 1: Employment Assistance Program for People with Disabilities

Under Commonwealth-State Disability Agreements the Commonwealth is responsible for employment services for the disabled (and the states for all other services including accommodation services). Special assistance to facilitate the employment of people with a disability was the subject of recommendations of the 1995 Baume report and an integral part of Labor's *Working Nation* active labour market policy (and before that, Commonwealth Disability Services).

However, from 1 May 1998, in line with National Competition Policy, the Commonwealth government moved into a competitive market for the delivery of all government-funded employment services, including services for those with a disability. The government's Commonwealth Employment Service (employing over 10,000 workers) was terminated and replaced by a new corporatized body, Employment National, which was established to compete with both commercial and not-for-profit non-government providers. All job-placement services were contracted-out following a national tendering process, with the group of successful bidders known as the *Jobs Network*. In the process, most previous labour market programs were cashed out and total expenditure for the employment services was reduced by approximately $1.8 billion over four years.[73] Many of the programs axed under these cuts were targeted at groups of long-term unemployed with special needs, including people with disabilities. One of the general trends following these dramatic funding cuts was the general shift from job training to job search. There were parallel cuts to Vocational Education and Training, with some states experiencing negative growth in expenditure and the Commonwealth criticized for not honouring its commitment to growth funding.[74] Emerging evaluations of the new *Jobs Network* note the focus of some commercially driven providers to offer little help apart from job search to the longer term, harder to place clients.[75]

As observed by the Australian Council of Social Services (ACOSS),[76] problems for access and equity have arisen as a result of the cashing out of previous labour market program funds in some areas of particular relevance to assisting those with a disability.[77] ACOSS was especially critical of the cashing out of funds for services such as mobility assistance, interpreter services, and disability access, and the lack of earmarked funds or specific performance requirements for such services in the new service agreements. It argued that provision of such services cannot be left to the market, and that there is a role for government.

The Commonwealth Review of Welfare Services is critical of the rise in government social security expenditure on Disability Support Pensions. An earlier paper flagged criticism of the rising incidence of people over 50 who are claiming income support (in particular the Disability Support Pension which is not an activity tested payment) the opportunities for early retirees to use up superannuation lump sums prior to pensionable age and the lack of mutual obligations on those receiving disability pensions.[78]

Critics of the new *Jobs Network* note its incapacity to respond to the diversity of labour market program needs of people with disabilities. A national peak advocacy organization, Women with Disabilities Australia, cites research showing that women have particular need for intensive assistance, that high effective marginal tax rates are a disincentive for those on pensions to work, and that women with disabilities have less access to and are less likely to use employment services than men.[79] A 1997 report highlighted the extent of unmet need for the employment focused Disability Reform Package; with provision for 27,000 places against estimated potential demand for 60,000 places per year.[80] By the year 2000, under its new name, the Competitive Employment, Training and Placement scheme, places had only increased to 28,500, despite the steep rise in need for such services.[81]

This case study illustrates the impact on a national program of funding cuts, shifts in program priorities, the impact of diminished capacity to service the special labour market program needs of people with disabilities, and the related impact of greater involvement of the for-profit sector.

Case Study 2: Workers' Compensation – A State Responsibility

Services for injuries in the workplace are a state responsibility, whereas Disability Support Pensions are a Commonwealth responsibility. On the face of it, whether responsibility for looking after a disabled person is a state or a Commonwealth matter should be straightforward; depending on whether or not the injury was work-related. However, this overlooks problems in determining whether an injury is work related (as e.g., with slow onset of injury or injury while travelling). Moreover, the needs of injured workers typically cross Commonwealth/state boundaries with demands on Commonwealth-funded programs including social security, medical and pharmaceutical services, rehabilitation and labour market programs; raising issues of cross payment between jurisdictions (e.g., the issue of brain injured younger people who are a state responsibility gaining access to Commonwealth aged-care funded nursing homes). There are also equity concerns, as the income benefits under state compensation schemes and under social security typically lead to different outcomes. From a national perspective, there is the added complication that compensation under state schemes varies from state to state (some states allow common law lump-sum settlements). These ambiguities regarding responsibilities and individuals' claims lead to accusations of cost-shifting from both levels of government, inefficient use of governments' resources, and to exclusion, poor servicing and inequities for injured persons. From a national perspective, workers' compensation is disjointed and fragmented, resulting in market interstate inequities.

Case Study 3: Home and Community Care – A Shared Commonwealth-State Program under the Commonwealth-State Disability Agreement

HACC was set up in 1985 to provide a comprehensive and integrated range of basic support services to older people, younger people with disabilities, and to carers: to enable people to live at home or in the community rather than in long-term residential care. It is an important part of Australia's response to the needs of people with a disability and is funded as a joint Commonwealth-state program, with the Commonwealth contributing 60 percent of funding. HACC is mainly concerned with services for older people, but has as another priority group, young people with moderate to severe disabilities; estimated at about 19 percent of HACC users.[82]

It relies substantially on a partnership model of government funding that in turn depends upon existing (women's) informal support networks in light of government's deinstitutionalization of aged and disability care. HACC funds are divided between the eight states and territories and then distributed by over 2,000 provider organizations nationwide.

Government policy has been driven by the twin objectives of the social benefits of maintaining people within the community and of cost-savings from transferring care of people with disabilities, the frail, and the dependent aged from long-term residential care to care within the community. Government has attempted to limit growth in nursing home bed numbers and has promised increased funding for community services; although unmet need for services for those with disabilities and their carers and government cuts to social and community services are sensitive issues.[83]

Some of the problems and policy challenges raised by the focus on HACC are outlined below and include shortfalls in appropriate levels of funding; the impact of tighter targeting, but increasing levels of unmet need; access to services; the impact of contracting-out and carers' issues.

Short Falls in Appropriate Levels of Funding

In Australia, the HACC program has not delivered the promised growth, due to lack of appropriate funding; although the 1998 agreement provided some recognition of population and wage-cost growth. At the start of the program, annual growth of 20 percent was promised, a rate that has not been met for the last ten years. The states have not met the matching requirements and the Commonwealth has continued to reduce its allocation.[84] The Commonwealth is committed to retaining a growth rate of 6 percent per annum in HACC funding, but this is partially funded by increased user fees and is well below the promised annual growth rate.[85] There is also the argument that funding for special new programs (such as the Staying at Home Package) has been at the expense of additional growth funds for HACC. However, there has been uneven regional and local distribution of funding; problems as a result of funding falling below service-delivery costs (requiring increased funding from councils); and the effect of expansion of linkages on demand and cost.[86]

Regarding funding for advocacy, a review of the National Disability Advocacy Program suggested the primary focus of advocacy funding should be directed toward the needs of individuals. This has been criticized by welfare bodies on the grounds that both individual and systemic advocacy "are essential partners in an effective strategy to improve access to and participation by, people with disabilities in community life."[87]

Tighter Targeting and Unmet Need for Services

As stated by the national welfare peak body, "The most recent national review of the HACC program estimated that it currently only meets 50 percent of the demand for services, and that this demand is growing at the rate of 2.7 percent per annum."[88] HACC illustrates the way that shifts to integrated targeted access to programs may undermine universalist assumptions about access and equity.

The State of Victoria serves as an appropriate example. Prior to the introduction of HACC in Victoria, a range of community support services was provided through generic agencies such as councils, non-governmental agencies, and district nursing services. These services had evolved largely in response to local circumstances since the 1940s, and were universally available. HACC specified its target group as frail older people, disabled younger people, and the carers of these people. Under HACC, funds are targeted to those at risk of admission to residential care.[89] It thus specifically excluded, or allocated to a "no-growth" category, other groups which historically had had access to community-based services. The use of increasingly tighter targeting strategies is now a key feature of community care.[90]

The AIHW estimated that 128,000 people in the "mild need" category, 12,700 in the "not determined category," and 10,600 in the "no handicap [sic] category," aged over 65, required assistance but did not get it for group two activities (moving around, home help, meal preparation, taking medicine or dressing wounds, financial management or shopping).[91]

According to some community activists, it is increasingly the case in Australia that those with lower needs in the context of tighter targeting and prioritizing are being excluded from subsidized care services and will either have to pay commercial rates, do without, or rely on the availability and willingness of unpaid help from families and friends.[92] This may also put at risk preventative aspects of the program. According to the national welfare peak body, "People with ongoing intensive care needs and those requiring post-acute care after (increasingly early) discharge from hospital are consuming more and more of the available resources."[93]

The Demand Study conducted as part of the review of the CSDA found "critical and urgent unmet need in virtually all areas of service provision."[94] In particular, it found that 13,500 people with severe and profound disabilities were in critical need of accommodation, accommodation support or respite services; 7,700 people with a severe and profound disability had a carer over the age of 65; and 7,000 carers of people with severe and profound disabilities said that they were unable to access respite care.[95] Significant under-use characterizes people with disabilities from non-English-speaking backgrounds and their carers; and further work is necessary into the needs of Aboriginal and Torres Strait Islanders with disabilities.

In terms of drawing out the broader implications of increased targeting, HACC both illustrates the move toward greater strategic control at the centre, and the complications and potential hazards of service rationalization. Clearly, increasing targeting is leading to bigger holes in the social safety net; with those clearly in need missing out on services, resulting in greater pressure on the community sector.

Access to Services

The main official criterion for access to both institutional and community services (even meals services), as well as certain cash benefits paid to the disabled or their carers, is "medical need." Many frail, elderly people, especially the mentally confused, do not qualify for a service in terms of strict medical need. Similarly, payment of a minimal cash benefit for home carers of the frail elderly requires a medical practitioner to certify that a patient has "a continuing need for nursing care." In fact, only a minority of carers receive this allowance, in large part because it is only paid when the elderly person also receives continuing care from a home nursing service.

Contracting-out

Transposed upon these changes is the shift from local council or non-profit organizations as service providers toward private (for-profit) providers, under policies of contracting-out. Unlike residential care, where the private for-profit sector has traditionally played a major role in service delivery, community care services have until recently been delivered by the public, not-for-profit sector, with a mix of government funding and heavy reliance on the contribution of informal care provided by family members (women) and the non-profit sector. With local government as a major traditional provider of home-care services, there are concerns about the impact of local government restructuring and the introduction of contractualism (especially in the State of Victoria, where the Kennett government mandated that 50 percent or more of services were to be contracted-out by June 1997 under local government Compulsory Competitive Tendering reforms).

Contracting-out raises issues of variations in standards, commitments, and quality of care, as state government funding flows to local government which then outsources service provision. Contractualism also shifts the goal posts in relation to consumer complaints and quality of service issues, with the erosion of the once essential building blocks of service quality (integration, cooperation, support, and a philosophy of public service and communal benefit). Contractual agreements rely on pre-specified outcome measures and performance appraisals, which frequently favour easily measured quantitative dimensions. Clear specification of outcome measures in the aged and disability care areas is difficult, given the varied client mix, the range of chronic and acute conditions, and varied formal and informal sector services.

At a general level, privatization and contracting-out have significantly shifted the nature of government community care programs and practices from public provision to market management under contractualism with declining budget allocations.[96] While competition may bring value for money, flexibility and choice, this may be at the expense of quality service outcomes and respect for rights and entitlements (such as access and equity considerations), service reliability, standardized quality and geographical availability, of home and community care.[97]

Findings from the *Compulsory Competitive Tendering (CCT) Research Project* on mainly women carers and service users of local government aged and disability services in the State of Victoria, found that contracts were won at the expense of workers' wages and conditions; there were minimal public consultations regarding the introduction of CCT; and some councils referred clients to private (fee-paying) services which they say they cannot afford. Finally, some services were reduced to the lowest common denominator with a reduction in the "less tangible human care and concern" and social support aspects of services.

Carer's Issues

Most chronically ill people living at home are not cared for by the community but by their female relatives. They are not kept out of institutions by the provision of formal community services. Rather, they receive substantial amounts of women's care — with or, more commonly without, formal support from community-based services. The state's dependence on families and in particular, on women as carers, is increased with the impact of changes to state-based provision of health care, such as hospital early discharge policies and "hospital in the home" in the acute-care sector and the shift from residential to contracted and privatized aged and community care services. Allocations to HACC and disability services fall far short of meeting a significant fraction of demand.

The costs to carers are often considerable. Economic costs include lost earnings and additional expenses, among others.[98] Over one-third of Australian carers give up paid employment in order to look after an elderly relative.[99] There are the costs of providing extra heating, transport, laundry, food, aids such as grip rails and bath chairs, and other house modifications. It is important to remember in this context that it is the very poorest elderly people who live with their adult children and, given income patterns in families, it is likely that their children will also be at the lower end of the income spectrum.[100] The costs of caring may well involve further pushing carers into poverty.[101]

Community services provide minimal support to family carers. Although the average elderly home-care patient living with his or her family is more disabled than the average frail older person living alone, two of the main forms of domiciliary care — home help and meals on wheels — are often not available to people living with relatives.

A report from the Victorian component of a national study of carers highlighted the problem of jargon-laden information; it also noted the inaccessibility to services for rural and outer suburban carers and persisting gaps in suitable respite options for carers. Noting some of the positive initiatives of a regional carer respite service infrastructure, recent neo-liberal reforms, local government amalgamations, increasingly restrictive targeting, cost-containment, and user pays policies "have seemingly all acted to constrain the beneficial impact of the various carer initiatives."[102]

As the review of the CSDA observed, in a sector that is under-resourced, complex, and heterogeneous, it is easy to be overwhelmed by the challenges of turning it into a better-managed and fairer service delivery system. As Lindsay observes, the disability services area is characterized by duplication, overlap, and gaps in the provision of, and access to, needed services.[103] State/territory and Commonwealth governments are responsible for home and community service programs established over many years, which have evolved in an ad hoc manner in response to needs and demands rather than coherent planning. "The result is a complex, fragmented maze of services, each with different administrative and funding arrangements and different target groups and each responsible to different levels of government."[104] Ambiguities in the division of Commonwealth and state responsibilities invite attempts to shift costs, as in the case of Commonwealth responsibility for aged residential care and the states' responsibility for accommodation support under the CSDA. The Commonwealth has argued that younger people with acquired disabilities should not be accommodated in its nursing homes and aged care residential accommodation and see this as cost-shifting on the part of the states. The Commonwealth argues that as they age, those with acquired disabilities should be supported in the community rather than in aged residential care. On the other hand, states argue that older people with lifelong disabilities should have equity of access to residential care with other aged people.[105]

It is at the point of service delivery that many of the above issues come to a head. It is often the case that similarly injured or disabled individuals are dealt with differently. A report from the State of Victoria questioned the capacity of the current system to offer access to appropriate services, service integration or continuity of care. With over 3,000 separate providers across its divisions of Disability, Youth and Family, and Aged, Community and Mental Health services, it noted fragmentation, lack of navigability and overspecialization as problems, along with service gaps in particular geographic areas and maldistribution of resources in relation to target populations.

ASSESSING AUSTRALIAN DISABILITY POLICY AND PROGRAMS FROM AN INTERGOVERNMENTAL PERSPECTIVE

How is Disability Policy Working?

In concluding this review of intergovernmental approaches to disability policy and service provision, there is a clear need to address overlap between disability and other policy areas such as aged and community care and state-based Workers' Compensation Schemes.

Yeatman noted the need to bring aspects of community and residential care for the frail and aged into strategic alliance with the disability services sector; involving, for example, disability aspects of the Home and Community Services Program and the Commonwealth Rehabilitation Service.[106] Yeatman notes that the disability sector is not reducible to service categories as aged care tends to be and highlights the needs of young children and adults throughout the lifecycle.

Duplication between governments can undermine effectiveness. Reviews of the CSDA have pinpointed the need for greater flexibility and coordination in service provision, lack of adequate planning, the need to improve assessment and service targeting; overlap and gaps in services, cost-shifting, lack of consistent data across the system, and lack of coordination between related services; significant inequities in service provision between regions and states; and failure to meet demand.[107]

Increasing consumer co-payments are concerning. One area where consumer out-of-pocket expenses are substantial is aids and appliances: with consumers expending over half the costs.[108] With approximately one-fifth of the population with a disability of some kind, this suggests consumers meet a significant proportion of expenses related to dealing with their disabilities.

Disability policy lacks a holistic approach. The CSDA tends to compartmentalize needs and responses with the consequence that services lack integration and inter-agency cooperation and thus waste resources and compound inefficiency. Some states such as New South Wales have proposed the use of a unified intake and assessment process for a range of aged care, community nursing, and disability support services rather than separate assessments for individual services.[109] With service provision at the state level, uneven standards and levels of innovation characterize the sector.

With acknowledged reliance on private provision of care, lack of appropriate access to carer support and respite has emerged as an important issue of unmet need. The CSDA review pinpointing carers with sustained negative coping experiences included those caring for a handicapped child (often with an intellectual or cognitive disability) and those in poor socio-economic circumstances with limited family support.[110] In the light of increasing demand for community support services, carers' issues are also picked up by other studies, highlighting the need to focus on the "care-giving unit" (rather than on the carer or care recipient) and on preventative and maintenance support services to all care situations in need (rather than on the "complex needs" end of the system).[111]

Despite the national agenda on disability policy and services, significant intersectoral issues still plague the area. There is a need to address the impact of other policy mainstream developments for those with disabilities and improvements to linkages between say, employment and other services.

The three case studies above and the foregoing analysis cannot be separated from the broader public and government policy context; in particular the reform thrust of the Coalition government in relation to welfare policy reform and the impact of the new goods and services tax in force from 1 July 2000.

Welfare Reform

Both sides of politics have pursued an economic agenda oriented to smaller government and curbs on social spending; although the differences between Labor and Coalition governments in expenditure growth in health, education, and community services are evident.[112] Both have sought to create the context within which competitive markets might facilitate efficiencies and deliver growth and trickle-down benefits, although there are discernible differences in policy responsiveness to evidence on growing poverty and increasing polarization of work rich and work poor families.[113]

In late 1999, the Howard government expressed its concern that income support payments (representing some 3 percent of GDP in 1998) are being provided to growing numbers of recipients with a disability, in proportions far higher than in previous decades.[114] Of the 2.6 million workforce age people receiving income support payments, 21 percent were in receipt of disability support pensions primarily because they have a disability that prevents paid employment.[115] This has been seen by many as a high rate, given Australia's population.

These figures partly reflect the aging of the population, but are largely labour-market driven. Over half of the new claimants of a Disability Support Pension comprise pre-retirement age older males (aged 55 to 64) with musculo-skeletal impairments. This combines the phenomenon of "worn out bodies" from prolonged periods of manual labour with the decline of manual jobs growth and recent trends of retrenchments among older, especially male, full-time workers. Disability Support Pension has picked up those marginalized by the labour market yet too young to qualify for the Age Pension. Given Commonwealth responsibility for social security pensions and benefits and labour market programs, this growth in expenditure has resulted in revised assessment processes from 1996–97 which do not appear to have substantially reduced the upward trend in disability pensioners.

The welfare review, (in fact more a review of social security and an attack on welfare dependency) focuses on controversial concepts of mutual obligation and government concerns regarding the sustainability of paying for the current system and "incentive effects associated with the design of social security payments."[116] The disability lobby has responded with the reposte that the proposed "participation support" framework for welfare reform needs a major injection of funding from the Commonwealth to achieve participation support.[117] The welfare sector has been vocal in its criticism of the review as victim-blaming and lacking in analysis of broader issues of social exclusion and inequality and poor jobs generation. The review also comes at a time of uncertainty regarding the short and longer term impacts of taxation reform with the implementation of a new goods and services tax (GST).

The New Goods and Services Tax

In terms of Commonwealth taxation, excise duties covered by section 90 of the Constitution, have been interpreted to include broad-based consumption or general sales taxes. This enabled controversial passage of federal legislation in 1999 to implement a new national GST, operational from 1 July 2000.[118] This has been described as the biggest shakeup for federal-state relations in Australia's history, as taxes collected under the GST will be treated as state and territory revenue. From 30 June 2000, revenue from a GST will replace General Revenue Assistance and some specified state taxes (including whole-sale tax, bed taxes, Financial Institutions Duty (FID) and debits tax).[119] Exemptions will be granted to various health, community, and charitable services: including aged care residential facilities, home-based aged care, and disability services. The flat tax on goods and services and personal tax cuts accompanying the introduction of the GST will impact disproportionately on low-income households, whilst advantaging those on higher incomes.

Whether or not states will be better off under the new tax package is currently open to speculation. Some argue that once the amended GST package is implemented, vertical fiscal imbalance will be worse than under the previous system; especially with predicted reduced revenue following amendments that exempted food from a GST; thus reducing the GST revenue flow to the states. Others run the counter-argument that the revenue-raising potential of the GST has been under-estimated. Welfare lobbyists have argued that the GST is a regressive tax, taking higher proportions of lower income household incomes. Although education and health are exempt, related products such as books are not and trade-offs against cuts in income taxation will not assist those on pensions and fixed incomes. Moreover, since people with disabilities face additional costs compared with the general population, the disability lobby argue a GST will add disproportionately to their tax burden. Not surprisingly, some states are now vocal in arguing that a GST will be inadequate in rectifying vertical fiscal imbalance, since it may signal both less income and less leverage with the Commonwealth. In the past, Premiers' Conferences have been a forum for states' demands for increases in General Revenue Assistance. When such funding is replaced by a GST based on states' proportionate GST earnings, this may largely preclude traditional haggling over general purpose funds.

States have argued that they lack the broad revenue base needed to respond flexibly to rising service delivery demands and that their reliance on other revenue sources, such as increasing taxes on business and gambling, may be counter productive for investment and growth or for equity.[120] In addition, some states, such as Victoria, have eroded their traditional revenue base by selling off state-owned enterprises under privatization agendas. These changes do not augur well for states' perceiving they have an adequate revenue base to deliver on national service priorities or on their own needs. On the other hand, if GST revenue increases, then it is likely that the Commonwealth will find ways of rolling back its commitments to the states made through SPPs under agreements timed for reconsideration around 2002–05.

CONCLUSION

In Australia, the disability policy area is characterized by attempts to achieve a nationally integrated system; efforts which are marred by inertia, funding difficulties in relation to unmet need and increasing demand, uneven commitment by the states on social spending; duplication and overlap of effort; cost-shifting between levels of government; and problems on the ground in terms of the governments' success at meeting the needs of people with disabilities and their carers.

The disability policy area has undergone some major shifts over the last 15 to 20 years. In brief, these encompass: a shift from residential institutional care to care in the community, and with that, a focus on normalizing and mainstreaming people with disabilities into community services, employment and recreation; shifts in employment for people with disabilities from sheltered workshops and Activity Therapy Centres to work in the community at standard rates of pay and conditions; efforts by governments to rationalize roles and responsibilities in the disabilities policy and services area; and efforts of governments at all levels to reduce their role in direct service provision and to become funders and/or purchasers rather than providers, of services in line with government-wide microeconomic reforms and National Competition Policy.

In terms of driving a national agenda on disability policy reform, Special Premiers' Conferences and COAG played a pivotal role in securing agreement between Commonwealth and states/territories on a major national reform agenda for disability policy and services delivery. In 1991, leaders and representatives agreed to proceed with rationalization of roles and responsibilities of disability services. There followed state legislation complementary to the *Commonwealth Disability Services Act* agreement about Commonwealth funding to the states to cover services transfer and growth of services costs and a division of responsibilities. The Commonwealth took full responsibility for employment and training and placement services for people with disabilities and the states took responsibility for accommodation support, information services, independent living training, recreation services and respite care; with joint responsibility for planning, priority-setting, and program evaluation.

These changes have come at a time of government undergoing monumental reforms under managerialist administrative changes and microeconomic reform agendas, designed to reduce government spending, and to enhance Australia's international competitiveness. This has entailed a government focus on re-defining policy responsibilities between various levels of government; government attempts to shift responsibilities back onto individuals in ways that are perceived by critics as punitive; reducing Commonwealth involvement in direct service provision by transferring services to the states/territories and to the community sector and to families; and the pursuit of microeconomic reforms based on a purchaser-provider split, contracting-out of services to the private sector, user charging, and public subsidy of privately provided services.

The problems and challenges outlined above are viewed by many with a degree of scepticism about the success of the current reform agenda. Those with severe or multiple disabilities have often been moved out into the community without sufficient resourcing or provision of appropriate supports; with the result that for women carers in particular, quality of life has deteriorated. Those with similar disabilities may be treated very differently under state and Commonwealth compensation schemes and those marginalized by structural changes such as labour market changes limiting employment opportunities, may be pressured to bear individual responsibility for their misfortunes. Commentators charge not only government with responsibility, but criticize service providers, advocates, and peak bodies for thwarting some of the attempts at innovation.

NOTES

[1]Apart from references to overseas useage, the term disability is preferred to handicap in Australian policy discussions. Australian Institute of Health and Welfare (AIHW), *Australia's Welfare 1995* (Canberra: Australian Government Publishing Service, 1995), p. 240.

[2]Brendon Gleeson, "Disability and Poverty," in *Australian Poverty: Then and Now*, ed. R. Fincher and J. Nieuwenhuysen (Carlton: Melbourne University Press, 1988), pp. 316-17.

[3]Commonwealth Department of Family, *The Future of Welfare in the 21st Century: What is the Welfare System and Who Uses It?* (Canberra: Commonwealth Department of Family, 1999); AIHW, *Australia's Welfare 1996* (Canberra: Australian Government Publishing Service, 1996); AIHW, *Australia's Welfare 1997* (Canberra: Australian Government Publishing Service, 1997); AIHW, *Australia's Welfare 1999* (Canberra: Australian Government Publishing Service, 1999); Anna Howe, *HACC Status Report for Victorian Local Government* (Melbourne: Municial Association of Victoria, 2000).

[4]The Australian Commonwealth comprises six states (Victoria, New South Wales, Queensland, Western Australia, South Australia, Tasmania) and two Territories, the Northern Territory and the Australian Capital Territory. In subsequent discussion, reference to states will be taken to include territories.

[5]Introduced in 1980, Invalid Pension was replaced by the Disability Support Pension in 1991 under the Labor government's Disability Reform Package.

[6]Martin Painter, *Collaborative Federalism: Economic Reform in Australia in the 1990s* (Cambridge: Cambridge University Press, 1998), p. 156.

[7]Local government typically encompasses cities, towns, shires, boroughs, municipalities, and district councils; with a focus on road and bridge construction and maintenance, water sewerage and drainage systems, health and sanitation services, building supervision and administration of regulations; along with some service provision in recreation, culture, and community services. Its revenue source comprises direct grants from the Commonwealth (about 20 percent of revenue), grants from state governments and local government revenue — mainly property taxes along with fines and service charges. In recognition of the significant role played by local government in areas such as health and community services, the Council of Australian Governments has included local government representation since 1996.

[8]H. Emy and O. Hughes, *Australian Politics: Realities in Conflict*, 2d ed. (Melbourne: Macmillan, 1991), p. 305.

[9]Federal-State Relations Committee of the Parliament of Victoria (FSRC) (Melbourne: Government Publishing Service, 1998), p. xvii. As well, for a summary of the background to federation, see Christine Fletcher, *Responsive Government: Duplications and Overlap in the Australian Federal System*, Discussion Paper No. 3. (Canberra: Federalism Research Centre, 1991).

[10]Brian Galligan, "What is the Future of the Federation?" *Journal of Public Administration*, 55, 3 (1996):78-79.

[11]FSRC, *Australian Federalism*, p. xx.

[12]Section 90 defines the exclusive powers of the Commonwealth government over coining of money, initiation of referendums for constitutional change, and customs and excise.

[13]Painter, *Collaborative Federalism*, pp. 6-7.

[14]FSRC, *Australian Federalism*, Vol. 2, p. 8-9.

[15]Several High Court decisions have expanded the scope for Commonwealth powers, including the Tasmanian dam case in 1983 and the Lemonthyme and Southern forests case of 1987–88, and later the Mabo (1992) and Wik (1996) cases relating to Native Title. Among the most controversial for changing the federal-state balance are section 51 (xxix) cases, dealing with the Commonwealth's power over external affairs. These cases concern the Commonwealth overriding the states in areas affected by Australia being a signatory to international agreements; although the use of section 51 is limited to agreements that are "genuine and not entered into simply as a contrivance to gain power over the States" and legislation cannot extend beyond the implementation of the treaty. See Brian Galligan, *The Politics of the High Court* (St. Lucia: University of Queensland Press, 1987); and Shane Solomon, *The Political Impact of the High Court* (Sydney: Allen & Unwin, 1992).

[16]In 1997, in the High Court cases of *Ha v. New South Wales* and *Hammond and Associates v. New South Wales*, the court struck down New South Wales tobacco licence franchise fees as an unconstitutional levying of excise; although the Commonwealth undertook to pay for lost business franchise licence fees in Revenue Replacement Payments (since franchise fees represent a substantial 12–13 percent of state taxation revenue.)

[17]The High Court of Australia has powers granted under the Constitution to review Commonwealth and state legislation in terms of its constitutionality. It thus influences the federal system and the federal balance of power through its interpretations. Importantly, several state challenges to Commonwealth dominance over uniform income taxation have failed.

[18]FSRC, *Australian Federalism*, p. xxii.

[19]D. James, *Commonwealth Assistance to the States since 1976*, Background Paper No. 5. (Canberra: Parliamentary Library. Parliament of Australia, 1997), p. 2; and FSRC, Vol. 2.

[20]T. Costello, *Budget Strategy and Outlook 1999/2000*, Budget Paper No. 1. (Canberra: Australian Government Publishing Service, 1999), Table 1; and Budget Paper No. 3, Chart 3.

[21]Commonwealth payments to the states and territories may also take the form of payments for recurrent or capital purposes, general purpose capital assistance (such as the Building Better Cities Program), loans to the states (the Loans Council Program was abolished by the Keating government in 1994–95) and National Competition payments, from 1995.

[22]General Revenue Assistance is paid as:

Financial Assistance Grants (FAGs) were put in place in 1942–43 to compensate states for Commonwealth wartime levying of income taxation. The level of grants is indexed to annual movements in the consumer price index and projections of population as at 31 December each year.

Special Revenue Assistance Grants to the Northern Territory and the Australian Capital Territory (0.07 of general revenue assistance); and National Competition Payments are conditional on states' compliance with the obligations of the 1995 COAG Agreement (2.3 percent of general revenue assistance).

General revenue assistance to the states comprised 51 percent of total payments to the states in 1998–99 (Budget Paper No. 3, Table 6).

[23]General Revenue Assistance comprises payments to the states with grant distributions based on principles applied by the Commonwealth Grants Commission. Financial Assistance Grants (FAGs) account for 97 percent of general revenue assistance. Horizontal fiscal equalization principles are embodied in the per capita relativities recommended by the Commonwealth Grants Commission, with the aim of improving equity for all Australians (see Costello, *Budget Strategy and Outlook 1997–98*, Budget Papers Nos. 1 and 3). States are not required to use the funds on specific areas of government activity; however, the Commonwealth can stipulate that states meet certain conditions for the receipt of funds. Under the 1995 Agreement on National Competition Policy and Related Reforms, the Commonwealth agreed to maintain a real per capita guarantee of FAGs on a rolling three-year basis, subject to states' progress in the implementation of National Competition Policy, monitored by the National Competition Council. Under the agreement, states are eligible for three tranches of ongoing National Competition Payments; paid on an equal per capita basis, with each state's payments conditional upon the National Competition Council's review of satisfactory progress on the implementation of specified reform conditions in the agreement (see Budget Paper No. 3, p. 12).

[24]Ibid.

[25]James, *Commonwealth Assistance to the States*, p. 1.

[26]Of the four programs relating to VET, two are specifically aimed at improving indigenous education outcomes, one is for English for Migrants and the fourth, allocating the major proportion of funds (over $865 million in 1998–99) is aimed at promoting a nationally identifiable and consistent vocational education and training system.

[27]These grants increased during the Whitlam Labor government from 25.8 percent of Commonwealth transfers to the states in 1972–73 to 48.5 percent in 1975–76. Under the Fraser Liberal government, they fell to 41.5 percent in 1980–81 and to 32.7 percent in 1981–82 and they grew again under the Hawke/Keating Labor governments to 52.8 percent in 1995–96. SPPs were reduced under the Howard Coalition to 50 percent in 1998–99, and are falling to around 49 percent of total payment to states in 1999–2000, see James, *Commonwealth Assistance to the States*, pp. 15-29; and Costello, Budget Paper No. 3, ch. 3, p. 17.

²⁸Painter, *Collaborative Federalism*, p. 153.

²⁹By way of brief description of the workings of the Australian political system, Australia has a bicameral system of government with upper and lower houses. Framers of the Australian Constitution saw the Senate as a means of protecting state/ territory rights from being dominated by political party influences. But as argued by numerous commentators, in reality, the Senate does not function as a states/territories' house, see J. Warden, "Federalism and the Design of the Australian Constitution," Discussion Paper No. 19. (Canberra: Federalism Research Centre, 1992). For policies to become law, bills must achieve a majority in the Senate as well as in the lower House of Representatives.

³⁰FSRC, *Australian Federalism*, p. xxi.

³¹Hawke's New Federalism is important for its commitment to responsiveness to local needs and the needs of regional diversity, delivery of quality cost-effective services (removing duplication between various government levels), a competitive national economy based on "competitive federalism," a guaranteed revenue base that matches states' and territories' expenditure responsibilities and a federation that is accountable through Parliament, see Leader's Forum, *Communiqué* (Canberra: Commonwealth of Australia, 25 November 1994). Four principles mark Labor Prime Minister Hawke's New Federalism: the Australian Nation principle; the subsidiary principle; the structural efficiency principle; and the accountability principle. See Kenneth Wiltshire, "The Directions of Constitutional Change: Implications for the Public Sector," *Australian Journal of Public Administration*, 55, 1 (1996):95-110. While these reforms are mainly discussed as cooperative federalism, Painter notes that recently, state government leaders have articulated a model of "competitive federalism" as a way of justifying their autonomy as a defence against Commonwealth domination of collaborative institutions, Painter, *Collaborative Federalism*, p. 7.

³²Martin Painter, "The Council of Australian Governments and Intergovernmental Relations: A Case of Cooperative Federalism," *Publius*, 26 (1996):101-20.

³³F.G. Hilmer, *National Competition Policy: Report of the Independent Committee of Inquiry* (Canberra: Australian Government Publishing Service, 1993).

³⁴E. Harman and F. Harman, "The Potential for Local Diversity in Implementation of the National Competition Policy," *Australian Journal of Public Administration*, 55, 3 (1996):111-17.

³⁵Governments signed the *Competition Code Agreement,* the *Competition Principles Agreement,* and the *Implementation and Funding Agreement,* commencing 1997–98. These were consistent with the six areas identified by the Hilmer report requiring action to remove barriers to competition in the Australian economy: limiting anti-competitive conduct of firms; reforming regulation that unjustifiably restricts competition; reforming the structure of public monopolies to facilitate competition; providing third-party access to certain facilities essential for competition; restraining monopoly pricing behaviour and fostering "competititve neutrality" between government and private business when they compete. See Hilmer, *National Competition Policy*, p. xvii.

[36]Prime minister and Cabinet played a central role in providing chairs of committees and working groups, drafting reports and communiqués and keeping track of business. See Painter, *Collaborative Federalism,* p. 67.

[37]Ibid., p. 6.

[38]Ibid., p. 89.

[39]P. Hendy, "Intergovernmental Relations," *Australian Journal of Public Administration,* 55,1:111-17, p. 112.

[40]National Commission of Audit, *Report to the Commonwealth/National Commission of Audit* (Canberra: Australian Government Publishing Service, 1996).

[41]L. Hancock and S. Cowling, *A Commitment to Public Service? Trends in Commonwealth Social Expenditure and Employment in the 1990s* (Melbourne: Centre for Public Policy, University of Melbourne, 2000), p. 14.

[42]National Commission of Audit, *Report,* pp. 47-48.

[43]Funding for disability services under the Commonwealth-State Disability Agreement is the major program relevant to disability.

[44]Disability is defined as those "who have any restriction or lack of ability (because of impairment) to perform an action in the manner or within the range considered normal for a human being; and hardship is differentiated into profound, severe, moderate and mild — indicating different levels of need," see Australian Bureau of Statistics, *Disability, Ageing and Carers: Summary of findings,* Cat. No. 4430.0. (Canberra: Australian Government Publishing Service, 1999). Disability referred to the presence of one or more of 17 restrictions, limitations or impairments identified by respondents. Australia follows international classifications of disability; recognizing the three dimensions of disability in the *International Classification of Impairments, Disabilities and Handicaps* followed by the WHO: body structure and function, activity and participation, AIHW, *Australia's Welfare 1999,* p. 214.

[45]AIHW, *Australia's Welfare 1999,* p. 219.

[46]Ibid.

[47]Australian Bureau of Statistics, *Disability, Ageing and Carers.*

[48]Ibid., AIHW, *Australia's Welfare 1999,* p. 221; Gleeson, "Disability and Poverty," in *Australian Poverty,* p. 324; Julie Nankervis and Joyce Rebeiro, *Carers Speak Out: A Consultation on Community Services with Carers in the Southern Metropolitan and Grampians Regions* (Melbourne: Carers Association of Victoria, 2000).

[49]AIHW, *Australia's Welfare 1997,* p. 304.

[50]The labour force participation rate of males reporting a disability (60 percent) is about 30 points lower than for males with no disability; and for females (46 percent) it is about 25 percent lower than the comparator for females without a disability, AIHW, *Australia's Welfare 1999,* pp. 49-52).

[51]Women with Disabilities Australia, submission to the federal government's Reference Group on Welfare Reform, WWDA, 1999.

[52]Since 1997, nursing homes and hostels have been brought together into a single residential aged care system. This includes a single instrument for classifying

residents according to care needs and the use of accommodation bonds, charges, and means-tested fees, see AIHW, *Australia's Welfare 1999*, pp. 208-09, 225.

[53]AIHW, *Australia's Welfare 1997*, p. 241.

[54]Ibid., p. 251.

[55]AIHW, *Australia's Welfare 1999*, p. 208.

[56]Commonwealth Department of Family, *The Future of Welfare in the 21st Century*; Women with Disabilities Australia.

[57]Australian Council of Social Services (ACOSS), "Reforming Welfare," *Impact*, February 2000.

[58]AIHW, *Australia's Welfare 1999*; see Appendix, Table 1 for a summary of formal services in Australia relevant to people with a disability and the sectors that provide funding and/or services; also see AIHW, *Australia's Welfare 1997*; Howe, *HACC Status Report*.

[59]Anna Yeatman, *Getting Real,* final report of the review of the Commonwealth-State Disability Agreement (Canberra: Australian Government Publishing Service, 1996).

[60]AIHW, *Australia's Welfare 1999*, p. 227.

[61]Commonwealth-State Disability Agreement (CSDA) funding goes to a mix of state and local governmental and non-governmental auspices. For every $1 of Commonwealth government transfers, state and territory governments received 62 cents; NGCSOs, 37 cents and local governments less than 1 cent, AIHW, *Australia's Welfare 1999*, p. 18.

[62]Department of Finance and Administration, *Portfolio Budget Statements 1998–99*, p. 199.

[63]Costello, *Budget Strategy and Outlook 1997–98,* Budget Paper No. 3, Table A6; Table 5 in the Appendix shows the 1998–99 Commonwealth budget expenditures on the above items.

[64]AIHW, *Australia's Welfare 1999*, p. 16.

[65]Yeatman, *Getting Real.*

[66]Ibid., p. 56.

[67]Ibid.

[68]Ibid., p. xiv.

[69]Ibid., ch. 5.

[70]Ibid., p. 99.

[71]Ibid., p. 100.

[72]AIHW, *Australia's Welfare 1999*, pp. 362-63.

[73]Tony Kryger, *Research Note No. 26 1997–98* (Canberra: Parliament Library, Parliament of Australia, 1998).

[74]Under the first three years of the Coalition government from 1995–96 to 1998–98, Commonwealth outlays on vocational and other education services only rose by 8.1 percent compared to the growth in funding of 66.2 percent under the last four years of the Labor government from 1991–92 to 1995–96. See Hancock and Cowling, *A Commitment to Public Service.*

[75]P. Pickering, *Altruism and Capitalism: Through the New Job Network?* (Brunswick: Brotherhood of St. Laurence, 1998).

[76]Australian Council of Social Services (ACOSS), *Budget 99: Making Good the Promise* (Sydney: ACOSS, 1999), p. 34.

[77]Analysis of budget shifts under the last four years of Labor and the first three years of the Coalition illustrate strong negative growth under the Coalition on real per capita underlying outlays on other welfare programs (–35 percent compared with –3.6 percent under Labor) and slower growth under the Coalition on social security and welfare expenditure on assistance to people with disabilities and to families with children, see Hancock and Cowling, *A Commitment to Public Service.*

[78]Commonwealth Department of Family and Community Services, *Older Workers, Disability and Early Retirement in Australia*, Background Paper, prepared for the Conference: "Income Support, Labour Markets and Behaviour: A Research Agenda" (Canberra: Commonwealth Department of Family and Community Services, 1998).

[79]Women with Disabilities Australia, Submission.

[80]Coopers and Lybrand, *Study of Unmet Demand* (Canberra: Department of Social Security, 1997).

[81]ACOSS, "Reforming Welfare," p. 3.

[82]Mary Lindsay, *Commonwealth Disability Policy 1983–1995*, Background Paper No. 2 1995–96. (Canberra: Parliamentary Library, Parliament House, 1996), p. 18.

[83]One of the most important policy developments in aged and community care has been the planned reduction of nursing home and residential care beds and a shift in emphasis to hostel and community-based home-care services. The period since 1985 has seen the restructuring of residential care in Australia, with further projected longer term decreases. Other changes include a national system of regulation for residential care; community care packages delivering home-based care; the merging of nursing homes and hostels; a stronger user-rights focus; expansion of brokered forms of community care; an accommodation bonds scheme for residential care; and, in terms of aged care financing, increasing emphasis on service user contributions, see AIHW, *Australia's Welfare 1997*, p. 261.

[84]L. Kumrow, "Community Care Outcomes from Casemix and Competition," *Health Issues*, 38 (1994):28-29.

[85]AIHW, *Australia's Welfare 1997*, p. 259.

[86]Howe, *HACC Status Report*, p. 2.

[87]ACOSS, *Budget 99*, p. 99. In June 2001, Senator Vanstone announced that the funding agreements between the national welfare peak bodies and the Department of Community Services would require 24-hour notice of all press releases, effectively silencing timely advocacy.

[88]Ibid., p. 91.

[89]Kumrow, "Community Care Outcomes from Casemix and Competition."

[90]L. Hancock and S. Moore, "Gender, Caring and the State," in *Health Policy in the Market State*, ed. L. Hancock (St Leonards: Allen & Unwin, 1999).

94   *Linda Hancock*

[91]AIHW, *Australia's Welfare 1997;* Howe, *HACC Status Report.*

[92]S. Moore, CCT, *Research Project Update* (Melbourne: Department of Management, RMIT, 1997); S. Moore, K. Hooper and I. Silva Brito, *Users' Experience of CCT of Local Government HACC Services* (Melbourne: Carers Association of Victoria, 1995).

[93]ACOSS, *Budget 99*, p. 91.

[94]Yeatman, *Getting Real*, p. xii.

[95]The study pointed out the likely increase in demand and shift in type of services required, with the aging of those classified as having a "severe or profound handicap" [sic] and in receipt of disability support services then aged 46-64 years of age, and the aging of their carers, see AIHW, *Australia's Welfare 1997*, p. 305; and R. Madden *et al.*, *The Demand for Disability Support Services in Australia: A Study to Inform the Commonwealth/State Disability Agreement Evaluation* (Canberra: AGPS, 1996).

[96]J. Alford and D. O'Neill, *Services and Assistance*, AIHW Cat. No. AUS8. (Canberra: Institute of Health and Welfare, 1999); and G. Hodge, *Contracting Out Government Services: A Review of International Literature* (Melbourne: Montech International, 1996).

[97]ACOSS, *Budget 99*; AIHW, *Australia's Welfare 1997*; Alford and O'Neill, *Services and Assistance*; Brian Costar and Nick Economou, *The Kennett Revolution* (Sydney: University of New South Wales Press, 1999); Howe, *HACC Status Report.*

[98]L. Rosenmann, "Older Women and Retirement," (University of Queensland, unpublished paper, 1994); Gleeson, "Disability and Poverty."

[99]Office of Disability, *Carers' National Agenda* (Canberra: Department of Health and Human Services, 1995).

[100]Rosenmann, "Older Women and Retirement."

[101]Gleeson, "Disability and Poverty."

[102]Nankervis and Rebeiro, *Carers Speak Out*, p. 9.

[103]Lindsay, *Commonwealth Disability Policy 1983–1995*, p. 4.

[104]Ibid.

[105]Commowealth Department of Family and Community Services, *Older Workers*, p. 75.

[106]Yeatman, *Getting Real*, p. xi.

[107]Lindsay, *Commonwealth Disability Policy 1983–1995*, p. 17.

[108]Sophie Hill, "Consumer Payments for Health Care," in *Health Policy in the Market State*, ed. Hancock.

[109]AIHW, *Australia's Welfare 1999*, p. 227.

[110]Yeatman, *Getting Real*, p. xii.

[111]Carer issues include significant waiting lists for case-managed service packages, problems resourcing complex care situations, the impact of rationing and targeting of HACC services to care situations with high or moderate needs, delays in carers accessing continuous support arrangements and difficulties for carers combining caring with part-time work or education, see Gill Pierce and Julie Nankervis, *Putting Carers in the Picture* (Melbourne: Carers Association Victoria, 1998), p. 11.

[112]Hancock and Cowling, *A Commitment to Public Service?*

[113]Andrew Burbridge, "The Polarisation of Families," paper presented to conference on "Earnings Inequality in Australia: Nature, Implications, Causes and Responses," Victoria University, 1999.

[114]In the late 1980s about one in seven people of workforce age was in receipt of government income support payments; compared to about one in five in 1999. The number in receipt of Disability Support Pension was around 600,000 people or 6 percent of the working age population in 1999, compared to 300,000 in the late 1980s, see Senator J. Newman, *The Future of Welfare in the 21st Century*. Speech to National Press Club, Canberra, 29 September 1999, pp. 5, 7.

[115]The Commonwealth Department of Family, *The Future of Welfare in the 21st Century* states that 31 percent were unemployed; 15 percent were students; 14 percent were lone parents; 9 percent were partnered parents, and 7 percent were the partners of age and disability support or other pensions; 3 percent were widows, carers veterans or on Special Benefit.

[116]Newman, *The Future of Welfare in the 21st Century*, p. 9.

[117]National Caucus of Disability Consumer Organisations, *Response to the Welfare Reform Interim Report*, 2000 <http: //www.wwda.org.au>.

[118]The Howard government tax package passed by the 1999 Senate, entails revenue collected from a 10 percent GST on goods and services (with exemptions for education, health, and some health-related products and, as added in controversial amendments, an exemption for certain items of food), to be collected by the Commonwealth and paid to the states after deduction of the costs of collection.

[119]Under the agreement attached to *A New Tax System [Commonwealth-State Financial Arrangements] Act* 1999, the following provisions will apply, Costello, *Budget Strategy and Outlook 1999–2000*, pp. 108-24).

- Payment of FAGs (Financial Assistance Grants) to states will cease on 1 July 2000;
- The Commonwealth will continue to pay SPPs to the states and has no intention of cutting aggregate SPPs as part of this reform process;
- Transitional arrangements to assist the states will include interest free loans July 2000–01;
- Any proposal to vary the 10-percent rate will need unanimous support of all states and territory governments and Commonwealth government endorsement with passage by both houses of Parliament;
- A ministerial council comprising Commonwealth and state treasurers will oversee the implementation of the agreement and consider ongoing reform of Commonwealth-state financial relations;
- The Commonwealth will distribute GST revenue grants among the states and territories in accordance with horizontal fiscal equalization principles and the pool of funding will comprise GST revenue grants and health-care grants (as defined under the *Australian Health Care Agreement*);

• A state's share of the pool will be based on population share and a relativity factor based on Commonwealth Grants Commission recommendations.

[120]Federal-State Relations Committee, *Report of the Register of Specific Purpose Payments Received by Victoria*, Fourth Report on the Inquiry into Overlap and Duplication, Vol. 2 (Melbourne: Government Printer).

3

INTERGOVERNMENTAL ASPECTS OF DISABILITY POLICIES IN BELGIUM

Johanne Poirier

INTRODUCTION

Over the last 30 years, the unitary Belgian state has gradually been transformed into a federation. Sophisticated and relatively generous disability programs had already been introduced when the movement to institute a federal system was initiated. This chapter attempts to find the fulcrum between this emerging federalism and disability policy.

State reforms were sought by the Flemish, Dutch-speaking, majority (60 percent of the population) essentially for cultural and linguistic reasons. On the French-speaking part of the country, the pressure to decentralize mainly reflected macroeconomic concerns (a fear that the majority would not make decisions beneficial to the declining economy of the south). Social policy in general, and disability policy in particular, were not part of the equation. They have, however, been significantly affected by the restructuring of the state.

The Belgian experience has given rise to a "federalism of the possible." Each successive constitutional reform introduced an additional centrifugal re-distribution of powers, sometimes in relation to matters that were not hotly contested. Decentralization was possible, so it took place. Sometimes, the devo-lution of closely related matters, desired by the Flemish or the francophone group, may not have occurred simply because no agreement could be reached between the two groups. On the other hand, some fields were devolved almost solely because they were easy to devolve. In those cases, devolution occurred because it satisfied a call for increased autonomy, or constituted a relatively costless bargaining chip. The area transferred may not have been a priority on the devolution wish-list. Regularly, devolution did not respond to public policy concerns.

This seems to have been the case with the jurisdiction over disability policy. In 1980, matters that affected individuals (such as state services) were devolved to the three cultural Communities (Flemish, French, and German). There were major exceptions to this devolution. The social-security system, for instance, remained federal. Hence, jurisdiction over disability policy, excluding financial allowances which constituted an integral part of the social-security system, were transferred to the Communities. This did not generate a lot of discussion or negotiation. It occurred, and it occurred early on in the federalization process, because it was relatively easy to do. This was not a contentious field of public activity. It affected a limited and relatively powerless group of persons. Moreover, visibility was not such that the federal government sought to preserve its control over this area.

Even today, disability is hardly ever mentioned in the context of state reforms or reflections on the federal system. Nevertheless, because programs for disabled persons were amongst the earliest programs subject to decentralization, they provide interesting lessons to the student of Belgian federalism. This experience shows that even when the matter to be devolved is not controversial, the transfer of jurisdiction takes time, adjustment, and a fair degree of good will on the part of public authorities. New financing mechanisms must be designed. Expertise, civil servants, and files must be shifted. This requires flexibility and a concern for detail, which may not be automatic when the shift occurs for wholly different political considerations.

The disabled person may well wonder what good this whole process has brought about. In a sense, this calls for an answer to the wrong question. The distribution of powers concerning disability policy was not policy-driven. It was driven by a desire for increased cultural autonomy and power by Belgium's main linguistic groups. Its success and failure must be assessed from that perspective. This does not, of course, preclude an incursion into the domain of program delivery, in order to examine the impact of the constitutional reform process.

In this context, it is interesting to observe that so far, decentralization has had very little impact on the actual content of policies. This is partly explained by the fact that distinct policy-making is relatively recent (while jurisdiction was essentially devolved in 1980, it took at least a decade for the transfer to occur completely). Moreover, despite a lack of formal coordination between the different orders of government involved, there is a fair degree of continuity in terms of programming. This may not be surprising since many of the actual decisionmakers have gone from the national (now federal) civil service to the administration of the federated entities.

In summary, disability was not an important factor in the constitutional transformation of Belgium. That transformation has had some impact on who conducts policy-making in the disability field, but not a significant impact on the actual policies, at least not so far. A detailed examination of the manner in which powers over disability have actually been redistributed in Belgium provides an interesting indication of the problems and complexities generated by a process designed for essentially cultural, not social policy, reasons. While the fulcrum between disability and federalism is not obvious, it is, upon closer study, quite revealing.

LEADING CHARACTERISTICS OF THE BELGIAN FEDERATION

The Federalization Process in Belgium: An Overview

Belgium was created as a unitary state in 1830. Despite the fact that a large portion of the population spoke Dutch dialects, the state institutions functioned only in French. Indeed, the elite in both southern (Walloon) and northern (Flemish) parts of the country spoke French. While the present institutions are extremely complex, this original language split remains a prevalent feature of the country.

Belgium federalism is recent. The first traces of the territorial divisions of the country, based on linguistic lines, go back to 1963. Major constitutional reforms took place in 1970 and in 1980, 1988, and 1993. It was only at that last stage that the Belgian constitution officially recognized the country as a federation. The gradual and incremental decentralization of a once unitary state required compromises that mark the institutions to this day.

Five major characteristics of Belgian federalism need to be emphasized.[1] First, it is *centrifugal* and the process toward more devolution is not over. Second, it is *bipolar* since the successive reforms were responses to conflicts between the two major language groups. Third, and paradoxically, it is also *multipolar*, since the bipolar nature of the conflicts did not generate a clear territorial division of the state into two entities, mostly because of Brussels, an overwhelmingly francophone city located in Flanders, and which could therefore not be attributed to the Flemish or the francophone entity. Moreover, Belgium has a small but generously recognized German-speaking community which also inherited institutions. In other words, while the logic of Belgian federalism is bipolar, the solutions designed to respond to different tensions, is multipolar. Fourth, and this is surely the most original aspect of the Belgian federal system, there are two types of federated entities, with distinct constitutional powers: the Regions and the Communities. Finally, the Belgian federation is asymmetrical. While powers are technically always devolved in a similar fashion to similar entities, those entities may organize, and do organize, their institutions differently. The most important distinction is the decision by the Flemish authorities to join the Flemish Community and Regional institutions, while such a fusion has not taken place on the French side of the country. This lack of symmetry makes the analysis of public policy, including policies toward persons with disabilities, a complicated endeavour.

From the beginning of the federalization process, envisioned solutions differed between the Flemish and the francophone sides of the country. Given their struggle to have their language and cultural rights recognized, the Flemish have always defended a devolution to the two major cultural Communities (the German-speaking Community being a beneficiary of this process). The Walloons have always favoured a territorial devolution to increase local autonomy over the economy. Indeed, the Walloons feared that the numerically superior Flemish would dominate institutions and take decisions detrimental to the declining heavy-industry Walloon economy. The Brussels francophones, who do not consider themselves Walloons, sought a large degree of institutional autonomy as well, in order not to be dominated either by the Flemish or the Walloons. Thus, there were incompatible demands for state reforms. While in Canada such divergences would likely have given rise to a stalemate, the original Belgian system attempted to satisfy everyone by creating a federation of both Communities (Flemish preference) and Regions (francophone preference), with a special status for Brussels and the German Community.

Communities were officially created in 1970. Regions were granted institutions in 1980. At that stage, however, legislative and executive powers of the federated entities constituted subgroups of national institutions. The status of Brussels was only resolved in 1988, when special, and very complex, institutions were introduced to create a regional entity (francophone request) in which both major cultural communities had a significant role to play (Flemish request). The French Community Commission (COCOF) is the legislative entity which governs social and cultural matters for the francophones of Brussels. It is composed of the French-speaking members in the regional legislature. The COCOF will re-appear in further discussion of policies toward persons with disabilities in Brussels because it functions independently from the Walloon Region and the French Community. There is also a Flemish Community Commission but it does not enjoy legislative power, it simply implements, in Brussels, policies designed by the Flemish Community institutions. Finally, there is, in Brussels, a Common Community Commission, which oversees policies in the social arena that affect persons of both language groups, such as bilingual hospitals.

In 1993, a new round of reform introduced direct elections of the members of the legislatures of the regions (except in Brussels, where this had occurred in 1989). The French and Flemish Communities are indirectly elected, as they are composed of members of regional institutions (this, of course, only really affects the francophone side of the country, since the Flemish institutions are combined). This direct election is likely to give rise to increasingly autonomous action on the part of the distinct entities and may lead to increasingly different policies developed in the north and south. We will return to this aspect later in the analysis. The 1993 reform also authorized the transfer of powers from the French Community to the Walloon Region and the COCOF. This was done in 1994, notably in matters of professional training, decentralized aspects of health-care policy and policies toward persons with disabilities.

The triple level of distribution of powers is surprising at first, but it follows a certain logic. Matters related to individuals, such as state services in education, culture, social services, are granted to the Communities. This has allowed the two main cultural communities to have jurisdiction over cultural policies for their own language group in Brussels. Matters that are more closely related to the territory, such as urban planning, the environment, housing, and public works have been devolved to the Regions. The federal level has maintained jurisdiction over defence, justice, fiscal and monetary policy (whatever has not been transferred to the European level) and, most importantly in the present context, the social-security system (though a large segment of social policy has been devolved).

The distribution of powers is extremely detailed, especially to a Canadian eye. The amount of detail leads to a conception of a largely exclusive distribution of powers, with very few areas of, theoretically, common jurisdiction. To give an example, preventative health is a Community matter, while health-care insurance is a federal matter. We will address the minute, almost lace-like, distribution of powers over policies regarding persons with disabilities later in the chapter.

In theory, the lack of concurrent powers (except in areas such as employment policies) should limit the risks of friction and overlapping. In practice, the delimitation between the detailed attributed powers can be quite problematic. This has recently given rise to a call, by the Flemish authorities, for a consolidation of related but so far scattered powers, in favour of the Communities (the Flemish authorities never discuss Regions, since they do not correspond to their preferred conception of the federal structure). There are very few areas of joint policy-making. The system is conceived of as a largely "disentangled" one, even if the closely related powers often mean that different actors will be involved in a particular policy field, such as disability.

The different conceptions of the Belgian system, within the Belgian political and constitutional circles is such that there is no agreement even on the actual number of federated entities. Without contest there is the joined Flemish Community and Regional legislature and executive, those of the French Community, of the German Community, of the Walloon Region and of the Brussels Region. Whether the COCOF, which enjoys legislative power, is actually a federated entity is the subject of certain controversy. It is, without doubt, a significant player in the area of social policy in Brussels.

Such a complex system is bound to generate tensions. Conflicts concerning the constitutional distribution of powers are settled by three different federal judicial institutions. First, the legislative section of the Council of State, a federal institution with separate language chambers, must give its opinion on all proposed legislation (but not regulation) whether it emanates from the federal Parliament or the federated legislatures. As its advice is not binding, it is sometimes ignored, but at a political cost. Second, there is an *a posteriori* control of legislation by the federal Court of Arbitration, consisting of six Dutch-speaking and six French-speaking judges. Half of these judges are former politicians, half are professional magistrates. Finally, regulations may be challenged after their adoption before the administrative section of the federal Council of State.

Another original institution in the compromise and balance-prone federal Belgium is the Concertation Committee. It is composed of the federal prime minister, five federal ministers, and six members of federated governments (on the multipolar model). It is also perfectly divided between French- and Dutch-speakers (on the bipolar model). Its role is to solve politically what is called "conflicts of interests," that is, actions by one order of government in the federation that affect another order. The typical case would be a proposed legislation by one entity, while another fears it will be affected negatively. In that case, the latter party can refer the matter to the committee. This course of action will automatically suspend the debated decision or legislation for 60 days, during which time a solution by way of consensus is sought. If no consensus arises, the legislation can be adopted. Ironically, the Concertation Committee is rarely used. A simple threat to refer a matter to it will often be sufficient to prevent some conflicts at the political level.

Ronald Watts has noted that two-member federations are highly unstable.[2] It is true that the bipolar nature of the Belgian federal structure gives rise to a high degree of frustration and polarization. The complex, multipolar, system tends to slightly limit this polarization, but with increasing difficulty. Flanders has unified institutions, a vigorous cultural identity, and a strong economy. It is increasingly frustrated with its contribution to equalization and to implicit transfer payments through the social-security system which it makes to French-speaking entities. At this stage, the francophones do not seek further devolution of powers and are mystified by the constant demand to renegotiate the terms agreed upon a few years earlier. Directly elected legislatures in the federated entities could pave the way for further demands for autonomy, or even separation. Consensus is increasingly difficult to reach in this complex centrifugal and asymmetrical federation.

Institutional Asymmetry

From the previous description, it should be obvious that the system has permitted the development of asymmetrical forms of governing in different policy areas, including policies regarding persons with disabilities. This asymmetry is not vertical, however. The asymmetry is between the way the Flemish and the French-speaking entities have organized powers transferred from the central government. The former "merged" the institutions of the Flemish Community and Region in 1980. There is only one Parliament and one administration. It is basically territorial, but with powers over the Dutch-speaking institutions in Brussels. The latter have maintained the complex division of powers between Community and Region (which even includes a transfer of jurisdiction from the first to the second). In other words, this is not the case of some infra-state entities being granted more powers in a particular area (on the Spanish constitutional or the Canadian administrative-agreement models), but of entities "inheriting" similar constitutional powers from the federal government and having the constitutional latitude to organize these powers as they see fit.

Characteristics of the Partisan Political Process

National political parties have all split along linguistic lines over the last 20 years. There are no truly federal parties active at the federal level. Members of Parliament are all elected either by Flemish-speakers, through a Flemish language party or by French-speakers, through a francophone party. Voices for "the whole of Belgium" are consequently rare on the political scene.

Governments are, so far, made up of the same parties at the federal and regional levels (except in Brussels). The creation of the coalition government following the general election is a complex bargaining process lasting several months. With a short exception, since the Second World War coalitions have always been comprised of the Social-Christian (French and Flemish) parties, often with the Socialists (French and Flemish). Other parties play an important role: the Flemish nationalist party Volksunie; the Liberals; the francophone rights defence party; the Front des francophones; the extreme right (particularly strong in Flanders); and the Green parties.

As there are few mechanisms for joint decision-making of the scattered constitutional structure of Belgium, coordination and compromise often take place at the partisan political level. No major policy may be implemented without the approval of the major partners in the various coalition governments.

Financing the Federation and the Federated Entities

As can be anticipated, financing as complex a federation as Belgium is not a simple process. The following will therefore be extremely simplified.[3]

Generally speaking, Communities and Regions do not enjoy a large degree of fiscal autonomy. This could change in the next few months, as the major *Financing Act* is to be renegotiated. Moreover, the constitution of a new coalition government following the June 1999 election could depend on a series of compromises between the constitutive entities, including increased fiscal autonomy, high on the Flemish political agenda.

The federal government collects the most important taxes: value-added tax (VAT) and personal income tax. It also sets the tax base and rates. Part of the proceeds of these taxes are then redistributed to the Communities and Regions following complex and evolving formulas.[4]

Communities may raise their own taxes. However, this power has never been exercised by the French or the Flemish Communities because it would require that the population of Brussels formally opts for one or the other community. This is assimilated to the selection of a "subnationality" and is taboo in Belgium. On the other hand, the German Community enjoys real autonomous fiscal power since it is assumed that all residents of the German-speaking territory are members of that Community.

The vast majority of Community resources are proceeds of taxes levied by the federal government. Proceeds of the VAT is redistributed on the basis of the number of children under 18 years of age in each Community, a needs criterion. This benefits the poorer French Community and is the source of Flemish recrimination. Proceeds of the personal income tax transferred to the Communities correspond to their respective share of that income. In the ever complex situation of Brussels, 80 percent of the proceeds are attributed to the French Community, and 20 percent to the Flemish Community. In addition to these major forms of revenue, Communities raise revenues through special licences linked to their areas of constitutional jurisdiction (a radio-television fee, for instance).[5]

Apart from the implicit redistribution that occurs through the needs criteria of the VAT distribution, there are no redistribution mechanisms in place for the Communities. The situation is different for the Regions.

Again, most of the regional resources come from a portion of the personal income tax levied by the federal government and "refunded" to the Regions. When the *Special Financing Act* was first adopted in 1989, the amount transferred to the Regions corresponded to their share of expenditure (based on their areas of jurisdiction). Starting in 2000, Regions will obtain a share of the personal income tax which corresponds to their respective contribution (as in the case of the Communities). In other words, Flanders, the richest Region will henceforth receive a larger amount per capita than the poorer Regions, since its contributive capacity is larger.

The *Special Financing Act* allows the Regions to impose an additional rate, or a reduction, on the federally levied income tax. So far, no Region has taken advantage of this possibility. This seems surprising given that Flanders is so actively seeking increased fiscal autonomy. This may be explained by the heavy negotiation procedure required and by the fact that Flanders would prefer increased autonomy for the Community (following a bipolar model, and to maintain close links with Brussels), rather than the Region.

Like the Communities, the Regions can raise non-fiscal revenues linked to their own jurisdiction (licences on lumber, gambling and games, road user fees). Regions also benefit from exceptional conditional transfers from the federal government in order to pay unemployed persons hired by regional public services.

An equalization mechanism has been introduced in favour of poorer Regions. A Solidarity Fund benefits the Regions where the personal income tax is lower than the national average. In 1997, for instance, the Walloon and Brussels Regions received 21.5 billion BEF and 120 million BEF respectively from this fund. The richer Flemish Region does not benefit from this Solidarity Fund. This redistribution mechanism is heavily criticized in Flanders.

In discussing social policy, it is also essential to consider the financing of the social-security system. The social security budget is distinct from the federal budget, although social-security is still under exclusive federal jurisdiction. A paragovernmental institution, the National Office of Social Security collects contributions from employees and employers, a federal transfer and the special Solidarity Fund.[6] It then redistributes the funds to the different branches of the social-security program: unemployment insurance, pensions, health care, family allowances, work injuries and disability benefits, and — of interest in the present context — allowances to persons with disabilities. The social-security budget is extremely important. It is equivalent to the federal budget, and makes after-tax refunds to the other levels of government.[7] It is generally recognized that the French-speaking population of Belgium (both in Wallonia and in Brussels) is a net beneficiary of the system, while the Flemish, who tend to have lower rates of unemployment, long-term illness, and higher salaries (who thus pay higher contributions) are net contributors. There are massive disagreements about the degree of north-south financial transfers, but there are no doubts that such transfers do take place. This is one of the reasons for the desire on the part of a number of the Flemish political parties to partially split the social-security system between the two major Communities (again, on the bipolar model). All francophone parties are opposed to such decentralization since it would imply an end to the implicit solidarity between all Belgian citizens which the current system implies. Negotiations to constitute the next coalition government will no doubt include discussions on that issue.

In summary, federated entities do not enjoy a high degree of fiscal autonomy in Belgium. The system of conditional grants, well-known in Canada, is a rare phenomenon. Organizations receive most of their resources from federally-levied taxes. Almost half of the federal revenues are redistributed to the federated bodies and the social-security system.[8] Certain solidarity mechanisms ensure a degree of redistribution to the poorer Regions and Communities (all French-speaking), a fact increasingly decried in Flanders. The (still) federal social-security system also ensures a degree of north-south financial transfers and is therefore currently under attack because of this.

DISABILITY IN FEDERAL BELGIUM

Constitutional Distribution of Powers Concerning Policies Related to Persons with Disabilities

The Belgian constitution does not per se deal with the legislative powers relating to persons with disabilities, although different constitutional Acts adopted since 1980 have decentralized important aspects of legislative and administrative authority in this area. Before launching into a description of the gradual constitutional decentralization of powers, it might be useful to briefly review policies developed by the unitary Belgian state, from its inception in 1830 to the 1980s.

During that period, the unitary state obviously had sole legislative authority, while some of the services were offered by provinces (administrative divisions of the unitary state) and municipalities. Certain benefits had been set up for disabled persons in the nineteenth century and specific legislation was introduced in 1929 which provided a means-tested allowance for persons between the ages of 14 and 40 with a permanent work incapacity.[9] The age limit was raised to 60 years of age in 1937.

The most important legislative initiatives dealing with services and allowances for people with disabilities were taken in the 1960s. Legislation was passed by the still unitary government in 1963 to create a national rehabilitation fund for persons with disabilities.[10] Then, in 1967, a fund was set up to be responsible for the medical, residential, and pedagogical care of persons with disabilities. Its main task was to develop and accredit day centres and full-time residential institutions both for children and adults.[11] In 1969, a new and comprehensive Act concerning monetary allowances was adopted.[12] The responsibility of the central government in all three areas remained unchanged through the first wave of constitutional reforms in 1970.

From the early 1960s, and for about 20 years, policy-making in this area went through a golden age. For one thing, the rehabilitation fund had an autonomous source of revenue: an extra premium on fire, car, and work-related injury insurance policies. The insurer collected the premium, so few civil servants were required to administer this part of the project. Since the insurance business was expanding during that period, revenues rose regularly, enough to allow for the introduction of new services. And since the state did not need to finance the program, the paragovernmental rehabilitation fund had a fair degree of latitude with which to conduct policy experiments and development.

In 1980, a special Act of Parliament (adopted with a two-thirds majority and a single majority in each of the Flemish and French-speaking groups) transferred (amongst other things) important aspects of the legislative power regarding people with disabilities to the three Communities (Flemish, French, and German).[13] This included responsibilities for residential institutions as well as rehabilitation, professional integration, and training (from the 1963 National Fund). As with all constitutionally attributed powers in Belgium, these transferred powers are deemed to be exclusive. In other words, from that point on, legislative authority regarding housing, training, and general services for disabled persons were the responsibility of one of the types of federated bodies in Belgium: the cultural communities. This important transfer of responsibility over this aspect of social policy did not give rise to much debate. This was not a highly symbolic area with the different levels of government seeking to control. Moreover, while some reorganization of the service-delivery system was required, this restructuring did not challenge the social-security system, which remained a sole federal responsibility. It appears, in fact, that the constitutional decentralization of powers concerning disablement policy was a fairly successful early attempt at transferring powers to the Community level. It could be seen as a testing ground for other areas of social policy to be decentralized in the course of the federalization process.

Despite this relative ease of transfer from a political point of view, it is interesting to note the more complex and protracted implementation of the transfer. The moving of policies regarding persons with disabilities to the Community level illustrates fairly well the complexity of the constitutional devolution process in Belgium: even when there is a substantial amount of agreement over the domain to be devolved, and regarding which of the federated entities (Regions or Communities) should receive the new powers, the actual process of devolution takes time and will require a certain degree of coordination.

The actual transfer of responsibilities over residential institutions occurred rapidly and relatively smoothly since the residential fund was actually part of the national administration. It did require the movement of files and some civil servants. At that stage, such a transfer was not too difficult since the federated bodies did not have an independent civil service. Hence, employees did not fear losing their advantage by placing the program into the hands of the Communities, and the unions also did not resist.

This was not the case for the transfer of responsibilities for rehabilitation. The rehabilitation fund, a paragovernmental agency as opposed to a department in the national administration, was dissolved in 1991, after three Communities had finally created their own funds to take over the responsibilities that they had been granted in 1980.[14] In the meantime, policies regarding rehabilitation continued to be legislated and administered by the federal government. There seemed to have been more resistance from the paragovernmental rehabilitation fund and the employees' union in that case than in the case of the governmental fund responsible for residential care. There was little experience with paragovernmental agencies of either the Communities or the Regions. Invalidity funds were, in a sense, charting new territory. Moreover, while the old Fonds-81 was completely transferred to the Communities, the National Fund's mission was to be split between the federal administration and the community. Indeed, before the Communities actually assumed the legislative powers in regards to the integration of persons with disabilities, medical and individual rehabilitation services were transferred to the *federal* Institut national de l'assurance-maladie-invalidité, by legislation adopted in 1988. It only came into force in 1991. This was coherent with a decision to maintain health services at the federal level, while making rehabilitation policies a Community responsibility.

In brief, then, responsibilities over residential care went straight from the federal administration to the Community administration, a transfer facilitated by the fact that despite the existence of a distinct legislative authority, there was a unified civil service. In other words, the boss changed but the employees remained the same. In the case of policy-making for rehabilitation, the situation was more complex as it involved the creation of a Community paragovernmental agency (a new feature of Belgian federalism at that stage) and the maintenance of part of the program at the federal level, which needed a much higher degree of negotiation.

Then, in 1993, only two years following the effective communautarization of policies regarding the social and professional integration of persons with disabilities, the French Community transferred the exercise[15] of some of its constitutional powers to the Walloon Region and to the Commission communautaire française (COCOF) of the Brussels Region.[16] In other words, the exercise of some community powers have now been *regionalized* in the French part of the country. This new transfer includes responsibilities for institutions as well as rehabilitation policies.[17]

This last transfer was motivated by *financial*, not policy, reasons: the financial resources of the French Community did not enable it to meet its constitutional responsibilities. The Walloon and the French part of the Brussels Region were willing to contribute, but requested control over both spending and policy development. Through all these modifications, the federal government retained legislative authority relating to the financing and paying of allowances to those with disabilities. The federal medicare system manages, through the paragovernmental Institut d'assurance-maladie-invalidité (INAMI) and mutualities, the medical and paramedical services to disabled people.[18]

It must be noted that the successive transfers of legislative authority were accompanied by a transfer of civil servants: from the central government to the Communities in 1981 (although this involved few people), from the central government to the Flemish, the German, and the French Communities in 1991, and finally, from the French Community to the Walloon Region and to Brussels' COCOF in 1993.[19] Property, contractual rights, and obligations were also transferred to the succeeding authorities.

The picture that emerges is a fairly complex one. Both the federal and the federated levels are involved in policy-making with regard to persons with disabilities. Moreover, despite an official devolution of powers to Communities, Regions are also actively involved in the area. Table 1 summarizes the authorities with constitutional powers over this policy area.

Although complex, the actual division of powers seems to be satisfactory. While the authorities in Flanders are calling for a constitutional devolution (called de-federalization) of medicare and of family allowances, further devolution of policies concerning persons with disabilities is not on the agenda. Some maintain that this is simply because the division of powers works in this area, that each entity has enough freedom and autonomy to adapt its policies to its specific needs. Cynics could argue that devolution is not on the agenda in this regard simply because not enough money is at stake.

It is clear, however, that the system is in process of consolidation: it is new, and the lack of cooperation is creating some problems. Overall, however, this would seem to be an area where federalization has worked.

TABLE 1
Constitutional Distribution of Powers Concerning Policies Related to People
with Disabilities

Federal

- *Allowances specifically for persons with disabilities*
  Income replacement allowance
  Integration allowances

- *Other social security provisions*
  Workers' Compensation benefits
  Unemployment insurance
  Additional family allowances for families with parents or children with disabilities
  Health care (reimbursement of medical, hospitalization and drug costs)
  Rehabilitation treatment
  Pensions

- *Some aspects of employment policies*
  Certification of collective agreements, including those with incentives to hire persons
    with disabilities
  Labour law
  Hiring quotas in federal public service and agencies
  Recruitment for all public administrations, including those of the federated bodies

- *Justice system*
  Labour law tribunals (also have jurisdiction for judicial review of decisions made by the
    various funds of federated bodies regarding integration of people with disabilities, and
    in some cases for decisions regarding institutions)
  Civil law protection for persons and property

- *Transportation (aspects of): parking permits for anywhere in the country*, train and plane
  accessibility and reduced-pricing

- *Fiscal and Value-Added-Tax (VAT) deductions*

- *Subsidized public utilities*
  Telephone, gas, electricity

Communities

- *Categories of handicap for their own services*

- *Formal education*
  Kindergarten to university

- *Leisure and culture*
  For example, a theatre company

- *Audio-visual*
  Books on tape, sign-language television programs

... continued

TABLE 1
(continued)

The following are also Community powers, which are now exercised by the Walloon Region and the Commission communautaire française on Behalf of the French Community. In the case of the Flemish and German communities these have remained fully "Community powers"

- *Institutions*
  Full residential or day centres, for children and adults

- *Professional integration*
  Employment incentives, adaptation of work environment

- *Professional training*
  In "ordinary" or "specialized" centres, on-the-job training

- *Material and technical aids*
  Wheelchairs, guide dogs, adapted telecommunications instruments, Brail bars

- *Home care*
  Including 24-hour "electronic alarm" system; help with daily living

- *Information and support services for people living outside institutions*

- *Financial help for adapting a house or car*

- *Early childhood support for families having a child with disabilities*

- *Guidance for families with an adult with disabilities living at home*

- *Out-of-school pedagogical support*
  Tutoring, interpreters

- *Financial assistance for transport or housing to students or people in training*

- *Subsidized transportation costs (for individuals)*

- *Reduction of radio-TV taxes*
  Though they are collected by the federal government

- *Hiring quotas in regional public administration and public organizations*

Regions

- *Social housing*

- *Norms of accessibility to buildings open to the public*

- *Public transit*
  Both regular and adapted (except trains)

- *School buses*

- *Professional "regular" placement services*

- *Hiring quotas in regional public administration and public organizations*

Demographics, Attitudes, Organizations

It is difficult to evaluate the number of persons with disabilities with precision. One indication comes from the number of persons who benefit from federal allowances. This number has now reached about 200,000 for a population of ten million.

Federal allowances are both residual and means-tested. As they are reserved for those with no other source of income, it is arguable that a certain stigma attaches to the receipt of those benefits. Nevertheless, the fact that Belgium has a well developed and generous system of social programs, arguably makes banal the reception of benefits and limits the degree of stigma attached to receiving benefits.

As we will see later, each federated body has established a paragovernmental fund responsible for the implementation of most of the policies toward persons with disabilities. Moreover, an impressive number of organizations defend the interests of those with disabilities, and these agencies can also be mandated to represent individuals in their dealings with government.[20]

For instance, at the federal level, the National Council for Persons with Disabilities[21] is comprised of a large number of groups acting on behalf of persons with disabilities, both Dutch- and French-speaking. It makes nonbinding recommendations to the federal government on any regulation concerning allowances. Note that to sit at the Conseil national, associations representing persons with disabilities must be national in scope. Since many of these associations have split over linguistic lines, it appears that they sometimes maintain a national group in order to participate (for instance, the National Association for Mentally Handicapped Persons has a Dutch-speaking section and a francophone section, the latter subdivides again into a Walloon and a Brussels section). While the common front may seem cosmetic, it could be argued that this requirement of national character imposes a certain degree of concertation between associations representing people with similar needs, irrespective of their linguistic groups, before they make representations to the Conseil national.

Similar consultative groups exist for the Walloon Region and French-speaking Brussels. On the Flemish side, the participation of associations takes a different form as they actually sit on the board of the paragovernmental fund.

In Belgium, major labour policies are negotiated by social partners. That is, labour unions (the rate of unionization is very high in Belgium) and employers' representatives will agree on policies such as the minimum wage, labour standards, and so on. Surprisingly, in this very divided society, those social partners still function on a national, *federal*, basis, although language-based subdivisions exist. This explains why the Conseil *national* du travail approves collective agreements, including those applicable to "adapted work enterprises" which are under the jurisdiction of federated agencies.

The social safety net is very high in Belgium. Talks of privatization in the social arena are still marginal. Yet, in a sense, there has always been an important role for non-state actors in services for persons with disabilities. Institutions such as residential homes, day centres, adapted work enterprises, and training centres are mostly run by non-profit organizations, although a few public adapted work enterprises exist in Wallonia. They are accredited, controlled, and financed by the different funds, but not run by them.

Yet, many services are still offered by public employees: individual counselling and guidance. In fact, at least in the case of francophone Brussels, the trend seems to be toward more public intervention. For example, the Fonds bruxellois francophone has just taken over the Service d'aide technique that was previously offered by the Red Cross. This is essentially information on technical products, a show room, and a loan system to test products.[22] Similarly, the Vlaams Fonds sees its mission evolving from a simple transmission line between public money and different types of social and non-profit organizations, to an agency more directly involved with citizens.

In short, new management theory, popular in Anglo-Saxon countries, is not an important item on the public agenda in Belgium.

SOCIAL POLICY AND FEDERAL PRACTICE: SERVING PERSONS WITH DISABILITIES IN FEDERAL BELGIUM

Definitions

Four orders of government intervene in public policy regarding persons with disabilities. While there are common criteria of entitlement to services, each entity has some jurisdiction to determine who is a disabled person for the purpose of the services it offers, as well as under what conditions they will extend services to persons with disabilities domiciled in another part of the country.[23] So far, the definition of a disabled person has remained fairly similar across the country and resembles the once unitary and now federal definition used to grant allowances. Amongst other criteria for getting services, the following is perhaps the most central: a person must have a limited possibility of social or professional integration due to a reduced physical ability of 30 percent or mental ability of 20 percent.[24]

Most programs are offered to nationals, recognized refugees, European Union employees working in Belgium and their dependents, or people who have resided in Belgium for five years consecutively (or for ten non-consecutive years). The federal government and federated bodies could independently modify these criteria, but so far have all maintained similar ones for their own programs.

Policies and Programs

This section briefly deals with some of the substantive policies developed by each order of government. In the case of federated bodies, I have insisted on legislative and constitutional authority, since it is already complex, using policy examples to illustrate the distribution of powers. Summaries of specific policies developed by federated organizations are found in Table 2.

Policies Developed by Federal Authorities

Nowadays, the main federal public policy takes the form of monetary allowances. I have, however, also outlined less visible, but very tangible fields of federal intervention, for they provide an image of how closely interwoven the actual distribution of powers is in this area.

Allowances. The federal government, which has retained exclusive jurisdiction over social security in Belgium, offers two kinds of allowances specifically for people with disabilities, for which the payment of social-security contributions is not required:[25] income-replacement and integration allowance.[26] The allowances are means-tested and spousal income is considered.[27] They are supplementary to other contributory regimes such as workers' compensation schemes.

The *income replacement allowance* is obviously based on one's decreased ability or inability to earn a living. Hence, it does not compensate for the handicap itself, but for the economic loss that results from the handicap. The *integration allowance*, provides compensation for lack of autonomy. It may be spent on any service or good by the recipient. The first is more or less equivalent to the "minimal level of subsistence." The latter is proportional to the severity of the handicap. This second allowance provides a certain level of

TABLE 2
Policies Developed by Federated Entities

Criteria for entitlement to most services
(Although federated entities could adopt different criteria, so far they have remained almost identical.)[1]

- Belgian national, stateless person, recognized refugee, European Union (EU) worker (spouse or children of EU worker), persons who have resided in Belgium continuously for the last five years, or for ten years altogether.

- Residence in the territory of the entity offering the service, unless there is a cooperation agreement (which exists between all federated entities except with the Flemish Community).

- Must be under 65 years old when filing first claim.

- Must have a limited possibility of social or professional integration due to a reduced physical ability of 30 percent or mental ability of 20 percent.[2]

General information service
Each of the four funds (agencies) provides information on services offered, as well as individual counselling.

Institutions for children and adults
(Most are non-profit organizations[3] accredited and subsidized by funds)

- Full residential care for children, generally run by non-profit organizations. A contribution of two-thirds of family allowances can be requested from the family.

- Full residential care (homes) for adults. Contribution according to means, all family revenues are considered. But at a minimum, individuals keep about $180 (4,300 BEF) of their federal allowance as pocket money.

- Residences for workers with disabilities, either in homes or in supervised group homes. Many are located near adapted work enterprises. Workers can keep half their salaries. At most, they pay 30,000 BEF per month.

- Day centres for children. A contribution of about 150 BEF per day may be requested.

- Day centres for adults. A contribution of up to 290 BEF per day may be asked.

- Foster families for children or adults (can house a maximum of five disabled persons). Contributions from the family are requested and all revenues are considered.

- Short-term institutions. Only in Flanders, day or night housing for limited periods (maximum three non-consecutive months per year). These essentially aim at providing support to families who have chosen to keep a person with disabilities at home.

- Protected housing. Autonomous living for persons with disabilities, with support by full-time educator (ration one for eight residents). Also available only in Flanders.

... continued

TABLE 2
(continued)

Early childhood support

- For families with a child with disabilities, under the age of six. A contribution of up to 6,000 BEF ($250) per year may be asked of the family.

Education

- From 2.5 to 21 years of age. In integrated or specialized classes. Some teaching is also done in hospitals. Integration into regular classes (with an interpreter for hearing-impaired) is increasingly advocated, but still quite limited. The proportion does not seem to be very different for the other communities.

- Adult education. Little structured help is provided. Funds are transferred to colleges and universities for social purposes (help with tuition, special programs, etc.) and institutions may, but need not, use that money to adapt buildings, or provide services to students with disabilities. This has not occurred on a significant scale. If the institution does not provide the service, there is no legal means of forcing them to, no appeal panel or tribunal. This is perceived (by institutions) as a fairly marginal area, with few requests for help.

Pedagogical support

- Professional or educational orientation.

- Honorarium for interpreters (for visually or hearing impaired). For the visually-impaired, up to 450 hours per year, at 663 BF per hour in Brussels. For hearing-impaired, 600 hours per year, at 663 BF per hour. The FBF and the AWIPH only pay for after-school help (since schooling is a Community matter). The Vlaams Fonds offers 900 hours of interpretation which may be used during or after school hours.

- Tutoring outside class.

- Financial support for housing or extra transportation costs for students.

Professional training

- Specialized centres, particularly popular in Wallonia and Flanders. There is only one in Brussels for visually-impaired persons.

- Integration in regular training programs, increasingly promoted, particularly in Brussels where there are few specialized centres.

Professional integration

- State recruitment services, done through the federal Recruitment Secretariat for the federal civil service, as well as other federated bodies.

- Regular placement services must extend their services to persons with disabilities.

- Quotas, set by all entities for their own public service and organizations. One federated agency sought to introduce quotas into the private sector, but the federal State Council considered this an infringement on the exclusive federal power over employment contracts.

... *continued*

TABLE 2
(continued)

Work-incentive programs for employers

- Adapted work enterprises used to be called protected workshops. The philosophy behind these non-profit organizations, introduced 35 years ago, was to provide work, social relations, and a certain economic independence for those who could not function in a regular work environment. The new "integration philosophy" seeks to use these workshops as training for regular employment whenever this is possible. In Brussels, there are 15 of them, all French-speaking, employing 1,500 persons with disabilities, and with a joint income of 960 million BEF in 1997. In Wallonia, over 5,800 disabled persons work in those workshops. Adapted work enterprises do mostly subcontract work in mailing, packaging, food services, horticulture, textiles, production of books in Braille, laundry, and office work. Employees have a regular contract of employment or a *contrat d'adaptation* (*infra*). Funds cover up to 65 percent of salaries and social-security premiums for employees. The salaries of managers are subsidized by up to 25 percent (and up to 66 percent for managers with disabilities). Funds provide some capital investment. A new Walloon law requires that at least 20 percent of managerial positions be occupied by persons with disabilities.

- Collective Agreement No. 26. This federal work-incentive program, described in the text, is only available in the private sector. It is a duplication of services now offered by the federated agencies. The program is administered by a federal labour inspector, who determines the rate of contribution (depending on reduced rate of productivity). It is mentioned here because the financial contribution is actually paid by the funds of the federated entities even though the entitlement is assessed at the federal level.

- "Compensation" or integration benefits. This is a similar program, with contributions toward the salary of an employee with disabilities, based on the rate of reduced productivity. In Brussels, for instance, the FBF can pay up to 65 percent of the employee's salary and social-security premiums in either a regular work environment (in a private or a public organization) or an adapted work enterprise.

- Financial assistance to adapt a working environment. To cover the costs of purchasing computer Braille-bars for visually-impaired employees, adapting washrooms, or providing wheelchair ramps. Available to private and public sector.

- Professional adaptation contract. On-the-job training for a maximum of three years, depending on the individual's adaptation needs. Public contribution is digressive: employers pay 40 BEF per hour (less than $2) the first year, and 60 BEF per hour after that. Funds pay a complementary daily benefit to the trainee of about 160 BEF ($6).

Work incentive for persons with disabilities

- Help with extra travelling costs, if person needs someone to accompany him or her, the fare for that person will be paid; if adapted public transit is not possible, taxis can be paid, or the cost of adapting a private vehicle reimbursed.

TABLE 2
(continued)

- Installation benefit, for persons with disabilities who want to start a business or open their own professional offices.

Services aimed at promoting the autonomy of persons with disabilities

- Information and support to individuals who live outside institutions *Accompagnement*. Services often offered by non-profit organizations accredited by funds and partly funded by them. They provide help with administrative processes, housing, advice on how to adapt a house, find work, plan holidays and leisure, help with medical follow-up, and budgeting, etc. A contribution of up to 500 BEF ($20) per month can be requested.

- Individual material or technical aids, to the extent that they are not paid by the federal *Institut d'assurance-maladie-invalidité*: wheelchairs, walkers, guide dogs, telecommunications equipment, adapted computers, Braille bars, etc. Some agencies request a contribution (10 percent is requested in Brussels by FBF, for instance). Note that if the price of adapting a vehicle is supported by funds, the purchase itself depends on the individual's financial means.

- Help with daily living. Home care, as well as 24-hour help for people with mobility problems living in their own home. Connection to electronic devices (televigilance). Housing must be located within ½ km of the service. Participation of up to 1,000 BEF ($40) per month may be requested.

- Personal assistance budget. This is a pilot-project of the Flemish Fund. It provides a budget for integration for an individual, who then hires an assistant in order to maximize his or her autonomy. In 1997, 12 persons benefited from this service.

- Guidance service. This is also offered by the Flemish Fund and provides support for families with a disabled member in order to help them find solutions to problems, services, etc. This initiative, like an extension of the early childhood support program, seeks to help families caring for a person at home and will thus limit the number of unnecessarily institutionalized persons.

Rehabilitation services

- Rehabilitation centres are accredited by the Communities (or Regions, in the case of Wallonia), which also cover their capital expenditures and operating costs. Note, however, that the majority of these services are located in hospitals, which are almost exclusively governed by federal legislation. Individual treatments (and thus a large part of salaries) are paid for by the federal social-security system through the Institut d'assurance-maladie (INAMI). Transportation to receive treatment seems to fall between the cracks of the division of powers, since INAMI refuses to pay, positing that this is not part of the medical services covered, but that it constitutes a support for integration, which is a Community (regionalized on the French side) power. Not everyone agrees, and so far, these costs are not covered at all by the Walloon Fund, although they are reimbursed by the Flemish Fund and in francophone Brussels.

... continued

TABLE 2
(continued)

Radio-television fees exemption

- Sensory-deprived individuals, and others with an 80 percent rate of invalidity (50 percent for war invalids), who cannot leave their home without help are exempted from paying this fee.

Housing

- Means-tested help provided to purchase a house, or with moving costs. Adapted units are reserved in some social housing projects.

Accessibility

- A 1975 (national) law concerning access has been or is being revised by all regional Parliaments. Note that new norms, as with the old ones, do not require modifications of older buildings, unless an application is made for a renovation permit.

Transportation

- As mentioned above, the federal government provides parking permits, and is responsible for accessibility and reduced-pricing on trains and planes. Regions have introduced adapted bus services (with a two-day reservation, prices are the same as public transit). In Brussels, the subway is now accessible to visually-impaired travellers, but few stations are accessible to wheelchairs. Also in Brussels there is a project to help taxi companies purchase vans that can accommodate wheelchairs. As mentioned above, Communities (or the regionalized funds of the COCOF and in Wallonia) provide help with *individual* transportation costs.

Administrative or judicial review of decisions by the federated entities

- With a few exceptions (notably in Wallonia), this has remained a federal responsibility.

Notes: Federal policies are discussed in the main text. Here are some of the major policies developed by the Communities and Regions. Distinctions in programs will be noted, otherwise, programs offered by all federated entities are relatively similar.

1. In the case of the Walloon Region and the COCOF, who exercise the constitutional competencies of the French Community, the latter has maintained full legislative authority over the determination of categories of handicap entitled to services. In other words, the Walloon Region and the COCOF cannot alter these categories. This way, the French Community has ensured a certain harmonization of criteria for all French-speaking persons with disabilities.

2. This 20–30 percent rule is found in unabrogated sections of the national legislation of 1963. So although federated entities have developed less rigid definitions in their own legislation, technically, this numerical one still applies. Why the bodies have not abrogated this national rule (or incorporated it into their own legislation) is unclear.

3. With a significant number of institutions affiliated with Catholic institutions, particularly in the north of the country.

autonomy since it may be spent on any good or service, and not only on those listed by governmental agencies. Note that the integration allowance is reduced by one-third if the person is institutionalized.

The two kinds of supplementary federal allowances for persons with disabilities are significant. The federal government spends over 36 billion BEF/ year (C$1.4 billion) in this area, and the number of beneficiaries went from 97,000 to 203,000 between 1984 and 1996. This increase can partly be explained by the aging population and cuts in other forms of social services such as welfare payments (while allowances for persons with disabilities were maintained) and a generally better informed public. Note that there are interesting geographical disparities in the number of allowances granted, but they do not necessarily correspond to the Flemish-francophone split.[28]

Social Security Provisions. Disability is taken into consideration in the calculation of pensions,[29] unemployment insurance,[30] and family allowances.[31]

Individual physiotherapy, speech-therapy treatments, as well as prosthesis are reimbursed by health-care insurance policies, through the federal Institute of Health and Invalidity Insurance. User fees apply. Transportation costs to and from rehabilitation centres are not covered by the federal programs and different federated bodies have adopted different strategies regarding these costs.[32] This apparently minor detail illustrates the lack of uniformity that is gradually developing across the country. This provides another example of the complexity of the system; while individual treatments are reimbursed, the federal health-care system, the certification of rehabilitation services, as well as capital and operating costs, all fall under community jurisdiction.

Some Aspects of Employment Policies. Specific collective agreements. Despite the successive waves of constitutional reforms and the decentralization of important aspects of employment policies, in Belgium collective agreements are still negotiated at the federal level, for every activity, by national trade unions and national employers' organizations. Once a collective agreement is reached, it is certified by the federal-level Conseil national du travail and rendered compulsory by federal regulation.

Two major collective agreements contain special provisions regarding disabled employees. *Collective Agreement No. 26*[33] provides for renewable financial incentives for private employers to hire workers with disabilities. A federal labour inspector will assess the rate of reduced disability and determine the size of the public contribution that will be offered to the employer.

This can reach 50 percent of both salary and social security premiums.[34] Of interest, is that responsible federated bodies execute this decision and will make the actual payment to the employer. While the organizations do not determine the contribution, the federal inspector must obtain their advice prior to fixing the public contribution. This seems to be little more than a formality to ensure a certain amount of cooperation. As we will see later, however, some federated entities have created, or are about to create, their own incentive programs for the private sector — designed, administered and financed. It is likely that in the foreseeable future, these programs will have an impact on the prevalence of the federal incentive program. For now, however, they are quite popular: in 1997, there were over 2,400 persons employed under this program in Flanders and Dutch-speaking Brussels; 850 in the Walloon Region (excluding the German-speaking territory); 48 in that very territory; and 134 in Francophone Brussels.[35]

Collective Agreement No. 43 provides that all employees in regular employment must receive at least the minimum wage set by sectoral collective agreements. It has traditionally included an exception for persons with disabilities who work in what used to be called "protected workshops" and are now referred to as adapted work enterprises. In 1992, this special minimum salary was increased to 80 percent of the average monthly minimum income in 1996,[36] and it reached 100 percent in 1998.[37] While these increases were negotiated on a national basis, as we will see later, the adapted work enterprises are accredited and subsidized by agencies of responsible federated bodies. A complex federal-community-regional refinancing mechanism was thus renegotiated to help agencies deal with the increased cost of both the subsidies for salaries and direct grants to adapted work enterprises who had to face significant increases in their operating costs without having had any input into this policy development.[38]

Quotas in the federal administration and agencies. Quotas were set up in 1972, before constitutional decentralization in this policy area.[39] As civil servants were transferred to federated agencies, quotas followed. Now, entities can set their own quotas, or even abolish them. Note that while the federal State Council had no problem with a regional entity setting quotas for its own civil service and public organizations, it was prevented from introducing quotas in the private sector, stating that this constituted an infringement on the exclusive federal power over labour legislation.[40] There is no plan to introduce quotas for the private sector at the federal level. Indeed, the imposition of quotas at the federal level would require a consensus between the Flemish and the francophone components of the state. The Flemish Community tends to be more neo-liberal on economic issues and would favour incentives for employers to hire persons with disabilities. This is an example of the difficulties to which the bipolar nature of the federal system can give rise. In other words, the Walloon Region is precluded from implementing a particular policy because of a disagreement with the Flemish group. The opposite is also often the case.

Recruitment for all public administrations, including those of the federated entities, is done by a federal secretariat with the cooperation from the entities who transfer files of potential candidates with disabilities. An interesting (non-legislative) initiative of this recruitment service, at least as it applies to the federal public service, it that it will give priority to visually-impaired applicants for a receptionist position.

Special arrangements for public servants caring for people with disabilities. Federal public employees can have up to five days paid leave per year to accompany a person with disabilities on a subsidized vacation.

Transportation. In Belgium, jurisdiction over some areas of transportation has been transferred to the Regions, while others have remained a federal responsibility. This gives rise to a scattered distribution of powers. The federal government provides special parking permits for persons with disabilities for anywhere in the country. Value-added tax exemptions on the purchase of private adapted vehicles, and a VAT reduction on repairs are offered by the federal government, following European Union norms. Note that these reductions are indirectly shared with the Communities who receive a return on federally collected VAT. The federal government also exempts adapted vehicles from road user fees.[41] Finally, access and reduced pricing on trains fall under the federal jurisdiction, including the free passage for the person escorting a disabled individual. Finally, reduced pricing on planes is also a federal competency.

Reduced Prices on Public Utilities. There are means-tested reductions on telephone, gas, and electricity rates. While the reduction is provided by the utilities companies, proof of invalidity is established by the federal Department of Social Affairs. There is no actual government subsidy.

HANDYTEL. A 24-hour telephone service in three languages (Dutch, French, and German) provides general information, as well as information concerning individual allowance cases.

Tax Rebates. Since the vast majority of state revenues are raised by the federal government, and the federated agencies have not used their limited fiscal powers to reduce taxation rates, deductions and credits for people with disabilities are awarded by the federal government. For instance, the tax exemption for a child with a disability is about twice the rate of another child. Real estate taxes are doubled in the case of a disabled dependant. Since 1995, work done to adapt a private home is subject to a reduced VAT rate. Note that the two types of federal allowances are tax-exempt and need not be reported.

Justice and Administrative Appeals. Labour law and labour administrative tribunals are still under federal jurisdiction, even for employers who are now organized and subsidized by federated agencies, such as "adapted work enterprises."

Judicial review of administrative decisions emanating from federal and federated entities. Federal Labour tribunals have jurisdiction over most aspects of social law. At least three federated bodies now responsible for the integration of persons with disabilities have attempted to create administrative review boards to hear appeals from their decisions. The (federal) court of arbitration and the legislation section of the (federal) State Council[42] declared these attempts unconstitutional, since they infringed on the exclusive federal power in justice matters, and since no specific derogation had been introduced by the *Special Institutional Reforms Act.*[43]

A federated entity cannot, directly or indirectly, abrogate the jurisdiction of the Labour Tribunal to hear challenges to decisions made by the administration or the funds of federated bodies. Recent case law, however, allows a federated agency to modify the Judicial Code to add to the jurisdiction of the Labour Tribunal. Moreover, on some limited issues, a federated agency can set up a parallel but purely administrative review board, so long as people still have access to the Labour Tribunal.[44] Given these constraints, federated bodies have organized slightly different review processes, but all involve appeals to the federal tribunals. Hence, the Flemish Community, after failing to establish a distinct review process for all decisions, has amended the (federal) Judicial Code to add to the Labour Tribunal's jurisdiction: henceforth, that Tribunal will hear decisions on integration issues (as it always could) as well as decisions made by the Flemish Fund concerning residential care, which were not previously subject to review. In Wallonia, the federal Labour Tribunal maintains its classic jurisdiction over integration decisions, but a distinct Appeal Commission, whose decisions can only be challenged before the federal

State Council (administrative law section) hears appeals concerning residential care, as well as early-childhood support decisions.[45] This, again, illustrates the gradually divergent paths taken in the management of this policy area north and south of the linguistic border.

Civil law protection of persons and property. In federal Belgium, both the civil law and the Justice systems have so far remained under federal jurisdiction. Consequently, procedure to designate a tutor or to put a person under a special protection regime are uniform across the country.[46]

Policies Developed by Federated Entities

The next section deals with the constitutional powers and some of the policies developed by the Belgian federated bodies. Most of the policy work is done through funds, established by the different governments,[47] which have taken over the role of the previous national funds. The following is admittedly complex, but such is the reality of Belgian federalism! To avoid too many repetitions, Table 2 summarizes policies.

Flemish Community. The Vlaams Fonds[48] is responsible for the integration of persons with disabilities who reside in the Flemish Region, as well as for residents of Brussels who wish to receive services in Dutch.[49] It administers and finances policies to promote the social and professional integration of persons with disabilities (ordinary or special training, incentives to hire disabled workers, and adapted work enterprises) as well as individual assistance (information, orientation, accompaniment, home care, early childhood support for families with a disabled child, etc.). It provides individual help with transportation (such as subsidized fares to school, training or work, or the adaptation of a car). It also accredits and subsidizes different types of day centres and residential institutions. It has initiated a new program of "protected housing" in which a minimum of eight persons with disabilities live independently, with educators (one teacher for eight individuals). There are around 800 people living in 36 of these homes in Flanders.

The Flemish Community is also responsible for providing special schooling and for integrating children with disabilities into regular classes. This is not done by the Flemish Fund, however, but is a direct responsibility of the Flemish Department of Education.[50] Since education is a community power,[51] the Department of Education has jurisdiction over Dutch-speaking schools located in Brussels. The same is true of audio-visual programs (sign-language, television, etc.).

French Community. Policies regarding disabled persons were officially devolved to the Communities in 1980. As we saw, the transfer was readily effective as far as institutionalized care. The effective transfer of rehabilitation policies, however, only occurred in 1991. At that point, a Fonds communautaire pour l'intégration sociale et professionnelle des personnes handicapées was created.[52]

As explained above, only three years later, in 1993–94, the exercise of the French Community's constitutional jurisdiction for policies concerning disabled persons was transferred to the Walloon Region and to the COCOF. At its dissolution, personnel chose between the new Brussels francophone fund or the Walloon Fund. A new transfer of files occurred. Supplies, library facilities and so on were split between those two agencies.

Since this regionalization of the community powers concerning policies related to persons with disabilities, the French Community's responsibility in the disability area is essentially limited to formal education, through either special or regular classes. Although integration into regular classes is now seen as a desirable option, in the French Community, it only helps one disabled student for every 100. There seems to be a fair amount of resistance, both from overworked teachers — who do not receive specialized training — and parents.

At the postsecondary level, there is no legislative provision for either specialized or integration policies. Each institution is responsible for providing support to disabled students. As a result, integration is quite haphazard: some have translated course work into Braille, others will allow sign-language interpreters, but do not pay for them, some will do very little. It is often argued that there is very little demand for these kinds of services! But, of course, one could argue that there is little demand, because there is little on offer.

The French Community is only responsible for the education of students 21 years of age and under. After that, the Walloon and francophone funds will reimburse the cost of maintaining the students in schools.[53]

Given its constitutional powers in cultural matters, the French Community can develop cultural programs for persons with disabilities. For instance, it has introduced sign-language translation for many television programs on one of the public television stations, most importantly the daily news. It also provides audio-visual materials though public *mediathèques* (books on tape, etc.).

As we will see, costs not covered by the French Community, such as individual help with extra transportation or residential costs, or particular pedagogical tools or tutoring, will be covered by either the now regionalized funds in Wallonia or in Brussels. In fact, responsibilities for pedagogical aid offered outside schools, colleges or universities have been regionalized on the French side of the country, but integration inside educational establishments have remained with the French Community. Again, this illustrates the complexity of the distribution of powers in this area.

German-Speaking Community. The German office for the integration of disabled persons[54] is responsible for institutionalized care, the social and professional integration policies, as well as special and integrated education of persons with disabilities in the German-speaking community. In other words, none of these competencies has been regionalized as in the French Community.

Regional powers regarding accessibility to buildings open to the public, public transit, and social housing are dealt with by the Walloon Region in the German-speaking Community, which is constitutionally enclosed within the Walloon Region. Policies developed by the German-speaking Community are quite similar to those developed by other agencies.

Flemish Region. The Flemish Region (whose institutions are merged with those of the Flemish Community) is responsible for regional matters affecting persons with disabilities, such as improving access to buildings open to the public as well as public transit. So far the pre-devolution policies of the federal government are generally still being applied, but the legislative power to modify them lies with the Flemish Parliament. As this is a regional power, it does not apply in Brussels, but only in Flemish territory, contrary to helping individuals with transportation, for instance, which is considered a "personal assistance" matter, falling under Community jurisdiction and for which Flemish institutions can extend support to Dutch-speaking disabled Brusselers.

Walloon Region. Apart from the education policies relating to people with disabilities (over which the French Community has jurisdiction), the powers of Wallonia are similar to those of the Flemish Community-Region. Some of them are true regional powers and are thus governed by the Walloon Parliament and administration. As we have just seen, those also apply to the German Community and include social housing, norms regarding access to public buildings, and public transportation.

Powers transferred by the French Community in 1993–94 regarding integration policies, however, apply to the Walloon Region, *minus* the German area. These powers are exercised by a "para-regional" fund: the Agence wallonne pour l'intégration des personnes handicapées (AWIPH), created in 1995.[55] See Table 2.

Brussels Region and the Commission Communautaire Française. While the foregoing might appear quite complex, the worst is yet to come! Institutions and legislative powers in Brussels are very intricate. This is partly due to the paradox of the city. It is a Region like the two others, with a regional legislative assembly and an executive. However, the jurisdiction over "community" matters in Brussels belongs to subgroups on these regional institutions: either the French-speaking members, sitting as the French Community Commission, or the Flemish-speaking members, for community matters of interest to Dutch-speaking Brusselers, or a combination of all of them (which means exactly the same people as in the regional Parliament, but wearing different hats, and this time called the Common Community Commission) in the case of Community matters (as opposed to regional ones) which affect both groups in Brussels. Those are called bi-community issues.

Hence, five different agencies, in addition to the federal and municipal levels, intervene on issues regarding persons with disabilities in Brussels: (i) the Region of Brussels, (ii) the Flemish Community, (iii) the French Community, (iv) the Common Community Commission (over bilingual social institutions),[56] and (v) the French Community Commission.

For all disabled residents of Brussels, regional powers (such as access to public transit or buildings and social housing) fall under the jurisdiction of the regional Legislative Assembly of Brussels (which has representatives of both linguistic groups).

The *Flemish Community* has not transferred any legislative power to the Flemish Community Commission.[57] The latter only has regulatory powers over Flemish cultural matters in Brussels. As regards disabled persons, policies designed by the Flemish government through the Vlaams Fonds will apply to Flemish institutions in Brussels as well as to the Flemish Region. In fact, there are no Dutch-speaking adapted work enterprises in Brussels, and only one Dutch-language residential institution.

The *French Community* plays the same role in Brussels as it does in Wallonia: it is essentially responsible for formal education, as well as for cultural issues. Again, a francophone, disabled student — from primary to university — will be subjected to French Community policy while in school (but not for help getting to school, or after school). For that, the student needs to turn to the Fonds bruxellois francophone of the French Community Commission.

The *Common Community Commission* (COCOM) is responsible for bi-community institutions in Brussels, that is, institutions that offer services to both French and Flemish residents of Brussels. While Brussels is officially a bilingual region, *bicommunautaire* institutions are the exception, not the rule. In Brussels, only 14 institutions catering to disabled persons are officially bilingual, and thus governed by COCOM. They are all full-time residential institutions or day centres for adults. There are no bilingual adapted work enterprises in Brussels.

The *French Community Commission of Brussels* (the COCOF) exercises the powers that were transferred by the French Community to the Region in 1993–94.[58] It is important to underline that inhabitants of Brussels do not, per se, have what is referred to as a French or a Flemish sub-nationality. It is the institution to which they turn that is linguistically tied and thus falls under the jurisdiction of the Flemish, the French, or both communities. For example, a Flemish-speaking, a francophone, and a Spanish immigrant, all domiciled in Brussels,[59] and who want to follow professional training in Flemish in Brussels will be governed by Flemish Community legislation. If the same people want to work in a French-speaking adapted work enterprise, they will be governed by the COCOF.[60]

In summary then, for Brussels: general social housing, including the designation of a number of units for persons with disabilities is a regional matter, while policies regarding individual help to modify a house, or to move to a more adequate one, is a Community matter (a regionalized Community matter for the francophone side). In Brussels, it is thus the responsibility of either of the Fonds bruxellois francophone (FBF), or the Vlaams Fund. Providing individual help for transportation to and for an adapted work enterprise is a Community, or regionalized community, responsibility, thus a responsibility of the FBF or the Vlaams Fund, depending on the language of service, but public transportation, including adaptation of buses for wheelchairs etc., is regional. Individualized programs of professional integration and professional training are done through the FBF or the Vlaams Fund, but regular placement policies and structures are regional. In the French-speaking part of the country, pedagogical support after school hours for a student with disabilities has been regionalized, but integration into regular classes and specialized education is still the responsibility of the French Community.[61]

An example of the intertwined constitutional responsibilities in this area is: a visually-impaired francophone student domiciled in Brussels would be taken to school by a service provided by the Region of Brussels (i.e., school buses are regional). At school, that student would be subject to French Community legislation and policies. Any after-school tutoring or special translation would be offered by the FBF (i.e., by COCOF). But if the student went to the mediathèque at night in order to borrow a CD, any particular help he or she would receive there, would be offered by the French Community. Note that if the individual took the subway to get to the mediathèque, he or she would benefit from the access policies developed by the Region of Brussels. But if it was the train, the federal government would have provided help with access! If someone was needed to accompany the student, that person's subway fare could be paid by the FBF, but if they took the train, the companion's fare would be paid by the federal government. This example shows the very complex intertwining of responsibilities of different public actors in this sector. While in Canada services will be under the authority of either the federal or the provincial order of government, in Belgium the number of responsible bodies is much larger. This is particularly striking given that Belgium is about the size of New Brunswick. Moreover, the situation in Brussels, officially bilingual but over which both unilingual Communities have claims, in addition to the federal government, is a disorienting puzzle. The complexity regarding policies that apply to persons with disabilities is only one example of the impact of the federalization process over public life over the last 20 years. This complex scenario is repeated in all areas of public policy, which has had to adapt to the evolving multi-layered federal system.

The decentralized system provides for a degree of asymmetry in services rendered. For instance, the list of "material aids" paid by distinct federated entities differs; hearing-impaired students can have 600 hours of interpretation outside classes in francophone Brussels, while the Flemish Community offers 900 hours which can be used in or outside classes. The way in which certain institutions are financed differs as well.[62] Yet, the differences remain quite minimal. As one policymaker in this area noted: you do not rewrite 30 years of unified policy-making in just a few years of policy-making power decentralization, especially since in many cases the personnel who now manage this policy area for the federated agencies used to work together for the federal government. There is thus a fair degree of continuity. Gradually, however, more visible distinctions in services will likely occur, particularly since the regional parliaments are now directly elected. The momentum for autonomous governance is likely to increase. The next few years may see the emergence of increasingly different services, both quantitatively and qualitatively in the north and the south.

Funding and Redistribution

Certain benefits offered to people with disabilities are directly financed by the "classical" social-security mechanisms (health and rehabilitation services, pensions, family allowances), and the two specific federal allowances are financed from the social-security budget, although the benefits are, exceptionally, not contributory. User fees are imposed for health services and rehabilitation. Other services, however, are paid from the general revenues of both Regions and Communities.

Tax deductions are available to those who care for a person with disabilities at home. Employers' contributions toward the social-security system (which generally correspond to about 26 percent of an employee's) are subsidized (by federated entities) for disabled employees, and management (with or without disabilities) of adapted work enterprises. As mentioned above, allowances themselves are exempt from income tax.

The old national rehabilitation fund was partly financed through a special premium on fire, car, and work-related accident insurance policies. In 1988, when responsibilities for individual rehabilitation and medical services were transferred to the federal medicare agency (INAMI), that agency acquired the proceeds of these special taxes. In other words, these specific insurance taxes are still being ear-marked. However, they are no longer solely aimed at persons with disabilities, but at all users of medical services.

As for services offered by the Communities and the Regions, they are financed from their general revenues. Within their envelope each entity has the authority to grant advantages or benefits to persons with disabilities in the framework of its own jurisdiction, to the extent that it has the financial means to pay for them.[63] So far, as noted, the differences have remained marginal.

Both federal allowances are financed through the regular social-security system. They are means-tested and, exceptionally for a social-security benefit, non-contributory. Integration services offered by the federated entities are offered regardless of income, but the contribution requested may vary for certain services depending on income. This ensures a certain degree of vertical redistribution.

To the extent that there are general financial transfers between the north and the south of the country, through the federal, social-security, tax and equalization systems, a certain amount of implicit interregional or intercommunity redistribution operates. With regards to disabled persons, it appears that there are more francophones receiving the income replacement for those 21–65 years, plus integration federal allowances (in absolute numbers), but more Flemish-speaking people in the over 65 category. It is thus difficult to assess whether part of the country receives more than another in this specific policy domain. Of note, however, are the distinctions in services *within* federated entities, depending in part on the economic well-being in the area. For instance, the poorer province[64] of Hainault in Wallonia suffers from a serious lack of full-time residential institutions for adults, while the province of Namur, also in Wallonia, has nearly half of its institutions occupied by people from other parts of Wallonia.[65]

The Intergovernmental Process

The foregoing descriptions indicate that all orders of government are involved in offering services to persons with disabilities. A certain amount of coordination is therefore required to ensure that services are properly rendered. Some users complain of being shifted from one government agency to another. Several services are offered by the federated bodies on a subsidiary basis, so that an application must first be filed with, for instance, the federal Institut d'assurance-maladie-invalidité. As mentioned above, there are gaps in the financing of transportation costs to rehabilitation treatment, when neither order of government feels responsible for a particular aspect. Another small detail, but one that illustrates the lack of coordination: Communities used to pay for maintenance of all wheelchairs. Now, the Walloon Fund refuses to pay for the maintenance of equipment paid for by the federal INAMI (as part of the rehabilitation program).

Some modifications to federal policies can have a direct impact on the federated agencies. That was the case in the decision by the social partners at the national level to remove the exception that permitted the payment of less than the sectorial minimum wage to persons with disabilities. The cost of this decision was borne by the federated bodies. This led to important intergovernmental negotiations.

Several public servants, when asked: "How do people find their way around this rather complex system?" responded that they get help from organizations that have had to keep up-to-date! There is a recognition that the restructuring of the state has had an impact on the way services are delivered. There is also an awareness that very little structural coordination occurs between the activities of the different public actors. In fact, it is interesting to note that while some of the funds have International Affairs sections, none of them have one specifically in charge in Belgian intergovernmental issues. The degree to which federated organizations ignore each other's work is truly surprising (especially across the linguistic border). One interesting form of cooperation across this divide took place in the judicial arena, the Flemish Community bringing its support to the Walloon Region in the latter's unsucessful attempt to convince the federal State Council that it had the constitutional power to create its own judicial review board in order to hear appeals of administrative decisions concerning rehabilitation.[66]

Nevertheless, cooperation is slowly evolving, and it takes different forms.

Cooperation Between Administrations. In Brussels, people can only register with one fund in order to obtain services: the Fonds francophone or the Flemish Fund. To avoid duplication, information is shared between these two bodies.[67] This is a purely administrative unwritten arrangement. Otherwise, the sharing of information seems to occur on an ad hoc basis, between individuals — who often used to work together in the same organization and who now work for decentralized ones — rather than between institutions. There are no formal discussion meetings, or regular transmission of information on programs, and so on. Occasionally, Flemish and francophone policymakers will discover what the others are doing in the context of a European-based forum. What I would call "active" cooperation is not very common with the federal authorities, since responsibilities are fairly well defined (despite some identified gaps). Cooperation is sometimes difficult between the Flemish and the Walloon parts of the country, largely due to the linguistic divide. On the other hand, cooperation between the Walloon Agency, the COCOF, and the German Community, which all occurs in French, is quite regular.

Formal Cooperation Agreements.[68] In the section on evaluation and assessment, I address the issue of formal cooperation agreements between federated organizations. Such agreements, which in Belgium enjoy constitutional status, have been concluded between the francophone and German-speaking bodies, but not between those and the Flemish Community-Region, which creates some gaps in services for a segment of the disabled population.

Interministry Meetings are informal and irregular. More frequent are meetings of ministers of health, which can deal with issues relevant to persons with disabilities. There are no secretariats or agencies to ensure continuity. Of note though, ministers responsible for policies regarding persons with disabilities in Wallonia, the German-speaking community, and Brussels have for a long time been members of their respective socialist parties. It is difficult to surmise what would have happened otherwise, but one can presume that cooperation is facilitated in such a situation. By contrast, in Flanders, in addition to the linguistic barrier, the minister responsible for policies for those with disabilities is from the Social-Christian Party (CVP). This may partly explain the obstacles found in the negotiation of free-mobility cooperation agreements between Flanders and other entities.[69]

Cooperation Induced by European Institutions. Belgium will now send several delegates, representing the different agencies responsible for a particular issue, to the meetings of the international organizations. For example, at the Council of Europe committee on discrimination against disabled people, Belgium sends four delegates (French Community, French Community Commission, Flemish Community, and Walloon Region). The German Community could send a representative, but does not. Occasionally, the Council of Europe will request a national report. In such a situation, one of the federated organizations (more rarely the federal government) will collect information and write on behalf of all other public actors.[70]

By contrast, the European Commission normally insists on having only one national spokesperson for some of its programs. This requires a certain amount of cooperation and coordination within Belgium. There are a few examples of "European-induced" cooperation. For instance, a program of the European Commission in place between 1993 and 1996 had four main lines of intervention: rehabilitation, integration in the education system and the economy, social integration, and the promotion of autonomy.[71] For this program, the French Community and the COCOF were represented by the Walloon Region member and there was alternate representation by the Flemish Community and the Walloon Region. In that case there was intra-francophone cooperation and representation across the linguistic divide.

In the case of another European program, a multilingual database on available services, the different federated bodies created a non-profit organization to provide a single Belgian spokesperson. This is a form of "cooperation through incorporation."[72] However, after a while, the Flemish and French data collecting organizations, part of the association, worked completely independently, often dealing directly with Europe. By the end, they were receiving their funds directly from the federated agencies (for the Belgian part) rather than through the non-profit organization, which gradually became an empty-shell. In other words, this form of cooperation was a partial success.

A more recent European program also requires only one official spokesperson per country. This has led to intense negotiations within Belgium.[73] The Flemish prefer to alternate yearly between the Flemish and francophone bodies (on the bipolar federal model), while the francophones favour a rotation between the four federated entities active in the area of policies for persons with disabilities (on the multipolar model). The issue is still unresolved.

On the other hand, here is a counter-example of European-induced cooperation. The Horizon program of the European Commission co-finances projects in employment-related areas. A sector deals with the professional integration of persons with disabilities. In order to get financing, government agencies must collaborate with an agency from another country (or entities composing these states). Hence, the Walloon Agency has projects with other public institutions in Portugal, the United Kingdom, Italy, Spain, Germany. However, it cannot collaborate with the Flemish Region for European financing. A Walloon official explained that at one meeting at which everyone presented projects, in the hope of finding groups in other countries interested in filing a joint application for European funds, she discovered that the Flemish Region had a very similar project, obviously designed to answer similar needs. They had never shared the information before, nor did they do so after. They could collaborate indirectly, if both received funding to work with the same organization from the same third country, but not if they worked together. In this particular case, no tripartite cooperation project emerged.

In the end, it appears that cooperation depends on the entities involved. Overall, the bipolar nature of Belgium remains prevalent even in the European context: The Flemish Community, on one side, and the francophone (and sometimes German-speaking) agencies on the other. Europe encourages dialogue in this divided country, but the unity is sometimes cosmetic. Moreover, when it is not required, it often simply does not occur.

The European Commission works on collecting and sharing information.[74] There is no strategy, at least at this stage, to harmonize legislation and policies on most social issues, including those affecting persons with disabilities. Europe is still too heterogeneous in culture and in wealth.[75] The emphasis is on developing common orientations, reflections, but not yet common policies.[76] Nevertheless, as recommendations become more precise, there could be a convergence of policies within Belgium, which would partly counteract the probable divergent paths that will evolve due to the direct election of the regional parliaments. This impulse could also come from other international organizations, but it is unlikely to be rapid.[77] In any event, this "convergent" action may not even result from increased cooperation, but simply from parallel but comparable policy-making.

Leading Developments in the Field

One policy issue currently being discussed raises several constitutional questions, this is the suggestion of "dependency-insurance" or sometimes "autonomy-insurance." It would cover assistance to persons suffering from a lack of autonomy and would be through homecare, day centres, institutional care, and so on. While the main target group is the elderly, the insurance would also benefit persons with disabilities.

This insurance could be considered protection against "social" risk, and thus a new area of social security, a clearly federal jurisdiction. Or it could be considered another aspect of assistance to persons, and thus a community responsibility. While the 1993 constitutional reforms transferred residual powers from the federal state to the federated bodies, this provision will not come into force until decrees have determined which of the Communities or the Regions will inherit this power. In the meantime, it remains federal. Hence, some could argue that this is a new field of public intervention, and that in the current constitutional state of affairs, only the federal Parliament has the power to legislate in this area.

In fact, a few years ago, the federal government launched the idea of such an insurance in its Loi-program. The Flemish Council reacted strongly, threatening to pull the *sonnette d'alarme* and set the concertation process into motion. The federal initiative was abandoned. Recently, the Flemish Parliament adopted an Act that re-introduced the idea. The insurance would cover the population of Flanders. As for Brussels, people could choose to opt into the program, regardless of their mother tongue. The constitutionality of this legislation will almost certainly be challenged before the Court of Arbitration.

The Situation as it Appears to Governments

Unlike health care, policies concerning persons with disabilities are not a hotly debated issue. The gradual redistribution of powers in this area has worked fairly well and in a sense, it could be argued that it illustrates how social policy could evolve within a state in the process of major constitutional transformation. Apart from relatively minor disagreements, and a limited degree of cooperation on the

European front, orders of government ignore each other. While services to the disabled population are developed and protected in a country with generous social programs, this is not a field that raises major concerns at the political level.

The Situation as it Appears to Persons with Disabilities

The situation is, however, disconcerting for users of the system. On the one hand, it can be argued that the constitutional and institutional changes have not profoundly altered the content of the policies, so that clients remain relatively unaffected by the transferring of responsibilities over the last 20 years. On the other hand, however, it can also be argued that the system, as most aspects of public life in Belgium, has become extremely opaque for citizens. There is little doubt that such a system gives rise to overlapping, gaps, confusion, and problems of accountability.

EVALUATION AND ASSESSMENT

Policy Comprehensiveness and Efficiency

Generally, a shift in philosophy has developed in the last few years. The 1963 and 1967 national legislation put the emphasis on the creation of parallel institutions (special classes, protected workshops, institutions), rather than on integration. Following important reflections which arose from the 1981 International Year of Disabled Persons, the emphasis is now more on integration, although the parallel programs and institutions remain very important, even predominant. The recent legislation adopted by the federated bodies puts more emphasis on reducing exclusion and promoting autonomy, as well as offering adequate services in housing, education, rehabilitation, and training, but there is still a gap between policy objectives and results.

Belgium has one of the lowest poverty rates of the OECD countries. This would suggest that even those living on basic income-replacement allowances, such as the federal disabled-allowance, fare relatively better than disabled people living in most western countries. Moreover, individual help in professional orientation and training, housing, transportation, and education, is available to all persons with disabilities.

But is it sufficient? Can one live or only survive on the *Mimimex*? Are cities accessible to everyone? Is integration really a priority? The National Council for Disabled Persons has raised several concerns.[78] It feels that the two federal allocations are insufficient to allow an individual to lead an autonomous life. The first one is aligned on the minimum level of subsistence, designed as emergency, last resort minimal benefits. The integration allocation is not linked to the extra costs caused by the handicap, but to family income. Moreover, the amount of the allowance varies depending on the cause of the handicap. Hence, persons receiving workers' compensation and war victims receive more than those suffering from a congenital disability who receive the residual allowance. The Council also complains that the entitlement to the equipment required to lead an autonomous life is not legally guaranteed and that access to such equipment has been severely cut in recent periods of economic recession.

Regarding housing, several experiments have taken place to encourage people to stay in their homes, but funding is limited and does not cover all costs. While rules of construction of social housing provide for a certain number of accessible units, these rules are not sufficiently enforced. Similarly, few means of public transportation, apart from trains, are accessible to people with disabilities. [79] Legislation dating from the mid-1970s relative to the accessibility of buildings being open to the public was not well-known, and certainly not enforced.[80] Furthermore, it had no retroactive effect, so that many city halls, cultural centres or train stations built before 1975 (which are many in Europe) are still not accessible. The Council notes that non-accessibility is sometimes even invoked to preclude access by disabled people, that is, their very presence is considered a fire hazard in cinemas, restaurants, theatres, etc., which, of course, justifies their exclusion. Accessibility to public buildings[81] is now a regional matter in Belgium. Regional entities have taken advantage of newly acquired legislative powers to rejuvenate policies. The question of effectivity and enforcement is still open, however. To a non-expert eye, it seems like there is still a need for progress to be made in making public space more accessible (trams, subways, cobbled streets, raised sidewalks, stairs, etc.).

The Council has concluded that the number of slightly disabled persons employed in adapted work enterprises, who could integrate into a regular normal working environment, is overrepresented.[82] It also underlines that the numerous work-incentive programs managed by the different orders of government do not pay particular attention to the needs of persons with disabilities.[83]

Cooperation Agreements Concerning Mobility

The federalization of policies and the creation of community and regional funds have produced problems for mobility. A person domiciled in Flanders has to register with the Vlaams Fonds to receive services. What if this person wants to attend an institution in Brussels? There is no problem if the institution is Flemish-speaking since it will be administered by the same fund. But what if the institution is French-speaking?[84] Similarly, what if a Walloon wants to work in an adapted work enterprise in Brussels? Or what if a resident of Brussels seeks to be admitted into an institution in Wallonia or Flanders? Or if a resident of the German-speaking Community needs to be admitted to an institution in Wallonia? To state the obvious, Belgium is a very small country and mobility is particularly important.

In 1993, when the French Community devolved the exercise of its jurisdiction to the COCOF and to the Walloon Region, it retained its legislative authority to determine the categories of handicap which are entitled to different types of services, in particular different types of institutions.[85] Yet, the year after, the Walloon Region sought to *add* a residency criterion for access to its services. This would have precluded residents of Brussels from receiving services in Wallonia.[86] The French Community Commission set off the alarm system, setting into place a concertation process[87] and threatening to go the Cour d'arbitrage to challenge the Walloon decree, were it to be adopted. Finally, a compromise was reached. The Walloon residency requirement was maintained, but "subject to" the adoption of cooperation agreements. Those were soon concluded both with the COCOF[88] and the German-speaking Community[89] ensuring mobility between these entities.

The residency requirement episode between the Walloon Region and the COCOF shows that tensions are not limited to agencies representing different linguistic groups. However, the fact that an agreement still has not been reached between the Flemish Community and other organizations shows, if not the depth of incompatibilities, at least the lack of political will to find a quick solution. In fact, different versions for an agreement between Flanders and the other federated bodies have been produced since 1994. They have not, however, been concluded yet.[90]

The lack of cooperation between Flanders and the rest of the country has definitely led to a denial of services to which some people had access previously, although the number of affected persons is difficult to estimate. To give an example, for *integration* services, applicants must register with their residential fund. Hence, all residents of Flanders must first register with the Vlaams Fonds. However, the Vlaams Fonds will not subsidize a resident of Flanders who attends a French adapted work enterprise in another part of the country.[91] Theoretically, a francophone from the Flemish periphery of Brussels could work in a French-speaking adapted work enterprise in Brussels or in Wallonia. But he or she will not receive a salary subsidy from Flanders, nor from the other agencies in which he or she is not a resident. So, in effect, a person in that situation would not be accepted by the French-speaking adapted work enterprise, which needs the financial contribution. In other words, francophones from the periphery are deprived of a service to which they were entitled previously.[92] While the reverse is theoretically also true, in reality there are far fewer Flemish residents of Wallonia who would seek services in Flemish.

The consequences of these barriers to mobility are barely discussed in Belgium outside the disability circle. However, in my view, they constitute a warning of the risks involved in the Flemish proposals to transfer jurisdiction over health care to the Communities. In some respect, persons with disabilities have paid the price of a decentralization process that was driven by a desire for increased autonomy, not a concern for the quality, or continuity, of services.

Federalism Principles

Yet, despite the gaps in communication and the difficulty experienced by some people in their search for services in their preferred language, the disability domain respects a fairly clear distribution of powers. Other policy areas, such as health care or employment, contain so many exceptions to the official transfer of jurisdiction that the decentralization is either cosmetic or at least, partial. In the case of health care, the transfer of powers to the Communities has been so limited that it has given rise to a Flemish movement to partially split the federal social-security system. In the case of employment policies, there are so many actors involved that the lines of responsibility are blurred and effective policy-making is a real challenge.

Policies regarding persons with disabilities illustrate the difficulties generated by a decentralization process, but they also illustrate that this process *can* function without completely endangering service delivery. This policy area could provide lessons for policymakers regarding the impact of federalization on concrete aspects of governmental services.

Most aspects of policies concerning persons with disabilities are clearly "disentangled." Often, the actual policies remain relatively similar, regardless of the federated body responsible for designing, implementing, and financing them. This appears to be more a result of habit and coincidence than coordination. The different federated entities enjoy a large degree of autonomy in the field of disability policy. Similarly, the federal government can act quite independently of the federated bodies (to modify allowances, for instance). It is important to bear in mind, however, that the federal institutions are essentially bipolar and consequently that any action on their part automatically takes into consideration the preferences of each major cultural community.

The general trend in Belgium is toward more decentralization. The only federal policy regarding persons with a disabilities that is currently under discussion by the autonomy-seeking Flemish authorities is the integration allowance. It is argued that this financial contribution is so closely tied to integration policies currently under Community jurisdiction that it should also be managed by the Communities. Again, this appears to be a matter of institutional coherence (bringing related jurisdictions together) rather than a policy-driven request. This is not, however, a hotly debated issue compared to the topic of decentralization of health care, for instance.

Overall, the disability policy arena is disentangled, yet remarkably homogeneous across the country. This is not surprising since some aspects were only truly transferred less than ten years ago. Distinctions are likely to appear in the years to come, as autonomous, elected legislatures develop new programs. In this regard, it is worth mentioning that the Flemish Community tends to look to the Netherlands and other Germanic countries for models of social and economic policy, while the French-speaking side of the country tends to draw its inspiration from France.

CONCLUSIONS

Intergovernmental relations in the sector of policies regarding disabled persons in Belgium is in transition, largely because the division of powers is so recent. In some cases, the ink was not even dry on the papers and the files hardly transferred before a new agency became responsible for this area. Powers have not stabilized, and a *fortiori*, nor have intergovernmental relations.

The complexity of the division of powers in this area, the labyrinth in which an individual finds him or herself, are particularly taxing for organizations that represent people with disabilities. Yet, despite this complexity, particularly acute in the French part of the country, the division of powers in this area is sufficiently clearly defined for entities to independently develop coherent policies. Moreover, the competencies that have remained with the federal government, while important in financial terms, do not preclude the institutions from legislating in a fairly autonomous manner. This, I believe, is quite different from the employment or health-care sectors, where, despite a theoretical transfer of powers, the exceptions to transferred competencies are so numerous, important, and varied, that the agencies either do not know exactly what they can do, or know that they cannot do very much.

There is in Belgium, an impressive array of programs and policies related to persons with disabilities. There are some differences on the margins in some of the federated entities, but many are still similar across the country. Action is parallel, but relatively comparable. This is quite interesting, given the few formal means of information-sharing.

There are a few gaps concerning services which no order of government wants to offer. There is also some overlap: work-incentive programs organized by federal institutions, but paid for by other bodies compete with programs totally organized and financed by those bodies. There is also some "federal dumping": the maintenance of wheelchairs bought by the federal INAMI used to be paid for by the Communities, now the Walloon Fund has stopped paying. The restrictions on the creation of administrative panels to review decisions by federated agencies can create some frustrations, but to the extent that the federal tribunals work efficiently (which in this area they seem to do) and work in both languages (which they do), the frustration has not led to too much acrimony.

As far as policy-orientation is concerned, the trend toward integration, as opposed to "protection," has been incorporated into the public policy rhetoric, as well as some of the legislation, but it has not so far translated into substantial changes in practice. To give but one example, in the Walloon Region in 1996, only four people were involved in regular professional training courses, while 694 were registered in specialized centres.

Without spending power, the federal government cannot get involved in matters that have been transferred to Communities or Regions. Likewise, Regions cannot spend in matters that have not been attributed to them. As a result, if they do want to "spend" on an issue, they will try everything to demonstrate that it falls outside their jurisdiction: the dependence-insurance debate illustrates this point quite clearly.

In conclusion, there is a fair amount of complementary action on the part of different orders of government, although often this seems to have occurred by chance, without coordination. In other words, there has not been a great deal of discussion on who should do what. Policy-making is largely disentangled, but ironically, quite compatible. This is no doubt due to the residential momentum of the still recent unitary system. Divergences are likely to appear as the decentralized state structure is consolidated.

NOTES

[1]This section greatly benefited from a paper written by Kris Deschouwer for the workshops held at the Institute of Intergovernmental Relations in Kingston, in September 1998.

[2]Ronald Watts, *Comparing Federal Systems*, 2d ed. (Montreal and Kingston: School of Policy Studies, Queen's University and McGill-Queen's University Press, 1999).

[3]This section is largely inspired by Philippe Cattoir's analysis.

[4]See Loi spéciale de financement du 16 janvier 1989, as modified by the Loi spéciale du 16 juillet 1993 visant à parachever la structure fédérale de l'État.

[5]Although this fee is set by the federal government, it is collected by the federal government and then redistributed to the communities.

[6]Fonds pour l'équilibre financier. This is a very schematic version of the social-security program that applies to salaried employees. Distinct programs exist for civil servants, self-employed persons, and members of specific trades.

[7]This is usually around 1,250 billion BEF. Ministère des affaires sociales, de la santé publique et de l'environnement, *Vade Mecum*, (Belgium: Budget des la Sécurité sociale, Contrôle budgétaire, 1996), p. 77.

[8]Also to the European Union. Total revenue transferred in 1997 (estimates): 1085,2 billion BEF. This is based on analysis by Philipe Cattoir.

[9]Loi du 1er juillet 1929, Arrêté d'exécution 22 avril 1929

[10]Loi du 16 avril 1963 relative au reclassement social des handicapés (M.B. 23.4.63).

[11]This fund is often referred to as the "Fonds-81," which comes from the regulation's number, but the name is still commonly used today to refer to institutional care services, and will be referred to later in the text. A.R. no. 81, 10 novembre 1967 (M.B. 10.11.67).

[12]Loi du 27 juin 1969 relative à l'octroi d'allocations aux handicapés (M.B. 15.07.69), et A.R. du 17 novembre 1969 portant règlement général relative à l'octroi d'allocations aux handicapés (M.B. 19.11.69).

[13]Loi spéciale de réformes institutionelles du 8 août 1980 (M.B. 15.08.80), s. 5 (1)(II)(4).

[14]Note that the 1980 Loi spéciale transferred those powers from the federal government to the Communities with a suspensive clause: Community decrees had to be taken before this transfer became effective. The National Fund for the social rehabilitation of handicapped persons of 1963 was thus dissolved by the Arrêté Royal du 3 juillet 1991 and replaced by the Vlaams Fonds, (M.B. 08.08.1990) and the Fonds communautaire pour l'intégration sociale et professionnelle des personnes handicapées, Décret de la Communauté française du 3 juillet 1991, (M.B. 30.07.1991). For the German-speaking Community, see Décret du 19 juin 1990 portant création d'un

"Dienststelle der Deutschsprachigen Gemeinschaft für Personen mit einer Behinderung sowie für dies besondere soziale Fursorge" (Office de la Communauté germanophone pour les personnes handicapées ainsi que pour l'assistance sociale spéciale) (M.B. 13.11.1990).

[15]The transfer of the exercise of the constitutional powers is really a constitutional transfer of legislative authority. In fact, the use of the term "exercise" is quite semantic, since the Walloon Region and the COCOF have complete normative authority over the transferred domains, and must approve any "retrocession" of the exercise of these powers to the French Community: see M. Leroy and A. Schaus, "Les relations internationales," in *Les réformes institutionnelles de 1993, Vers un fédéralisme achevé* (Bruxelles: Bruylant, 1994), p. 41. The term was used, however, to make it clear that the new authorities were limited in the exercise of these new powers as the French Community had been: in other words, while the Walloon Region Assembly has jurisdiction over the whole Walloon Region for regional powers (such as urban planning or public transit), it only has jurisdiction over the French-speaking parts of the Walloon Region in the exercise of the transferred community powers (i.e., the Walloon Region *minus* the territory of the German-speaking Community).

[16]Décret II de la Communauté française du 22 juillet 1993 attribuant l'exercice de certaines compétences de la Communauté française à la Région wallonne et à la Commission communautaire française, and corresponding decrees in the Région wallonne and the COCOF, taken pursuant to s. 138 of the constitution. With this transfer of legislative power, the COCOF has become, for many analysts, a federated entity. See, for instance, B. Blero and F. Delcor, "Les transferts de compétences de la communauté à la région," in *Les réformes institutionnelles de 1993: vers un fédéralisme achevé?* (Bruxelles: Bruylant, 1994), p. 100.

[17]I mention this distinction, because despite the recent constitutional transfer, the 1960s distinction between the two funds affects the way the new legislators can act (particularly with regard to appeal mechanisms).

[18]Note that reimbursement for medical services is done through health-care "mutualities" with which individuals register. The federal Institut d'assurance-maladie-invalidité receives funds from the Institut national de la sécurité sociale (ONSS) and transfers money to the many "mutualities" who reimburse their members.

[19]See, for instance, Arrêté du gouvernement de la Communauté française du 8 décembre 1995 transférant des membres du personnel du Fonds communautaire pour l'intégration sociale et professionnelle des personnes handicapées à la COCOF, (M.B. 10.02.96); Art. 73 of the Décret du Conseil régional wallon du 6 avril 1995 relatif à l'intégration des personnes handicapées, (M.B. 25.02.1995); Arrêté du Collège de la COCOF du 18 juillet 1996 portant équivalence de certains grades des fonctionnaires du Fonds bruxellois francophone pour l'intégration sociale et professionnelle des personnes handicapées (M.B. 18.9.96).

[20]In Brussels, however, the COCOF is about to modify its policies to permit organizations to attend meetings with the administration with the disabled person

requesting services, but not in lieu of them. This is presented as another way of promoting the autonomy of the person with disabilities.

[21]Created by arrêté royal 09.07.81 (M.B. 21.08.81).

[22]Along the same lines, until recently, the evaluation of a person's level of autonomy and professional integration was decided jointly between the person's social worker and the manager of the adapted work enterprise. Now, it is done solely by the former, since it is thought that managers could be in a conflict of interest position, seeking to maintain a person's low level of integration to justify a higher public subsidy (which is proportional to the rate of reduced productivity).

[23]For details, see the section on the intergovernmental process.

[24]This 20–30-percent rule is found in unabrogated sections of the national 1963 legislation. So, although federated bodies have developed less rigid definitions in their own legislation, technically, this numerical one still applies. Why the bodies have not abrogated this national rule (or incorporated it into their own legislation) is unclear.

[25]This is not the rule, as most social-security programs (health, unemployment insurance, workers' compensation, pensions and family allowances) are not financed through general tax revenues, but through premiums linked to salaries.

[26]The Loi du 27 février 1987 (M.B. 01.04.87) is a complete revision of the 1969 Act. Certain amendments were adopted in1993, including (i) the elimination of the definition of reduced capacity to earn an income as one-third or less of what an able-bodied person can earn; (ii) and the express inclusion of social-security benefits in the calculation of income (to avoid "double-dipping"); and (iii) the introduction of a distinct calculation of income-replacement allowance and the integration allowance.

[27]With an exemption of 60,000 BEF for the spousal income.

[28]For instance, 1.9 percent of the residents of the provinces of Brabant and of Flemish Anvers, as opposed to 3.3 percent for Western Flanders and 3.9 percent for Hainault (in Wallonia) receive allowances. These distinctions can be explained by differences in income and health in those areas.

[29]This covers pension rights accumulated through work in adapted work enterprises and the inclusion of days of incapacity to work in the entitlement to a pension.

[30]For instance, workers with a 33 percent permanent disability or more are entitled to 35 percent of their previous salary after 15 months of unemployment and for an unlimited time, which is more generous than the regular entitlement.

[31]Family allowances are substantially increased in the case of a disabled child or parent. If a child is institutionalized, two-thirds of the family allowance is transferred to the institution.

[32]The Walloon Fund (*infra*) refuses to pay for this transportation (though it pays for transportation of disabled persons to school, training, etc.). It maintains that this is an integral part of federal responsibility regarding rehabilitation. The francophone Brussels and the Flemish funds (*infra*) pay for these costs, however. Of course, before the domain was de-federalized, the National Fund paid for both general transportation (now community-regional) and rehabilitation (now federal), so the problem did not arise.

[33]Concluded by Conseil du Travail (15.10.75). Note that an employer cannot fire an employee in order to benefit from this program.

[34]It would be 40 percent in the German Community.

[35]Conseil de l'Europe, Comité pour la réadaptation et l'intégration des personnes handicapées, La législation anti-discriminatoire à l'égard des personnes handicapées, Rapport établi par la délégation belge – février 1997, pp. 14-15.

[36]Convention collective no. 43 septies du 02.07.96.

[37]"Augmentation du salaire minimum dans les ETA," *Le Soir*, 24 avril 1998, p. 3.

[38]The federal contribution takes the form of a generalized reduction in social-security premiums that adapted work enterprises must pay, see Loi du 6 décembre 1996 (M.B. 24.12.96).

[39]For the federal public service, A.R. du 11.08.72, as modified by A.R. 10-06-75 (M.B. 29.07.75), A.R. 29-11-76 (M.B. 19.01.77) et A.R. 19-07-85 (M.B. 07-08-85). For public organizations, A.R. 05-01-76 (M.B. 03-03-76), as modified by A.R. 23-10-89 (M.B. 23-11-98).

[40]Opinion of the State Council, legislation section, concerning s. 12 of the *Avant projet de décret wallon portant une politique globale d'intégration des personnes handicappées* L. 23.478/2/V, 12-08-1994. The proposed quotas were aimed at private enterprises hiring 50 people or more. Quotas for the Walloon Region are found in *Arrêté de l'exécutif régional wallon*, 13-09-90 (M.B. 11-12-90).

[41]Here is another interesting initiative: a non-profit organization, Le Centre d'adaptation à la route pour automobilistes handicapés, will assess a person's ability to drive, will loan an adapted vehicle for driving lessons and exams and recommend equipment.

[42]The State Council is the major administrative law appeal tribunal.

[43]Voir arrêt 49/93, C.A. 24 June 1993 (French Community); 25/97, C.A. 30 April 1997 (Flemish Community). Note that in this case, the Walloon Region intervened to support the Flemish Community against the federal government's position.

[44]Opinion of the State Council, legislation section, no. 23,478/2/v, 12 August 1994.

[45]Art. 22 décret wallon 06.04.95: Appeal Commission (administrative, multidisciplinary, headed by a judge). It has jurisdiction over appeals concerning decisions to award benefits (financial or in-kind) by the Walloon Agency. Although documents say the decision made by such a body is final, it can always be reviewed by the administrative section of the federal State Council.

[46]See *Civil code*, ss. 487-515 and *Judicial Code*, ss. 1238-1253

[47]Flemish Community, German-speaking Community, the Walloon Region and the COCOF.

[48]Vlaams Fonds voor Sociale Integratie van Personen met een Handicap, créé par la Loi du 27.06.90 (M.B. 08.08.90).

[49]This year, only 57 residents of Brussels are registered with the Vlaams Fonds. Other residents of Brussels receive their services from the francophone fund.

[50]Note that the competency to set criteria for diplomas, from kindergarten to university has remained under federal jurisdiction.

[51]Education was developed in 1989, but ever since 1970, there have been two Departments of Education, one for each linguistic group, and each one has its own specific legislation.

[52]Décret de la Communauté française du 3 juillet 1991 relatif à l'intégration sociale et professionnelle des personnes handicapées, (M.B. 30.07.91).

[53]There is a convention between the Walloon Fund and the French Community providing for the payment of 370,000 BEF per year, per student. It is estimated that there are 400 to 500 students in that situation.

[54]"Dienststelle der Deutschsprachigen Gemeinschaft für Personen mit einer Behinderung sowie für die besondere soziale Fürsorge," créé par Loi du 19.06.90 (M.B. 13.11.90).

[55]Décret du Conseil régional Wallon du 6 avril 1995 relatif à l'intégration des personnes handicapées, (M.B. 25.05.95).

[56]While Brussels is officially a bilingual region, *bicommunautaire* institutions are the exception, not the rule. In Brussels, only 14 institutions catering to disabled persons are officially bilingual, and thus governed by the COCOM. They are all full-time residential institutions or day centres for adults. There are no bilingual adapted work enterprises in Brussels. Note that the COCOM is financed not by both communities, but through federal transfers.

[57]It has been delegated administrative, not legislative, powers. This is not relevant in the present context, Loi spéciale du 12 janvier 89, s. 65 and Constitution, s. 166(3)(2).

[58]The Fonds bruxellois des francophones pour l'intégration sociale et professionnelle des personnes handicapées is to be replaced by the regular civil service. Representatives of COCOF explained that they believe it preferable to integrate services for persons with disabilities into the regular civil service, rather than getthoize it in a separate administrative body. This approach is, of course, quite different from the one taken by the other federated bodies.

[59]The problem of people domiciled outside the territory of a particular entity and who want services from that entity is addressed below, in the section dealing with cooperation agreements.

[60]Note that there are no Flemish or bilingual adapted work enterprises in Brussels.

[61]Note that for Dutch-speakers in-and-out of school, support is provided by distinct bureaucracies (the Department of Education inside schools, or the Vlaams Fond outside schools) but under the responsibility of the same federated entity, that is, the Flemish Community.

[62]Entreprises de travail adapté are discussed below.

[63]It is unclear, however, whether a federated entity could "subsidize" user fees. This would likely be seen as an infringement of exclusive federal power over social security.

[64]In the past, provinces were administrative divisions of the unitary state. They are now administrative divisions of the federal order of government, and not federated entities. They have no legislative power, for instance.

⁶⁵Agence Wallonne pour l'intégration des personnes handicapées (AWIPH), *Rapport d'activités 1996* (Wallonia: AWIPH, 1996), p. 59

⁶⁶See discussion on judicial review in the section on federal policies.

⁶⁷The problem does not arise in the other Regions since people must register with the fund in their area of residence.

⁶⁸"Cooperation agreements" as envisaged by s. 92 of the Loi spéciale du 8 août 1980, have constitutional status, are legally binding and can be interpreted and enforced by an ad hoc arbitration tribunal. Note that none of these tribunals has ever been constituted.

⁶⁹The problem is not so acute in the other direction, since there are far fewer Flemish-speakers in Wallonia (and in Brussels, Flemish-speakers can get services through the Vlaams Fonds).

⁷⁰See, for instance, the 1997 report on anti-discrimination legislation by the Belgian delegation to the Council of Europe.

⁷¹See HELIOS II, Guide européen de bonnes pratiques pour l'égalité des chances des personnes handicapées, C.E., Office des publications officielles, Bruxelles, 1992.

⁷²ASBL Handynet Belgique. The association also channelled the work of two data-collecting organizations, a Dutch and a French-speaking one.

⁷³High Level Committee on policies related to disabled persons.

⁷⁴Over 80 organizations collaborate with the European Commission to share information. This permitted the publication of good working practices on employment, education, integration and the functional readaptation of persons with disabilities.

⁷⁵For information on policies developed by the EU, see Brian Doyle, *Disability, Discrimination and Equal Opportunities: A Comparative Study of the Employment Rights of Disabled Persons* (London and New York: Mansell, 1995), pp. 55 ff.

⁷⁶Commission des communautés européennes, "Livre blanc: politique sociale européenne – une voie à suivre pour l'Union," 27 juillet 1994.

⁷⁷See United Nations, General Assembly, *Standard Rules on the Equalization of Opportunities for Persons with Disabilities*, 20 December 1993.

⁷⁸Conseil supérieur national des handicapés, *Non-discrimination et égalité des chances pour les personnes handicapées,* Rapport du colloque organisé le 29 nov. 1996 (Bruxelles: Point de vue du Conseil supérieur des handicapés, Administration de l'intégration sociale, Ministère des Affaires sociale, de la Santé publique et de l'Environnement, 1997).

⁷⁹Efforts are being made in this area. See, for instance, proposed legislation by the Parliament of the Brussels Region.

⁸⁰In fact, even the Belgian delegation to the Council of Europe notes that the 1975 legislation is not enforced, Conseil de l'Europe, Comité pour la réadaptation et l'intégration des personnes handicapées, *La législation anti-discriminatoire à l'égard des personnes handicapées, Rapport établi par la délégation belge*, février 1997, p. 12.

⁸¹This is a larger category than simply "public buildings."

[82]It also seems like specialized training if the individual is only prepared for adapted work enterprises, and not for regular employment, even when this is a realistic possibility.

[83]Conseil supérieur national des handicapés, Rapport d'activité 1997, copy of a letter dated september 1997 and addressed to State Secretary Jan Peeters.

[84]This would be particularly acute for francophones living on the periphery of Brussels. On this issue, see Association nationale d'aide aux handicapés mentaux, "Les difficultés rencontrées par des personnes handicapées dans une des régions et voulant être prises en charge dans une autre," Mai 1994. Note that the problems of mobility outlined in this chapter have been solved, except as regards Flanders.

[85]The 1967 National residential fund introduced 14 categories of handicap. When this fund was replaced by the Fonds communautaire in 1991, those 14 categories were maintained. In the subsequent transfer to the Walloon Region and to the COCOF, the French Community did not transfer the competence to modify these categories. S. 3(7) of the 1993 French Community decree states that policies toward persons with disabilities are transferred, except for norms establishing categories of persons with disabilities (Décret II de la CF du 19 juillet 1993), (M.B. 10 septembre 1993). These categories are important because residential institutions are accredited to receive individuals from certain determined categories of handicap.

[86]Projet de décret prédécent celui du 6 avril 1995.

[87]Article 62 of the constitution.

[88]Décret portant approbation de l'accord de coopération du 19 avril 1995 entre la Commission communautaire française et la Région wallonne visant à garantir la libre circulation des personnes handicapées, (M.B. 14.06.96).

[89]Décret portant assentiment à l'accord de coopération du 10 avril 1995 relatif à la prise en charge des frais de placement et d'intégration sociale et professionnelle des personnes handicapées (M.B. 06.11.96).

[90]A projected cooperation agreement between the French and the Flemish Communities to iron out these kinds of difficulties was developed in 1990, but never signed. It also provided for a regular exchange of information, contacts between institutions and advisory bodies, a civil servant responsible for "liaising" between the Communities. In fact, it is even more complicated than that: francophones from the periphery of Brussels can register directly in a residential institution or a day centre in Brussels or Wallonia. For those services, the person's domicile is not taken into account. In that case, the COCOF will subsidize them, that is, residents will have to pay a day fee, just as other residents (which can be paid from allowances), but they are not charged for extra operating costs.

[91]I was told that one adapted work enterprise located in the periphery "unofficially" functions in both languages, and will admit francophones.

[92]Note, however, that people who were admitted to services before the dissolution of the National Fund have a kind of *droit acquis* and are not moved out of their institution or work environment. The problem arises for new registrations.

4

CANADA'S FEDERAL REGIME AND PERSONS WITH DISABILITIES

Sherri Torjman

INTRODUCTION

At a major international conference, an august panel was asked to address, from their unique cultural perspectives, the topic of "the elephant." The speaker from England went on at length about "The Elephant and the Empire." The representative from France talked about "The Wine Preferences of the Elephant." The US delegate focused upon "Building a Bigger and Better Elephant." The Canadian presenter spoke about, not surprisingly, "The Elephant: Federal or Provincial Jurisdiction?"

Indeed, federal-provincial issues are never too far from the surface of any debate in Canada. Many discussions, tensions, and conflicts arise over the issue of who does what — and more important — who *should do* what in the political arena.

And so it goes with disability. In fact, the federal-provincial struggle and the rethinking of federalism in Canada have become the major concern of the disability community. There are two reasons for the marrying of these issues. Disability is on the federal agenda because Ottawa is trying to forge a new set of working relationships with the provinces. It has identified disability as a major focus for this work.

At the same time, federalism is on the agenda of the disability community which has long advocated the need for a strong federal role to protect its issues and advocate its interests. This championship role has been seen as the natural purview of the federal government; for the past two decades, the disability community has pinned its hopes on the federal government because of the human rights protections that Ottawa introduced in the early 1980s. These protections were seen as the key to opening all other doors, including employment opportunities and access to disability-related supports, that would lead to full citizenship. Moreover, federal constitutional protection takes precedence over all other laws, which means that these would have to conform to the requirements of the federal statute. A wide range of laws, policies, and programs would have to be changed in order to make concrete and real the national commitment to human rights.

But in recent years, the disability community has been deeply concerned that current shifts in federalism in Canada, embodied in a document known as the Social Union Framework Agreement (discussed below), will transform fundamentally the power balances in this country. The community worries that changes to the current "rules of the game" could undermine progress on the disability front. The fear is that the disability agenda could suffer a serious setback under new federal-provincial arrangements. While disability is a key item on the federalism agenda, the new federal-provincial relationships inadvertently could end up impeding progress on disability issues. In order to understand this irony and how it evolved, it is first necessary to look at the structure of the Canadian federation and current discussions to change its shape.

CHARACTERISTICS OF THE FEDERATION

Constitutional

Canada is a federated structure whose governance framework is set out in the *British North America Act* (BNA) of 1867. The framework was supplemented by the introduction of the *Constitution Act* in 1982.

Under the BNA Act, the federal government was designated as responsible for the "peace, order and good government of the country." The Act confers implicitly a federal spending power that allows the federal government to make payments to individuals, institutions or other governments for purposes that Parliament does not necessarily have the power to regulate. Ottawa claims that this constitutional interpretation gives it the power to spend money and attach conditions to the money even if the purposes fall within the clear purview of the provinces.

This interpretation resulted in the following division of powers. Ottawa has jurisdiction over areas that affect the well-being of the entire nation, including the armed forces, international trade, and communications. The federal Department of Human Resources Development is responsible for several national income security and employment training programs, although the latter recently have been devolved to the provinces. (The province of Ontario has not yet signed a bilateral labour market agreement with Ottawa.) Both the federal and provincial governments are involved in the areas of justice, finance, revenue, and transportation.

Constitutional responsibility for health and welfare-related issues, by contrast, was accorded to the provinces. "In 1867 provincial jurisdiction in the health and welfare field could be inferred from the specific headings of Section 92 of the BNA Act that granted them authority over "hospitals, asylums, charities and 'eleemosynary institutions,' 'municipal institutions,' 'property and civil rights,' and 'all matters of a merely local or private nature in the province.'"[1]

More complex is the issue of income security, which basically became defined as a field in which both federal and provincial governments share an interest. From an area of virtual provincial dominance in the 1860s, income security began to emerge as an area of decisive federal dominance. "Given the local, private and municipal complexion of welfare in the 1860s, provincial responsibility seemed clearly based in the constitution, and this pattern was seldom challenged until after the First World War. In the early decades of the new century, judicial decisions confirmed the authority of provincial governments to regulate commercial insurance plans and to establish workers' compensation programs, and the federal government was quite content to accept provincial responsibility for welfare, and to restrict its initiatives in the field to assistance for its own client groups, such as veterans in the aftermath of world war."[2]

However, the transition to an industrial economy and the emergence of high unemployment in the Depression of the 1930s created a demand for income support that proved beyond the fiscal capacity of local governments. The scope of social problems facing the country and the demand for greater action set off a series of federal responses. The time was ripe for federal involvement — primarily because of the need for postwar rebuilding. The first stages of intervention came in the form of grants to provincial governments. A constitutional amendment was passed in 1940 to permit the federal government to become involved in the provision of unemployment insurance. Subsequent constitutional amendments allowed Ottawa to provide old age pensions in 1951 and survivor and disability benefits in 1964.

As the economy improved, however, the political tides began to turn and the provinces reasserted their authority in what they claimed as their areas of jurisdiction: health, education, welfare, and social services. But the constitutional waters had been muddied by the fact that the federal government was involved in these fields by virtue of its constitutional spending power. Ottawa used to transfer money to the provinces for health and postsecondary education under a block-funded arrangement known as Established Programs Financing (EPF). Moreover, the federal government had (and continues to have) authority to enforce the conditions of the national medicare system under the *Canada Health Act* and to withhold funds for contravention of its conditions.

Ottawa also used to share with the provinces in the cost of welfare and social services under the Canada Assistance Plan (CAP). EPF and the CAP have since been rolled into a new arrangement called the Canada Health and Social Transfer (CHST), described below. The fact that the federal government contributed funds to these so-called provincial areas of jurisdiction certainly has made far more complex the issue of federal-provincial boundaries. There is no question that provinces act as delivery agents in the provision of health, education, welfare, and social services. Tensions have arisen over the fact that the federal government has made substantial financial contributions in these areas and thereby wields the authority of the "purse."

To complicate matters, the federal government began in the late 1970s to make substantial changes to the financing arrangements, but did so unilaterally and without warning. These changes severely threatened the predictability of the provincial financing base. The introduction of the CHST in 1995 (which took effect in 1996) was seen as the final straw in an ongoing wave of federal cutbacks. It unleashed a series of events that led to a new set of federal-provincial negotiations.

Jurisdictional conflicts — especially around health, education, welfare, and social services — have gone on for years and continue to this day, although in somewhat quieter form due to the newly-signed Social Union Framework Agreement. The 1960s and 1970s, in particular, had "unleashed a flood of proposals for redesigning the basic elements of the Canadian constitution, including both the structure of the central government and the division of powers between the federal and provincial levels of government."[3]

Despite extensive constitutional debate, the *Constitution Act* that supplemented the BNA Act in 1982 did not substantially change the division of powers in the county. But the *Constitution Act* did incorporate a crucial dimension that had not previously been in place. It introduced a Charter of Rights and Freedoms that articulates the basic freedoms for all Canadians: democratic rights, mobility rights, legal rights, equality rights, and minority language educational rights.

The *Constitution Act* and its embedded Charter are considered to be the supreme law of the land. Legislation and policies at all levels of government and their respective agencies must respect and comply with the protections afforded in the Charter. The equality and mobility rights are of particular importance to persons with disabilities. The equality rights provisions include protection from discrimination on the grounds of physical or mental disability. More specifically, section 15(1) of the Charter affirms that: "Every individual is equal before and under the law and has the right to equal protection and equal benefit of the law without discrimination and, in particular, without discrimination based on race, national or ethnic origin, colour, religion, sex, age, or physical or mental disability."

The inclusion of physical or mental disability as a proscribed ground of discrimination was a pivotal moment in history for the disability community. The constitutional change resulted from a recommendation put forward by the House of Commons Committee on the Disabled and the Handicapped. The committee had been created in 1981 by the federal government in respect of the International Year of Disabled Persons as declared by the United Nations. Because of the anticipated constitutional amendment, the committee recognized that it was well placed to introduce some crucial proposals. It had a unique window of opportunity to recommend fundamental constitutional change that not only would represent a substantive advance for the country but also would place Canada as a leader on the world stage.

The inclusion of physical and mental disability as a proscribed ground of discrimination in the Charter of Rights and Freedoms was important for two reasons. First, it effectively set the federal government as a champion of the rights of persons with disabilities. Second and equally important, the provisions of the Charter explicitly and implicitly affect all jurisdictions. The Charter protections confer certain obligations on the federal government as well as the provinces to take positive steps to protect and promote equality rights.

In addition to equality rights, the Charter protects the mobility rights of Canadians. One of the federal government's key constitutional roles is to ensure that all Canadians are treated broadly in similar ways, irrespective of language or residence. This obligation is embedded in the constitutional commitment set out in section 36(1): "to provide essential public services of reasonable quality to all Canadians." Mobility rights, in particular, ensure that all Canadians can move freely to and take up residence in any province. The implications of mobility rights with respect to disability supports and services are discussed more fully later. The rights of persons with disabilities are also affirmed in federal and provincial human rights codes that apply to both the public and private sectors. Employment equity legislation and programs in some jurisdictions are designed to increase the labour force participation of designated populations, including persons with disabilities.

In addition to the general protection afforded in these codes, several jurisdictions set out explicit employer obligations in their respective employment equity acts. The new federal *Employment Equity Act*, which came into effect in October 1996, is intended to achieve equality in the workplace and to correct conditions of disadvantage, although the requirement to provide "reasonable accommodation" needs clarification and interpretation. Workers' compensation legislation in most jurisdictions also places a positive obligation upon employers to accommodate workers injured on the job.

Jurisdictional

In Canada, there are few areas around which there is a clean jurisdictional split. As noted, the federal government is responsible for issues of national and international concern. Primary federal areas of responsibility include customs, foreign policy, fisheries and oceans, communications, and transportation. Provinces, by contrast, are concerned with municipal issues and services to people such as health, education, welfare, and social services. But many areas overlap and there is shared responsibility in several fields. The transportation issue is a case in point. Here the distinction in jurisdiction is made along the lines of scale. Transportation concerns that apply to interprovincial or international travel lie in the federal domain. By contrast, provincial and, in some cases, municipal governments are responsible for local or intraprovincial transportation.

While most discussions of disability issues focus on supports, employment, and income, the transportation issue illustrates that there are no simple divisions when it comes to the federal and provincial governments. It is also worth noting that substantial progress with respect to transportation accessibility has been achieved in recent years. While the systems are by no means problem-free, the improvements are due largely to concerted federal investment in this area.

The split when it comes to income programs is more complex. In the disability field, the federal government has responsibility for income programs — namely Employment Insurance and the Canada Pension Plan (CPP) — deemed to be social insurances (described below). Even here, the issue is not "neat"; the province of Quebec runs a sister program called the Quebec Pension Plan (QPP). The provinces administer workers' compensation programs as well as last-resort welfare programs.

Disability supports in the form of health and social services fall primarily in the provincial domain. However, the federal government is involved in this area in three key ways. First, it provides tax relief through the income tax system for the cost of disability-related goods and services. Second, it is responsible directly for the delivery of health and social services to the Inuit and to Aboriginal Canadians on-reserve. Third, it transfers funds to the provinces for investment in health, education, welfare, and social services through the CHST.

Institutional

At the federal level, the Department of Human Resources Development assumes primary responsibility for disability issues. There is no designated minister responsible for this area; rather, the minister of human resources development is deemed to be the key minister to which groups relate on most disability-related issues. This designation is not to downplay the involvement of other departments such as Justice, Transportation, and Communications. It is simply that the human resources development portfolio includes key issues of importance to persons with disabilities, notably labour market training and income security. The Department of Human Resources Development houses an Office of Disability Issues. Moreover, the department has been actively involved in the social union negotiations.

In recent years, however, the disability community has focused its attention increasingly upon influencing the finance minister. Several changes to Canadian legislation since 1986 have made the Finance Department the major driver of government policy, especially with respect to health and social services. The feeling is that if the finance minister can be convinced of the need to spend in a certain program area, then the relevant department likely will come on board as a result. This shift in emphasis is explained more fully in a report entitled *How Finance Re-Formed Social Policy*.[4]

There are several public bodies expressly concerned with disability issues. The House of Commons is the primary legislative body with 301 elected representatives from across the country. The Senate is the upper house or body of "sober second thought." Its primary role is to review the laws passed by the House of Commons, although it can introduce legislation of its own. The Senate includes a total of 104 members who are political appointments, and it possesses all the powers of the House of Commons except that of initiating financial legislation. The House of Commons alone is constitutionally authorized to introduce legislation concerned with raising or spending funds.

Both the House of Commons and the Senate have a set of standing committees responsible for exploring issues of national concern. The House of Commons, in particular, has a Standing Committee on Human Resources Development which considers a broad range of social issues. The committee is composed of representatives from all political parties. It recently struck a subcommittee on Disability Issues that will focus explicitly on concerns relevant to persons with disabilities. It should be noted that, in the past, there have been standing committees on disability issues that had independent status and produced reports of their own.

The Canadian Human Rights Commission is the major national player responsible for enforcing the terms and conditions of the *Human Rights Act*. The provinces have their own human rights commissions to enforce provincial human rights codes. Several provinces have appointed advisory committees whose mandate is to provide specific advice on disability issues.

DISABILITY: A COUNTRY PROFILE

Social and Demographic Data

In 1991, the latest year for which national data are available, 4.2 million Canadians, or 15.5 percent of the population, had a disability. The 1991 figures indicate a significant increase from 1986, when 3.3 million persons or 13.2 percent of the population had some form of disability.[5] The increase reflects the fact that the incidence of disability rises with age, it is expected that this proportion will grow in the coming years. It is also possible, however, that some of the rise in numbers was due to increased reporting as a result of changes introduced in 1987 to the Canada Pension Plan.

Prior to 1987, contributors to the CPP were required to work and to have made CPP contributions for at least five of the past ten years before they could claim disability benefits. The eligibility rules were changed in that year to allow workers who had paid into the CPP for the past three years to qualify for disability benefits, provided they met the key requirement of having a severe and prolonged disability that prevented them from working.[6] Because many Canadians became beneficiaries of a long-term disability benefit in the key time period under question, more individuals could have reported that they had a disability.

Of the estimated 4.2 million Canadians with disabilities, 3.9 million live in private households and 300,000 live in institutions. Of those who live in households, 89 percent of young persons (defined by Statistics Canada as less than 15 years of age) with disabilities are mildly disabled, 8 percent have moderate disabilities, and 3 percent have severe disabilities. The profile is quite different for those between the ages of 15 and 64 who live at home. Of this group, 54 percent have mild disabilities, 32 percent have moderate disabilities, and 14 percent have severe disabilities. Seniors have the highest incidence of disability.

Adults with disabilities have average lower educational levels compared to adults without disabilities. Statistics Canada's Health and Activity Limitation Survey (HALS) found that 65 percent of persons with disabilities have completed only high school or less compared to 50 percent of the overall population. Only 6 percent of adults with disabilities have a university degree compared to 14 percent of other Canadians.

But education appears to be at least as important for employment for adults with disabilities as it is for others. The employment rate of adults with disabilities with university education (67 percent) is more than double that for persons with only elementary school education (30 percent). The educational profile of persons with disabilities improved marginally between 1986 and 1991. A higher percentage had at least some postsecondary education in 1991 (35 percent) than in 1986 (31 percent). Yet the highest level of schooling completed by young people (aged 15 to 24) with disabilities was still lower than for youth without disabilities. The education levels of young women, both with and without disabilities, was somewhat higher than for young men. Most children with disabilities (91 percent) attend school and most (62 percent) attend regular classes. They are at a disadvantage, however, because of their disabilities. Almost 40 percent either started school late, took longer to complete their schooling or had their education interrupted.

In 1991, 48 percent of working-age people with disabilities were employed, 8 percent unemployed, and 44 percent were "not in the labour force." People with severe disabilities are least likely to be in the labour force. The reasons for not joining the labour force most often cited by people with disabilities included losing their current income (21 percent), problems with training (16 percent), and no jobs available (15 percent).[7]

Persons with disabilities, particularly women, are concentrated at the bottom end of the income scale. About 60 percent of persons with disabilities have incomes below the poverty line.[8] Of adults with disabilities, 43 percent had an individual income of less than $10,000 per year and 26 percent had an income of less than $5,000. Adults with severe disabilities are much more likely to be poor than those with mild disabilities. These figures do not take into account the extraordinary costs associated with disability that can be substantial in many situations.

But disability affects far more than just a minority of the population. It touches everyone. All Canadians have some experience with disability through contacts with relatives, colleagues or friends with a disabling condition. A major social-security review that had been conducted in 1994 by the federal Department of Human Resources Development succinctly summarized this reality: "People with disabilities are our parents, brothers, sisters and spouses, as well as our colleagues, our friends, our neighbours and ourselves."[9] Moreover, most Canadians will experience some form of functional incapacity or limitation as a normal part of aging; the incidence of disability rises directly with age. Seven percent of children under age 14 have some form of disability compared to 50 percent of the population over age 65. The rate of disability for working age Canadians, aged 15–64, is 13 percent.[10]

The fact that this national profile is dated is itself a major issue with the disability community. Statistics Canada's HALS was supposed to be conducted every five years as a post-censal survey, that is, after the formal national census which is conducted every five years. The last census was conducted in 1996 and results are now being released. But due to budget constraints and "other priorities," Statistics Canada had decided that the HALS post-censal survey would not be carried out this time. The (then) minister of human resources development subsequently intervened and agreed to have his department assume responsibility for and help design the survey. Statistics Canada, however, will be conducting the actual survey on HRDC's behalf. The survey will be conducted after the 2001 national census.

Political Organization of Disability Groups

The political organization of disability groups tends to mirror the political structure of the country. There are national groups whose mandate is concerned mainly with issues of national and international scope. At the political level, they relate primarily to the federal government. Key national groups include: the Council of Canadians with Disabilities, the Canadian Association of Independent Living Centres, the Canadian Association for Community Living, the Canadian Paraplegic Association, the Canadian Council on Rehabilitation and Work, the Canadian Hearing Society, the Canadian National Institute for the Blind and the Canadian Cystic Fibrosis Foundation. This list is by no means exhaustive; rather, it is intended to illustrate the wide range of organizations that comprise the disability community.

Many national groups receive some core funding from the federal government although these grants have been cut in recent years. Groups have had to rely more upon other sources of funds including memberships, contracts and private donations from individuals and foundations. National groups typically have provincial offices. In some cases, the Quebec office has split from the national group and acts independently at both the provincial and federal levels. The disability organization representing the province of Quebec, for example, is not part of the structure of the Council of Canadians with Disabilities. Provincial groups, in turn, generally have local chapters. These work on issues at the municipal government and local service level. Most voluntary organizations in Canada conform to this federated structure. Their national office relates to the federal government; provincial and local branches deal with provincial and local governments, respectively. But groups working in the disability area, perhaps more than any other field, place a strong emphasis on the federal arena. This emphasis is the result of several factors.

The Charter of Rights and Freedoms lies at the heart of the citizenship agenda. The disability community has been keen to push this agenda because it believes that citizenship represents the key to all other doors: employment, disability-related supports and services, and access to transportation and communications.

A major factor in the preoccupation with citizenship is the recognition that an inordinate focus upon provincial health and social service policy would not effect associated changes in employment policy, education, transportation, and communications. These areas are considered crucial for promoting full participation in Canadian life. Another reason for pushing the citizenship agenda is to ensure that every government department and agency make provision for persons with disabilities in their respective policies, programs, and services. A focus upon health, services, income or any single issue for that matter would not create the sweeping, comprehensive change that the community believes is required. Moreover, the federal Charter of Rights and Freedoms overrides all other statutes, thereby requiring all jurisdictions to confer similar rights and to modify their current policies or provide appropriate services to ensure these rights.

Yet another explanation for the strong federal focus is the fact that persons with disabilities are seeking some semblance of national consistency with respect to the goods and services to which they have access. There is substantial variability throughout the country in the availability and delivery of supports and services for persons with disabilities. They see the federal government as at least helping to set parameters, if it cannot go so far as to impose formal standards, which would provide some national coherence.

The strong federal focus is not intended to imply that there is little substantial work under way with respect to provincial governments. Indeed, these governments have been the focus of much attention because they have primary constitutional responsibility for health and social services. But organizations representing persons with disabilities know that they must be careful in the strategies they employ; they do not want to fall into the trap of having their concerns classified solely or even primarily as health issues that require "treatment" through medical care or social services. They want to ensure that the issue of disability does not become medicalized as in the past. The medical framework that used to dominate the disability discourse tended to reinforce incapacity rather than ability and focused more upon rehabilitation than integration. The model of service delivery developed by the province of Quebec is regarded as an exemplary approach that most groups throughout the country would support.

Organizations representing persons with disabilities recognize, however, that they do have to modify somewhat the target of their efforts. They have had to struggle with how best to deal with the realities of recent changes to federalism which have shifted from a federal-only focus to a federal-provincial partnership. The new federalism has created challenges for all voluntary agencies. But the realignment has been especially difficult for persons with disabilities who always have considered the federal government the champion of their interests, even though Ottawa has been more of a champion in theory than in practice of late.

A related problem for all agencies, but again for the disability community in particular, is the fact that the new federalism involves extensive discussions in federal-provincial working groups involving government officials. While governments claim to be improving their accountability to the public (see, e.g., the Future Directions Strategy discussed below), the action has not yet matched the rhetoric. The voluntary sector is concerned that it will be left out of these federal-provincial forums altogether, or at best consulted after the fact.

The disability community has welcomed the recent action by the House of Commons to reinstate a parliamentary committee on disability issues, even if it is only a subcommittee of the larger Standing Committee on Human Resources Development. The disability community hopes that the new committee will provide a voice for their concerns. It also could help them bridge the gap with the federal-provincial working group composed not of elected representatives but of government officials to whom most groups feel they have little direct access.

SOCIAL POLICY AND FEDERAL PRACTICE

Scope of Field

This chapter discusses disability issues within the context of personal supports, employment, and income programs. It is essential to recognize, however, that this description cannot capture the scope of how persons with disabilities have defined their concerns. The disability community sees its issues as nothing short of complete inclusion in every aspect of Canadian life. Full citizenship is the ultimate goal. Needless to say, such a broad vision touches upon almost every aspect of the public policy agenda.

Definitions

Canada officially employs the definitions set out by the World Health Organization in 1980. "Impairment" refers to any loss or abnormality of a psychological or anatomical structure or function. "Disability" is any restriction or inability (resulting from an impairment) to perform an activity in the manner or within the range considered normal for a human being. "Handicap" refers to any disadvantage for a given individual, resulting from an impairment or a disability, that limits or prevents the fulfillment of a role that is normal for that individual.

While these official definitions are used, individual programs put forward their own definitions as to the term disability: especially to define what is meant by severe and long-term impairment. Clearly, the purpose of the more precise definitions is to restrict eligibility for certain programs. It is also important to note that the term "persons with disabilities" tends to be used by governments and in reports as though it refers to a single group of people. In reality, the represented population is highly diverse. The term includes physical, mental, and psychiatric impairments. It refers to persons whose disabling condition was present at birth and those whose condition arose at some point in their lives as a result of an accident, injury or normal aging.

The actual disability may be mild or profound, temporary or permanent. Its consequences may be very different: affecting physical functioning and stamina, cognition and memory, or visual and auditory communication. Some disabilities can be readily accommodated at home or in the workplace while others cannot. Some disabilities are constant while others are progressively degenerative. Still other conditions have periods of remission; given individuals may have periods of normal activity followed by periods of inability to function.

Policies and Programs

As noted, this chapter focuses upon the three policy and program areas: personal supports, employment, and income. First, there is the wide range of supports that enable persons with disabilities to live independently in the community and to participate in education and employment. Training and vocational programs comprise the second component of the disability income and supports system. Finally, a range of income programs provides financial assistance for workers whose earnings have been interrupted on a temporary or permanent basis, as well as for those with little or no attachment to the labour market. This focus is not intended to minimize the importance of the other related issues that contribute to full citizenship including human rights, transportation, and communications.

Disability Supports

Disability supports refer to the range of goods and services that help offset the effects of a disabling condition. These supports include:

- health-related goods such as medications, special dressings, oxygen equipment, dialysis equipment, surgical dressings, and medically-prescribed diets;
- attendant services that provide assistance with personal needs such as bathing, feeding, dressing, and grooming;
- homemaker services for help with household tasks such as cooking, shopping, meal preparation, cleaning, and home maintenance;
- respite services, which refer to assistance primarily for families caring at home for children with severe disabilities;
- interpreter, reading, and other communication services;
- technical aids and equipment (e.g., wheelchairs, visual aids, prosthetic appliances) to assist mobility, communications, and other areas of functioning;
- work-related supports such as scanners, TTDs (teletypewriter devices), large computer screens, and other special equipment;
- information and counselling services to identify, organize, and manage disability supports.

The availability of disability supports varies widely throughout Canada. Provinces (and municipalities in some jurisdictions) are responsible for their provision. In most cases, local non-profit organizations actually deliver the supports. Disability supports all have associated costs that are offset in different ways.

Health and Social Services

Disability supports that are primarily health-related in nature, such as attendant care, tend to be furnished through various health settings. User fees may be charged if the services are delivered outside a hospital, clinic or physician's office; Canada's medicare system provides coverage for services considered to be "insured" health services. By contrast, extended health-care services that typically are delivered outside a hospital or medical setting are permitted to charge fees. Given the trend toward the delisting of some previously insured health services (i.e., removing them from the list of health-care services), more health-related supports are being delivered at home with associated fees.

Home health care generally falls under provincial Ministries of Health, although the federal government is responsible for the provision of this service to the Inuit and to Aboriginal Canadians on-reserve. In some cases, however, it is difficult to distinguish between "pure" health and social services.

Attendant services combine both health and social service elements because
they can involve the administration of a health act, such as injection of a nee-
dle, as well as services such as bathing and grooming. Attendant services come
under the jurisdiction of provincial Ministries of Health or Social Services.
Supports that are clearly social in nature, such as homemaker services and
respite care, are usually provided, or at least paid for, by provincial Ministries
of Social Services. In some provinces, such as Ontario, these supports are the
responsibility of local levels of government. The services themselves typically
are delivered by non-governmental organizations, such as visiting homemak-
ers' associations, operating in local communities. User fees may be charged to
help offset the costs.

The province of Quebec, in particular, delivers these supports through a
unique approach that determines eligibility on the basis of need rather than
cause of disability or level of income. In 1978, Quebec established a special
office (l'Office des personnes handicapées du Québec) which effectively inte-
grates under one roof all programs and services for persons with disabilities.
Unlike any other province, eligibility for these programs and services is determined by the *presence* of a disability, regardless of cause or level of income.
This provision is based on the notion of the rights of citizenship; citizens with
disabilities have a right to special supports regardless of any other circumstances. Indeed, the Quebec model is the closest that any jurisdiction in Canada
comes to embodying the ideal of citizenship within the provision of disability-
related supports.

Technical Aids and Equipment

Technical aids and equipment refer to items that provide assistance with the
activities of daily living: moving, eating, hearing or speaking. The provision
of technical aids and equipment defies simple description. Patients in hospitals or special residences generally receive the aids and equipment they need
as part of their treatment.

Access is far more complex for those living independently in the community. Ministries of Education or Health usually assume the cost of technical
aids and equipment for children in public schools. Adults have access through
different routes, depending on the jurisdiction and types of programs in which
they are involved. Those participating in some form of rehabilitation or training program or through Workers' Compensation may receive these supports as
part of the program. Persons not involved in rehabilitation or training — e.g.,

they may be at university, seeking work or at home — generally make provision for special needs on their own.

Some jurisdictions operate programs designed solely for the provision of technical aids and equipment. These programs vary widely throughout the country. In some cases, they include a range of assistive devices. In other cases, only certain types of equipment (e.g., hearing aids, respiratory equipment or wheelchairs) are provided or only persons with certain conditions (e.g., paralysis, cancer or cystic fibrosis) can qualify for assistance under the program.

Tax Credits

Some disability supports are not delivered directly. Rather, their cost can be reduced by various benefits delivered through the income tax system, namely the medical expense tax credit and the disability tax credit. The medical expense tax credit helps offset the cost of a designated list of disability supports. Because the credit may be claimed in respect of the health-related expenses of an individual, spouse or dependents, it is available to all Canadians and not just to persons with disabilities. There is a long list of expenses deemed eligible for the medical expense tax credit. They include: payments to medical practitioners, nurses and hospital services; attendant care; nursing home care; medical devices (e.g., artificial limbs, wheelchairs, braces, eyeglasses and a list of prescribed devices); prescribed drugs; and home renovations. The medical expense tax credit is non-refundable; it reduces income taxes owing and does not benefit people with incomes below the taxpaying threshold.

The disability tax credit also provides some tax relief for the additional, but often hidden and indirect, costs of disability. These costs may include incidental expenditures related to disability such as higher utility costs for heat or air conditioning; additional transportation costs; higher prices for goods because of fewer shopping choices; and reduced capacity to earn income. In the case of the disability tax credit, however, there is no designated list of allowable expenses.

In order to qualify, claimants must have a physical or mental disability that is severe and prolonged which markedly restricts their ability to perform the activities of daily living. "Prolonged" means that the impairment has lasted or may be expected to last for a continuous period of at least 12 months. "Severe" and "markedly restricted" mean that all or almost all of the time the person is unable, or requires an inordinate amount of time, to perform a basic activity of daily living, even with therapy and the use of appropriate devices and medication. The specific diagnosis or condition is irrelevant. What is important is the impact of the condition upon the person's ability to carry out one or more basic activities. These include feeding and dressing; eliminating (bladder or bowel functions); walking; perceiving, thinking and remembering; and speaking so as to be understood in a quiet setting, by another person familiar with the individual.

The income tax system provides some limited relief for caregiving in the form of an infirm dependent tax credit and a caregiver tax credit. Certain medical devices are exempt from the national goods and services tax as well as some provincial sales taxes.

Welfare "Special Needs" Provisions

Persons with disabilities who have no access to required supports through an existing program must purchase these goods and services on their own. They may claim certain costs under the medical expense tax credit. Those who cannot afford to make the up-front payments generally must rely on provincial welfare programs for help with disability-related costs.

The primary role of welfare is to provide financial assistance for basic needs, such as food, clothing, shelter, and utilities. But welfare also plays the important role of helping offset the cost of special needs arising from health-related or disabling conditions, for example, wheelchairs, hearing aids, prosthetic equipment, medications or medically prescribed diets, special eyeglasses or other assistive devices for independent living or work.

Yet, there is no guarantee that welfare actually will pay for all, or even some, disability supports. If a province (or municipality in the case of Ontario) has exceeded its special needs budget prior to the end of the fiscal year, it may decide to stop providing support for special assistance until the next fiscal year. Or a certain item, such as a recreational wheelchair, may not be included in the list of permissible costs. Finally, special assistance is made available only when the applicant has no other resources or there is no appropriate program to offset these costs. Welfare is intended as a last resort.

Employment

Employment Assistance for People with Disabilities (EAPD)

The employment needs of persons with disabilities used to be met primarily through the *Vocational Rehabilitation of Disabled Persons Act* (VRDP). It allowed for the federal government to share with the provinces the cost of a wide range of vocational supports needed to help persons with disabilities enter or re-enter the labour market.

In 1997, the federal and provincial governments began to explore ways to improve the VRDP agreement. The new *Employability Assistance for Persons with Disabilities Act* also allows for the cost-sharing of a broad range of services including assessment, employment counselling, wage subsidies, and technical aids and equipment. But the current cost-sharing arrangement will be replaced by a federal allocation to the provinces on the basis of a set formula. Alcohol and drug treatments will not be included under the new agreement. It will cover a five-year period with provision for a review after the first three years and will incorporate an accountability framework with associated outcome targets.

Labour Market Agreements

In November 1995, the federal government made a commitment to withdraw from labour market and training policy in recognition that this field falls primarily within provincial responsibility for education. The commitment was reaffirmed in the February 1996 Speech from the Throne. On 30 May1996, the federal government presented the provinces and territories with a Labour Market Development Proposal that offered an opportunity to assume greater responsibility for the design and delivery of so-called "active employment measures" outlined in the *Employment Insurance Act* implemented in July 1996. The province of Ontario has not yet signed a labour market agreement with the federal government.

Active employment measures include targeted wage subsidies, that is, assistance to employers to encourage them to hire unemployed workers; self-employment assistance intended to help unemployed workers start their own businesses; job-creation partnerships; and skills and loans grants that provide unemployed workers with assistance to obtain employment-related skills.

The programs supported under these agreements will be available to individuals who are active claimants of Employment Insurance (EI), a contributory program paid for by employers and employees. The problem is that the programs are intended only for people who are EI claimants. Those who do not qualify for the program or have not contributed long enough do not have access to these active measures. This access problem is a major concern among employment development workers and the unemployed.

Opportunities Fund

The 1997 federal budget announced an Opportunities Fund worth $30 million a year for three years. Under this fund, federal dollars are allocated in proportion to the working-age population of persons with disabilities. A small portion of the fund (about 10 percent) was reserved for national initiatives. Its purpose is to work in partnership with organizations representing persons with disabilities and other sectors to reduce barriers to labour market participation and to support innovative approaches to employment or self-employment. The target population includes persons with disabilities who require assistance to prepare for, find, and secure work, and who are not currently eligible for EI-funded employment programming. The dollars may be used to assist persons who have participated in other labour market initiatives but are still unable to make the transition to employment.

The Opportunities Fund is intended to complement existing programming. Services such as employment counselling and job-finding clubs can be supplemented by special supports paid for by the fund. It can also build on pilot projects developed by non-governmental organizations. The various employment benefits supported under the fund include targeted wage subsidies to help offset the incremental costs of hiring a person with a disability; targeted earnings supplements; job-creation partnerships; self-employment assistance; training to help individuals take courses; and case management to support the development of personal action plans.

Aboriginal Programs

The federal government has entered into a series of bilateral National Framework Agreements with organizations representing First Nations to guide the devolution of federal funds to selected Band Councils. The agreements require that provision be made for equitable services for designated groups, including persons with disabilities.

These National Framework Agreements are intended to allow Aboriginal communities to design and deliver their own labour market programming. The initiative will help address a key concern: the labour market participation of Aboriginal Canadians is lower, on average, than the rest of the population. This problem is due partly to the fact that education levels are lower and Aboriginal Canadians face serious barriers to education and training.

Income

The current system of disability income support can be described more accurately as a patchwork of uncoordinated programs. Eligibility and benefits are based to a large extent on cause of disability — how and why the disability occurred — rather than on level of need. People with virtually the same functional capacity can receive very different types and levels of benefits depending upon the cause of disability. The disability income system is composed of categorical programs, social insurances, private insurance, and social assistance.

Categorical Programs

The purpose of categorical programs is to compensate for the effects of disability or injury related to specific causes or events. These programs include tort liability, automobile accident insurance, criminal injuries compensation, and war veterans benefits.

The introduction of tort actions in the last century allowed people who experienced a disabling accident as a result of someone else's negligence to seek redress through the courts. Tort liability is an important component of the disability compensation system except in cases in which the right to sue has been removed explicitly, that is, in workers' compensation programs and in provinces with no-fault accident schemes.

Partial no-fault systems of automobile accident insurance have been adopted in Ontario, Manitoba, Saskatchewan, and British Columbia; a full no-fault system operates in Quebec. Criminal injuries compensation is also available for people who are victims of violent crime. Federal veterans benefits may be paid to members or former members of the Canadian Armed Forces who are suffering from a disability resulting from an injury or disease attributable to military service in war or peace.

Social Insurances

There are three major social insurances in Canada: workers' compensation, Employment Insurance and the Canada/Quebec Pension Plan. These are referred to as "insurances" because they represent a pooling of risks in the event of earnings loss as a result of designated contingencies. These programs are social insurances in that contributions to the plans are compulsory and all workers who meet the required eligibility criteria are covered.

Workers' Compensation. Provincial workers' compensation replaces between 75 percent and 90 percent of lost insured earnings in the event of occupational injury, disability or disease. The variation is actually smaller than the numbers suggest because the programs with 75 percent replacement rate base the benefits on gross earnings while the 90 percent benefits are based on net earnings. Employees receive compensation in the event of injury but abrogate their right to seek legal damages. Benefits are determined by the length and severity of the incapacity. In addition to cash awards, workers' compensation plans include a variety of in-kind benefits, such as rehabilitation services. Employers pay 100 percent of the cost of this program.

Employment Insurance. Employment Insurance (EI) is a federally administered program that replaced Unemployment Insurance in 1996. EI provides income protection from temporary work absences arising from unemployment, illness, disability, or birth or adoption of a child. The risk for which EI offers protection must be a temporary interruption. Workers who are unemployed over a prolonged period may receive assistance under different programs, notably, CPP and welfare.

Employability enhancement is a major focus of the new program. EI redirected a substantial sum of money ($800 million) from income support to employability benefits. These include a package of active employment measures, noted earlier, to help workers prepare for and find a job. A three-year $300 million fund also was established to generate economic growth and create new jobs.

Canada/Quebec Pension Plan Disability Benefit

The purpose of the Canada Pension Plan is to protect workers and their families from a long-term or permanent interruption of earnings as a result of retirement, severe and prolonged physical or mental disability, or death. Quebec operates an analogous program.

There are three eligibility criteria for the CPP disability benefit. Contributors must be between the ages of 18 and 65. They must have paid into the program for four of the last six years. The third eligibility criterion relates to the disability itself that is both severe and prolonged and interferes with substantially gainful employment.

The disability benefit is a fully indexed, taxable benefit. It consists of two parts. All beneficiaries receive the flat-rate component — $339.80 a month in 1999. The second component is earnings-related and is equivalent to 75 percent of the retirement pension that the contributor would have received at age 65, up to a maximum $563.75 a month. The total maximum monthly benefit in 1999 is $903.55.

In April 1990, the CPP approved a limited pilot project to explore the rehabilitation provisions of the disability benefit. In 1991, this project was integrated with the National Strategy for the Integration of Persons with Disabilities. Although the project ended officially in March 1996, it remained active for an additional year. Its purpose was to identify suitable CPP beneficiaries and provide the necessary vocational rehabilitation services to allow them to return to work. The assessment and rehabilitation plans were determined on an individualized basis with the approval of the individual. Benefits were paid during rehabilitation and upon completion of the program to allow for a three-month job search.

Effective August 1995, the Department of Human Resources Development put in place several additional measures to encourage self-reliance and participation in Canadian society. CPP beneficiaries are not considered to be gainfully employed until they have returned to work for three months. They can have their work skills tested without fear of immediately losing benefits. Individuals continue to receive benefits while attending school or university. Those with recurring or degenerative disabilities have their CPP benefits reinstated on a fast-track basis if the disability recurs. Involvement in volunteer activities no longer triggers an automatic reassessment.

Private Insurance

Private group insurance plans also provide disability coverage. While these plans vary in the specifics of their eligibility coverage and associated premiums, they typically act as a top-up to other programs. Private insurers are rarely the first payers of disability compensation.

In 1983, the Canadian Life and Health Insurance Association estimated that 43 percent of workers were covered by some form of private disability insurance. By 1994, only 5.4 million Canadians, still fewer than half the working population, were covered under private group insurance for long-term disability.[11]

Welfare

Provincial social assistance, commonly known as "welfare," is the income program of last resort. It provides financial assistance to individuals and families whose resources are inadequate to meet their needs and who have exhausted other avenues of support. Persons with disabilities are a substantial group; in 1995, an estimated 20 percent of welfare cases (approximately 332,000) were headed by a person with a disability.

Each province and territory sets its own rules and regulations that govern eligibility, amount of basic assistance, type and amount of special assistance, enforcement policies and provisions governing appeals. Despite the differences, all jurisdictions have several features in common. Applicants must qualify on the basis of provincial definition. Provinces generally require that the disability be severe and prolonged and that the applicant with a disability be considered "unemployable" — i.e., unable to engage in remunerative employment. In addition, applicants must qualify for welfare on the basis of a needs test. The value of their liquid (i.e., cash, bonds) and fixed (i.e., house, car) assets must not exceed designated levels. Nor can their incomes exceed certain levels. In 1996 (the latest year for which national data are available), the maximum annual welfare incomes for single persons with disabilities ranged from a low of $6,698 in the province of New Brunswick to a "high" of $11,759 in Ontario.[12] These figures represented 47 percent and 73 percent of the poverty line, respectively.[13]

While it appears that a range of programs is in place with respect to disability supports, employment programs, and income programs, there are some serious problems which have been identified over the years.

PERSPECTIVE OF PERSONS WITH DISABILITIES

Persons with disabilities face a wide range of problems including lack of personal supports, high unemployment, and low incomes. In many cases, these problems are due not to the condition or capacity of the individuals themselves but rather to the barriers they face in gaining access to supports, education or training, and jobs. The barriers that confront individuals with disabilities are compounded for Aboriginal Canadians with any form of disability. Their lives are made infinitely more complex by jurisdictional disputes. They are often passed back and forth between jurisdictions depending on whether they are considered "status" or "non-status" according to federal law.

The federal government typically takes responsibility for Aboriginal Canadians considered to be status Indians living on-reserve or Inuit while provincial governments are supposed to provide services to non-status Indians and Métis. In addition to issues related to status and jurisdictional complexities, they face problems arising from geographic isolation and the lack of community supports and services.

Lack of Supports

Many Canadians who require assistance to live independently in the community or who want to participate in education, training or the labour market are unable to do so because they have limited access to disability supports.

The delivery of disability supports varies widely throughout the country. The goods and services that may be provided in one jurisdiction may not be available in another. The disability supports to which individuals have access are very much a function of where they live. In some cases, essential disability supports are simply not available. The problem is made more complex by the fact that disability supports need to be highly individualized. The delivery of these supports can be equally problematic. Many are provided to individuals in their own homes, but are not made available in schools, workplaces or recreation centres. Another difficulty arises from the fact that disability supports are often an integral part of the care provided in group homes, nursing homes or institutions. The individuals who require these supports become "tied" to these residential arrangements. Because the funds go to the residences, the services are not portable. They are not "attached" to the person but remain with the institution, making it difficult for residents to seek independent living arrangements.

Individuals also may be denied access to disability supports because of age; income; the nature, cause and severity of their condition; or their involvement in training or the labour market. In some cases, for example, medical diagnosis rather than functional ability is the primary eligibility criterion. Persons with disabilities may be denied access to a given support because they do not have the "correct" diagnosis even though their functional capacity may be almost identical to those with the designated condition.

Affordability also creates problems of access. The cost of disability supports can be prohibitive and, as noted, there is only limited assistance to help offset these costs. Some 36 percent of adults face costs related to their disability which are not reimbursed by any public or private plan.[14]

Welfare may provide last-resort assistance. But the provision of this "income-in-kind" then makes it difficult to move off the program for fear of losing essential disability supports. An improvement in financial circumstances through employment, inheritance or another source means that these individuals risk their security, and possibly their lives, if they cannot gain access to these supports.

Finally, even when disability supports are available or affordable, problems may arise around responsiveness. Consumers typically have little say in how services are delivered or managed. Some services operate as though they are needed only between regular working hours on weekdays. Services may not be available at the place they are required. Attendant services may be delivered at home but not at a workplace or school even though the same attendant would carry out precisely the same task. Consumers are often afraid to voice their concerns for fear of personal reprisal or of losing the service altogether.

High Unemployment

The lack of certain supports — notably attendants, readers, interpreters, and technical aids — makes it difficult for children with disabilities to function at school. Many school boards segregate these children into special education classes. Their problems continue at higher levels of education. Students in colleges and universities often encounter difficulties gaining access to the supports they require. Sometimes they cannot even "get in the door" of these institutions because the premises are physically inaccessible. The admissions policies may not make provision for students who are hearing or sight impaired. The course requirements may not be flexible, for example, allowing a student with a communication impairment more time for completion of the designated work.

There are also concerns with training.[15] Persons with disabilities are often relegated to separate programs rather than integrated within mainstream initiatives. As noted, most men and women with disabilities do not qualify for employment measures because they are ineligible for EI. They are ineligible for this work-related benefit due to their inability to get a job in the first place or to remain in a job for long enough.

Even within specialized programs, there are problems related to accessibility (often interpreted narrowly to address only physical access) and accommodation of training tasks to meet individual abilities. The duration of participation may be limited, for example, even though additional time may be required to learn a task.

Barriers in the education and training systems translate into employment problems later in life. Persons with disabilities have a lower than average rate of workforce participation, partly because of less than average educational attainment and lack of disability supports. These individuals also face a variety of physical, procedural, and attitudinal barriers.

Low Incomes

Canadians whose work is interrupted temporarily or permanently as a result of disability or who have no workforce attachment must rely on various income programs. There is no comprehensive disability income system. As noted, it is more a patchwork of uncoordinated programs. There are multiple assessments based on different criteria which add to the cost and complexity of the system. Until recently, there were few links among the programs. Some would say that this patchwork is necessary; diverse programs are required to address different problems, capacities, and varying degrees of labour force attachment. But the patchwork itself is also responsible for many problems.[16]

Eligibility for most income programs is determined by where and how claimants became disabled or by the nature or severity of their disabling condition. Those who do not qualify under existing eligibility criteria generally must rely on welfare for financial support. For the purposes of calculating benefits, most welfare systems classify persons with disabilities as long-term cases or as "permanently unemployable." On the one hand, it is to their advantage to be labelled in this way. They often receive higher benefits, have access to a range of goods and services, and are not required to show continuing proof of job search. They tend to be more financially secure than "employable" welfare recipients and are subject to fewer administrative reviews. At the same time, the classification of permanently unemployable virtually ties many persons with disabilities to the welfare system because they are deemed to have no employment potential. Yet, many so-called "unemployables" would be able to work if they had access to the appropriate supports.

These expectations regarding employability are somewhat dated. Many persons with disabilities can work, especially if accommodation is made to their needs through provision of an adapted workplace or special equipment, specialized training or restructuring of job descriptions.[17] Moreover, significant scientific, medical and technological advances in recent years have made it inappropriate, even incorrect, to equate disability with unemployability. The social security review undertaken by the federal Department of Human Resources Development heard in its extensive consultations that many more people with disabilities would like to work if they had the opportunity, tools, and appropriate supports.[18]

Other problems with disability income include the fact that persons unable to work must rely on income programs that are often inadequate to meet their needs. The majority of adults with disabilities live on incomes that fall below poverty levels. In addition, certain sources of disability income, including workers' compensation, social assistance, and employee-purchased disability insurance benefits, are exempt from income taxation while other benefits, such as EI and the CPP disability benefit, are taxable. For most recipients, the after-tax value of the latter benefits is lower than their face value.

CHANGES AND LEADING DEVELOPMENTS IN THE FIELD

The problems with respect to disability supports, employment and income are not new; they have been on the agenda of the disability community for many years. There is no shortage of reports that explore the various dimensions of these problems.

Canada has a legacy of federal, provincial, and federal-provincial studies that have explored the lack of disability supports, high unemployment, and low incomes. Some highlights of the major initiatives are presented below. While this chapter focuses primarily upon federal reports, the past two decades have also seen many noteworthy provincial initiatives.

Obstacles

The International Year of Disabled Persons is often cited as the landmark date for tracing the history of disability studies in Canada. Work had been carried out prior to this time, but no efforts were as sweeping and dramatic as those that took place in 1981. In respect of the international year, the federal government appointed an all-party Special Committee on the Disabled and the Handicapped to undertake a comprehensive review of federal legislation pertaining to persons with disabilities.

The committee produced the *Obstacles* report that put forward 130 recommendations on all aspects of public policy including human rights, income security, assistive devices, transportation, and communications. The major accomplishment of the committee was to ensure the inclusion of persons with physical and mental disabilities in the equality rights section of the Charter of Rights and Freedoms. The report also sparked attitudinal change that helped create a new climate for ensuring that persons with disabilities are treated as full citizens rather than passive recipients of service.

International Decade of Disabled Persons

Canada continued its work in this area in respect of the United Nations Declaration of the International Decade of Disabled Persons (1982–1993). In 1982, a major federal-provincial effort was initiated to propose options for disability income reform. In response to recommendations in the *Obstacles* report, social services ministers established a federal-provincial working group. The group conducted an exhaustive study which developed several costed options for income security reform. These proposals were published in a *Joint Federal-Provincial Study* issued in 1985.

Another major initiative was the appointment of a Royal Commission on Equality in Employment. The 1984 *Report of the Royal Commission on Equality in Employment* explored the duty to accommodate persons with disabilities and the elimination of overt and systemic barriers to equality. It pointed out that equality does not mean treating everyone the same way. In fact, in order to achieve equality, it actually may be necessary to treat people quite differently.

In 1985, the Parliamentary Committee on Equality Rights published *Equality for All,* which established an equality framework for meeting the needs of persons with disabilities. That same year saw the creation of the Status of Disabled Persons Secretariat whose mandate was to raise awareness and support the full participation of persons with disabilities in Canadian society.

National Strategy for the Integration of Persons with Disabilities

In the early 1990s, the federal government announced a five-year National Strategy for the Integration of Persons with Disabilities. Its purpose was to implement a cross-government initiative to bring persons with disabilities into the social and economic mainstream. The strategy focused upon programming in 12 federal departments and agencies to promote the objectives of equal access, economic integration, and effective participation.

A committee was appointed to coordinate individual departmental initiatives and encourage interdepartmental collaboration. Several key initiatives were undertaken as part of this national strategy. More than $14 million over five years, for example, was directed toward several provincial demonstration projects to support the movement of persons with intellectual disabilities from institutions to communities.

Mainstream Review

In 1992, the Conference of Federal/Provincial/Territorial Ministers of Social Services announced a mainstream review to develop a collective strategic framework for the full integration of Canadians with disabilities. Ministers also directed that the review explore whether governments and individuals with disabilities could agree upon a vision and statement of principles. The report of the mainstream review proposed the "open house" concept as a conceptual framework to support the shift from segregation to mainstreaming.

The open house concept emphasized the importance of persons with disabilities enjoying the same rights and benefits as other Canadians and participating fully in all aspects of life including school, work, and recreation. This participation is made possible by the removal of discriminatory social, economic, and physical barriers and the provision of supports that accommodate and respect differences. The report also explored the need to make generic programs, such as child care, training, and education, more open and inclusive.

Standing Committee on Human Rights and the Status of Disabled Persons

The Standing Committee on Human Rights and the Status of Disabled Persons, a committee of the House of Commons, actively promoted the equality rights of persons with disabilities. In its 1990 report, *A Consensus for Action: The Economic Integration of Disabled Persons,* the committee recommended that all federal departments, Crown corporations, and agencies be required to review and reform legislation and regulations in order to promote the integration of persons with disabilities. The report called for an effective mechanism to ensure ongoing and consistent monitoring of all policy, legislation, and regulations in relation to persons with disabilities. In its 1992 report, *Paying Too Dearly,* the committee highlighted the costs of the continued marginalization of persons with disabilities. The following year, the committee published *As True as Taxes: Disability and the Income Tax System.* The report explored various improvements to the tax system, for example, including more items within the medical expense tax credit, creating a new disability expense tax credit, and making the disability tax credit refundable. That same year, the committee produced the report *Completing the Circle* which highlighted the needs of Aboriginal Canadians with disabilities.

In 1995, *The Grand Design: Achieving the Open House Vision* further developed the open house vision that had been put forward in the mainstream review. The report assessed the successes and limitations of the National Strategy for the Integration of Persons with Disabilities. The committee recommended the appointment of a secretary of state with a mandate to coordinate federal activities related to disability, carry out an impact assessment of all proposed measures on persons with disabilities and prepare an annual report to be referred to the standing committee. The committee also proposed a set of protections within the Canada Health and Social Transfer to ensure minimum funding for disability supports.

Social Security Review

The social security review was launched by the federal Department of Human Resources Development in early 1994 and completed in 1995. It included a comprehensive exploration of options for reforming a range of social programs: child benefits, Unemployment Insurance, labour market programs, and other areas of social policy.

The review produced a series of background papers, one of which dealt with persons with disabilities. The paper put forward several proposals for reform, including a comprehensive earnings replacement program or a guaranteed annual income for persons with disabilities.

Task Force on Disability Issues

The federal Task Force on Disability Issues was established in June 1996 by the ministers of human resources development, finance, revenue, and justice. Its mandate was to define and make recommendations regarding the role of the Government of Canada as it relates to persons with disabilities.

The task force travelled extensively and organized 15 public consultations throughout the country. It commissioned a set of research papers on five key issues: national civil infrastructure/citizenship, legislative review, labour market integration, income support, and the tax system. In October 1996, the task force issued its report entitled *Equal Citizenship for Canadians with Disabilities: The Will to Act.*

The report proposed a comprehensive set of recommendations. These included a *Canadians with Disabilities Act* to ensure consistent action, coordination, and accountability at the federal level. It proposed a legislative review to establish an ongoing strategy to assess laws and policies for their impact on persons with disabilities. The task force recommended the incorporation of a "disability lens" in the development of all laws, policies, and programs. It also suggested an ongoing accountability mechanism to track government actions and the publication of an annual report; changes to existing labour market programs; and improved tax assistance to offset the costs of disability.

Federal-Provincial Working Group

The most recent initiative in Canada is a report by a federal-provincial working group on disability. It is entitled *In Unison: A Canadian Approach to Disability Issues*. This vision paper evolved as part of the social union process currently under way in Canada. The document is described below, following the discussion of the current political context, and more specifically, the social union negotiations.

Future Directions Strategy

In July 1999, the federal government announced yet another national strategy on disability entitled *Future Directions to Address Disability Issues for the Government of Canada: Working Together for Full Citizenship*. The document builds on the *In Unison* report and states that the purpose of the strategy is to affirm the federal commitment to action. The strategy focuses upon increased public accountability and improvements to policy and program coherence. It promises to strengthen the coordination of disability issues and to improve access to programs, services, and information by persons with disabilities. The federal government will engage in discussions with the provinces, Aboriginal representatives, and community organizations in order to meet these stated objectives.

SOCIAL POLICY REFORM

In the past two years, Canada has been engaged in discussions around a new framework for federalism referred to as the social union. The social union discussions focus primarily upon the "who does what" of social policy, that is, the respective roles of the federal and provincial governments, the associated financing arrangements, and the monitoring and enforcement functions.

In February 1999, the federal and provincial governments (except Quebec) signed a Social Union Framework Agreement which sets out some general rules for how these two levels of governments should work together in future. It is intended to promote a respectful and collaborative approach to resolving key social issues that are not clearly defined as exclusively federal or provincial. The agreement talks about, among other issues, the need to protect the mobility rights of Canadians and the importance of accountability: both key issues for persons with disabilities.

The agreement may provide an important basis for encouraging Ottawa and the provinces to work collaboratively on outstanding issues, such as the lack of disability supports. It also could be seen to require governments to act far more responsibly and responsively with public funds. Despite the potentially positive aspects of the Social Union Framework Agreement, the disability community is worried that the agreement could water down the federal leadership role if Ottawa becomes overly concerned with conciliation. It may not be free to take definitive action.

The concern is certainly valid, federal leadership on disability issues does appear to have waned in recent years. Yet it has weakened in other areas as well, such as social housing. Until the federal budget in February 1999 which announced $11.5 billion in new health-care spending over five years, the federal government actually had cut back and retreated from several social policy areas.

While it is too early to judge whether the new Social Union Framework Agreement will result in any measurable progress on disability issues, it potentially could lead to some positive results. It is not too early, however, to look at its history because there are some interesting events that occurred as the social union negotiations were under way and that also had taken place before the signing of the formal agreement.

As noted, jurisdictional issues have been debated for years in Canada, in fact, they used to take the form of constitutional wrangling. Some of the same issues are being considered, but this time in a new venue within a non-constitutional context. One of the more interesting questions relates to the factors that played a role in pushing the social union negotiations to the front burner. Two key factors are responsible: the failure of recent constitutional negotiations and, more specifically, the 1995 federal budget.

The federal and provincial governments have been embroiled for years in constitutional discussions. The negotiations that took place in 1986 and 1987 and led to the drafting of the proposed Meech Lake Accord were regarded as a failure. Crucial negotiations affecting the future of the country had been held in secret. Canadians deeply resented this "backroom" approach to nation-building and were unclear that the proposals on the table actually would strengthen the country. Parliamentary approval and the consent of all provincial legislative assemblies were necessary for the ratification of the Meech Lake Accord; it failed ultimately to be ratified within the three-year deadline set out in the constitution. Another round of constitutional talks also ended in failure. These talks produced in 1992 a set of proposed constitutional amendments known as the Charlottetown Accord. But like Meech, the Accord was never ratified, having been rejected in a national referendum.

Meech and Charlottetown were followed by the Quebec referendum in 1995 which nearly brought the country to the brink of break-up. The federal government, in particular, recognized that the old rules of the federal-provincial power game no longer would work. There was pressure to find a new way to do business, to renew the country outside a constitutional framework. Equally important, there was pressure, at least on the part of the federal government, to demonstrate that Canada is a viable federation. The social union discussions evolved as a way to renew and rebuild Canada outside a constitutional framework.

The notion of a social union incorporates two dimensions: the *substance* that it embodies and the *process* that it implies. The *substance* of the social union emphasizes the collection of laws, policies, and programs concerned with various forms of investment in people. But this body of laws, policies and programs is really no different than what used to be called "social policy" or the "welfare state." The factor that distinguishes the concept of social union from these other terms is the *process* that it implies. The social union process, at least in theory, has several distinguishing features. These include collaboration, asymmetry, and accountability.[19]

A key feature of the social union is that work in any substantive area should be conducted in a *collaborative* fashion. Ottawa alone no longer should spell out the rules with which provinces must comply to receive federal funds. Rather, the social union theory or intent implies that any rules, whether in the areas of funding, program delivery or reporting, should be set jointly by the federal government and the provinces.

The social union's intent was to consider Ottawa and the provinces as equal players in the social policy game. Equality does not negate the fact that one party may be a more appropriate delivery agent than the other in certain areas. The federal government, for example, is the most suitable level of government for supporting income programs because it is able to ensure the same benefits for all Canadians. Ottawa also has the capacity to generate the revenue to provide adequate and equitable benefits. The provinces, by contrast, are better at delivering health care and social services. These can be tailored to individual need and regional differences.

In short, the social union thinking that shaped the actual negotiations viewed federal and provincial relations as a process of "managed interdependence" in which both levels of government have an important role. In theory, the social union is intended to create a partnership approach to dealing with social needs.[20] Co-management effectively results in different responses to the same problem and can give rise to asymmetrical federalism. The ensuing variability throughout the country is seen, again in theory, not only as inevitable but also as desirable as jurisdictions work within their respective fiscal and political priorities.

While provinces may develop different responses to a given issue or problem, they jointly have been involved in a process in which they share a common vision and a set of values, principles, and objectives. This new federalism is sometimes referred to as a "pan-Canadian" approach. While the individual paths to addressing an issue may be different, the end point is the same. It should be noted with respect to asymmetrical federalism that Quebec is the one jurisdiction that has not formally participated in the social union discussions although it has monitored the process and has continued to accept federal money. But Quebec has always followed an asymmetrical route in terms of social programs. Moreover, it generally is regarded as a leader in social policy, especially with respect to disability policies and programs.

Another feature that distinguishes the concept of the social union from the past is the encouragement of "horizontal policy-making."[21] This term means that various levels of government and different ministries within the same jurisdiction should work together to tackle the issue at hand. In any given province, for example, the Ministries of Education, Social Services, Health and Justice should collaborate on issues pertaining to persons with disabilities.

This so-called whole-of-government approach was intended to address an important problem which had been prevalent in the past. Human needs tended to be divided into political jurisdictions or single ministries as though these needs could be compartmentalized into neat boxes. That approach not only exacerbated existing problems but often created new problems.

Yet another dimension of process inherent in the social union, at least in theory, is the concept of public accountability. All governments are seen as accountable both individually and collectively to the public and, more specifically, to groups that have a special interest in certain issues, such as supports for persons with disabilities. In looking for ways to rebuild the federation, the social union was viewed as an opportunity to open up public processes and make governments more accountable for their activity. The social union also provided a framework for actively engaging citizens in consultation and other forms of deliberative problem-solving. In short, the social union is intended to operate effectively in three spheres. First, it is concerned with revamping the laws, programs, and services that comprise the social policy envelope. Second, it is a means of renewing the federation through new forms of intergovernmental relations. Third, it is intended to encourage democratic engagement and public accountability.[22]

It was not long before the social union theory was seriously tested by political events. Prior to 1995, there were two major financing arrangements for social programs: EPF and CAP. As noted, the EPF arrangement was a block fund under which transfers were made to provinces for health and postsecondary education. The transfers were a combination of cash payments and tax points. Provincial entitlements were calculated on the basis of a formula that took into account growth in population and gross national product (GNP). The CAP, by contrast, was a cost-shared arrangement in which Ottawa shared 50 percent of provinces' costs for welfare and social services. Over the years, the federal government had been making changes to these two financing arrangements. The 1986 federal budget limited the indexation of the EPF transfers to the provinces to the annual increase in GNP minus two percentage points (the formula used to be the full increase in the GNP). The 1989 budget reduced the indexation of the EPF formula by yet another percentage point. The 1990 budget froze federal transfers for 1990–91 and 1991–92. The 1991 budget extended the freeze through 1994–95, after which the GNP-less-three percentage points formula was to kick in.[23]

In 1990, Ottawa also announced a freeze on sharing the cost of the CAP (the now infamous "cap on CAP") for the three so-called have provinces of Ontario, Alberta, and British Columbia. The freeze took effect just prior to the recession of the early 1990s — the most severe economic trough since the

Great Depression of the 1930s. Welfare caseloads were poised to skyrocket in response to the economic slump.

In the1995 federal budget, the government announced its intent to dismantle these two pieces of legislation and replace them with the Canada Health and Social Transfer. The CHST is a block fund that provides federal support to the provinces for financing health, postsecondary education, welfare, and social services. The new legislation would allow provinces more flexibility in how they spend federal money. But there would be far less money to spend. The CHST cut nearly $6.2 billion from federal transfers in its first two years alone. The removal of the legislative base of CAP was especially troubling. There would be less money for social services in particular and for supports to help persons with disabilities live independently in the community.[24] But the CHST did call for the federal minister of human resources development to engage in discussion with the provinces around the principles and objectives that would underlie the use of the funds. Not surprisingly, the new legislation was not well received by the provinces, which stood to lose considerable dollars in exchange for their newfound spending "freedom."

The provinces decided to respond to the federal initiative by planning a joint strategy. They formed the Ministerial Council on Social Policy Reform and Renewal. In 1996, the premiers issued a joint report (except for Quebec) that effectively became a blueprint for the agenda they intended to pursue with the federal government. Their report put forward several social policy proposals including a national child benefit, a national disability benefit, and labour market initiatives. There is no question that these proposals were intended to shift some costs back to the federal government. But at least the recommendations helped open the door to some renewed federal-provincial activity.

As part of their 1996 report, the premiers proposed a national income benefit for persons with long-term disabilities. A federal-provincial working group on disability issues was struck to consider this possibility as well as other common concerns, such as employment opportunities and supports for persons with disabilities. The working group has acknowledged the potential complexities involved in developing a single national income benefit. It likely will be some time, if ever, before such a program is introduced in Canada. But the federal and provincial governments did take a step forward in that direction. They agreed to harmonize their respective income programs, reduce inequities among jurisdictions, and remove the disincentives to work inherent in these programs.

The very fact that this federal-provincial process is taking place is crucial. Many problems which people with disabilities face arise from the fact that they are passed back and forth between jurisdictions. Ottawa often would try to get people to move from a federal benefit, such as EI or CPP, onto a provincial program, usually welfare. The provinces, in turn, would shift people from provincial programs such as welfare or workers' compensation to federal programs, in this case, CPP. At the very least, there is now a federal-provincial venue to address this problem. There is a process in which Ottawa and the provinces are recognizing explicitly that their delivery of income supports and services has been less than adequate in many respects and certainly has not met the needs of many Canadians with disabilities.

The harmonization of income programs is important from a service delivery perspective. But it is also linked intrinsically to the ability to move freely throughout the country. In fact, mobility is a key constitutional protection and is a central issue in the Social Union Framework Agreement. The harmonization of income security programs is intended to promote greater equity in all regions.

The federal-provincial working group also developed a vision paper entitled *In Unison: A Canadian Approach to Disability Issues*. The paper was released on 27 October 1998, after having been approved by the federal and all provincial governments (except Quebec).

IN UNISON: A VISION

The principles of inclusion and full citizenship comprise the foundation of the federal-provincial vision paper, *In Unison: A Canadian Approach to Disability Issues*. Citizenship can be achieved only through the adoption of a framework that clearly and explicitly ensures that persons with disabilities can participate fully in all aspects of Canadian society.

The exercise of full citizenship requires a commitment by governments to develop policies and programs that enhance the equality of persons with disabilities. It represents a national effort to provide the disability supports, employment opportunities, and income assistance necessary to overcome barriers and to give expression to society's collective responsibility to share in disability-related costs.

In Unison describes three building blocks — disability supports, employment, and income — in which changes must be made to promote full citizenship. Each building block sets out objectives and associated policy directions. These include: ensuring greater access to disability supports and off-setting disability-related costs, enhancing employment opportunities for persons with disabilities, and removing the disincentives to work in current income programs.

These objectives are intrinsically linked. Availability of and access to disability supports are required to promote employability. These supports allow access to education and training programs and ensure that persons with disabilities can get to and function in their workplaces. Access to paid work clearly has a direct impact upon earnings and the need to rely upon programs of income support.

In Unison commits all governments in Canada to work toward these objectives. Equally important, it encourages all governments to work *together* to reach these objectives. To date, several key issues have arisen out of the federal-provincial *In Unison* agenda. These include the protection of mobility rights, the harmonization of income security, the coordination of labour market initiatives, and accountability.

Protection of Mobility Rights

Mobility is a central component of Canadian citizenship. It entails the unimpeded movement of goods, services, and human and natural resources throughout the country. The right to mobility is enshrined in section 6 of the Charter of Rights and Freedoms. This right was reaffirmed in the 1996 Speech from the Throne in which the federal government committed itself to "protect and promote unhampered social mobility between provinces and access to social and other benefits, and [to] work with the provinces to identify new and mutually agreed approaches." The Social Union Framework Agreement addresses explicitly the need to remove barriers to the mobility of Canadians.

Mobility is a key issue for persons with disabilities. Because they rely on personal supports that typically are attached to residential or income programs, persons with disabilities are not free to move throughout the country. The *In Unison* document commits the federal and provincial governments to improved portability. Within the disability context, "portability" means that disability supports are attached to the individual. They go with the person who needs the supports, regardless of the region or setting in which they are required. The concept of portability moves well beyond geographic mobility. It implies that supports are portable across any and all sectors — home, school, work, and community. These supports also should be available in all regions so that access is not linked to place of residence.

One way to effect *In Unison*'s commitment to portability is to separate supports from income and from participation in any given program. A national commitment to portability would require each jurisdiction to develop a plan for how it will ensure access to disability supports. Each plan should include actions that articulate how disability supports would be detached from income and other programs and "assigned" instead to the individual. The availability of disability supports should never be an impediment to mobility.

Individualized funding provides a means to achieve the commitment to portability. This financing arrangement involves the transfer of dollars directly to individuals to allow them to purchase disability supports. Ideally, the primary eligibility criterion for individualized funding would be the presence of a disability. Factors such as age, employability, cause or nature of disability, or location in which the supports will be used would be irrelevant. Persons with disabilities would have access to the forms and levels of support they require in any part of the country without having to establish residency, undergo a waiting period or "present with" a certain medical condition. Of course, there are also weaknesses inherent in this form of financing arrangement.[25]

Harmonization of Income Programs

The federal-provincial working group on disability has set out as a major task the harmonization of income programs. As noted, interjurisdictional "buckpassing" often leaves many individuals falling between the cracks or being passed back and forth between programs with multiple assessment procedures.

An immediate way to improve the disability income system is to review and harmonize existing programs. The federal-provincial working group has committed individual jurisdictions to removing disincentives to work, reducing overlap and duplication, and minimizing interjurisdictional inequities. The process of harmonization involves the sharing of information which, in turn, is intended to promote comparable levels of essential services, another dimension of the Social Union Framework Agreement.

The federal and provincial working group has developed a framework for the harmonization of income programs. Jurisdictions are free to select the areas in which they plan to work with respect to removal of work disincentives, rehabilitation and labour market re-entry, and the streamlining and coordination of assessment/reassessment procedures. The federal and provincial governments are expected to produce an annual public report of their respective harmonization efforts.

Coordination of Labour Market Initiatives

As noted, there are several major labour market initiatives that affect persons with disabilities: Employability Assistance for People with Disabilities, federal/provincial labour market agreements, the Opportunities Fund, and the National Framework Agreements with First Nations. The fact that there is now a federal-provincial working group to address disability issues can encourage these initiatives to work in tandem and support each other rather than proceed independently.

A coordinated approach in which key players are at the "same table" also can promote a shift from segregated to mainstream programming. It can ensure that all mainstream programs make accommodation for persons with disabilities. Accommodation could include extending course completion dates, modifying the job description or work arrangements, and removing the age limit for youth programs to help students with disabilities successfully complete their training. Improved coordination also would reduce the numbers of individuals who "fall through the cracks" because they do not meet current eligibility criteria.

Accountability

Finally, *In Unison* commits the federal and provincial governments to an open and transparent accountability process. The accountability framework is still being developed. Federal commitment to an open and transparent process was affirmed in the newly announced *Future Directions* strategy. At the very least, there is an expectation of a public report of the activities that various jurisdictions have taken, both individually and collectively, to move forward the disability agenda. The federal-provincial working group also is expected to harmonize its activities with a Working Group of Aboriginal Canadians concerned with disabilities.

The commitment to accountability is intended to recognize the growing public demand for greater democratic engagement in the form of transparency and public participation. Public reports and ongoing consultation should provide citizens and organizations representing persons with disabilities, in particular, the information they require to assess whether the objectives set out in the *In Unison* document are being met.

But accountability can move well beyond reporting on the various activities of different government departments. It can also involve an active process of determining whether all government policies and programs are removing barriers to the inclusion of persons with disabilities and, equally important, promoting their participation as full and equal citizens. The formulation and implementation of government legislation, policies and programs could be examined, for example, through an "inclusion lens" in order to consider their potential impact on persons with disabilities. A high-profile mechanism could be designated or established within each jurisdiction to take responsibility for incorporating an inclusion lens within all government activities.

FUTURE CHALLENGES

There is now in place in Canada a clear action plan rooted in strong values to guide future federal-provincial action on disability. There are specific building blocks and clear objectives to pursue at the federal and provincial levels. But this is only the first step and could face serious challenges even before it gets actively under way. The problem is that this federal-provincial collaborative process could end up being smoke-and-mirrors rather than real substantive change. The challenges of the future arise around the issues of transparent decision-making, a lowest common denominator approach and lack of federal leadership.

Transparent Decision-Making

The recently announced Social Union Framework Agreement made reference to the importance of public accountability and transparency. It talked about the need to monitor and measure the outcomes of social programs and report regularly on their impact. This commitment to transparency is crucial, especially in light of the fact that the federal-provincial process leading up to the agreement was highly secretive and far from inclusive.

As noted, the working groups which have been struck as part of the social union process, including the one on disability, are expected to develop an accountability framework. This framework presumably includes some form of discussion or consultation with interested stakeholders and the public more generally. The danger is that the consultation process itself could become the major or only action taken by governments. It is easy to make all the "busy work" surrounding consultation become the end in itself when it is actually only the means to an end.

There are other problems associated with the accountability imperative: that implicit and explicit commitment to opening up the process and "democratizing" public policy development. There are uncertainties as to the stage at which this process should be open to public consultation. At what point and how frequently should the outcomes of federal-provincial discussions be shared?

The following example illustrates the problem. The federal-provincial working group on disability set up a reference group to keep consumers informed of the discussions and to receive their input on an ongoing basis. Questions arose around the *In Unison* document and the most appropriate stage for sharing the contents of this vision paper prior to its public release. Ideally, consultation should have taken place at a very early stage to test out the proposals before the document went to various governments for approval. However, officials on the federal-provincial working group were concerned that disability groups would be informed of the possible policy options in the vision paper before they had had an opportunity to brief their ministers — let alone obtain agreement from them on the proposed directions. The consultations eventually were held, but at a relatively late stage in the process.

There are also questions, as noted, as to how the new federalism affects the relationship between governments and voluntary groups. With much of the business of the disability agenda being discussed in federal-provincial working groups involving government officials rather than elected politicians, it is difficult for groups to know how they can relate to, let alone influence, this process.

Lowest Common Denominator Approach

Another potential problem is that the current federal-provincial working group process may encourage a lowest common denominator approach. On the one hand, it is invaluable to have all key parties working together to improve social programs. It is an essential step in promoting the availability and quality of income programs and disability services throughout the country. But there is serious pressure to make the arrangement work in order to prove that Canada is a viable union. In seeking to maintain harmonious relations, a federal-provincial group may decide to back away from a certain proposal if even one jurisdiction objects to any aspect — be it the price tag, a particular ideological perspective or a new way of addressing a problem. A given province, for example, may object to the scrutiny of its policies and programs through an inclusion lens. Important proposals can be lost if there is a sense that they may not be well received in a certain province. Rather than struggle with the problem and figure out a compromise, many issues could be pushed to the back of the agenda for another day, which may or may not come again.

There are also problems around the specific initiatives that have been carried out to date. Short-term harmonization measures go only so far. While they may improve the overall functioning of the income system, they still retain the diverse range of programs. This problem has led to calls over the years for comprehensive reform of the disability income system. But little action, other than more study, is expected in this area.

Weakened Leadership Role

The disability community is especially worried that the federal-provincial working group arrangement will water down the federal leadership role that, in the community's view, is so crucial to advancing the disability agenda. Ever since the heady days of Canada's new constitution and the introduction of a Charter of Rights and Freedoms which guaranteed the protection of disability rights, the disability community has regarded Ottawa as the champion of its issues. The current fear is that the federal government will abandon its leadership role in the name of constitutional conciliation and will be less prepared to take action that protects citizens' rights or introduce programs that will provide direct assistance to any given population.

CONCLUSION

The concerns that the disability community raises are relevant to all Canadians. There are questions about the future and ongoing role of the federal government, in particular, in social policy issues. Will Canada's national government be able to speak on behalf of the nation? Will its voice in representing the needs of all Canadians be able, if required, to rise above the "horizontal policy-making" that is reshaping the federation? Will it be able to act with leadership and authority without being accused of infringing its consensual commitments under the Social Union Framework Agreement? All Canadians should be concerned about these crucial questions that the disability community is raising on behalf of the entire country.

NOTES

[1]Keith G. Banting, *The Welfare State and Canadian Federalism*, 2d ed. (Kingston and Montreal: McGill-Queen's University Press, 1987), pp. 47-48.

[2]Ibid., p. 48.

[3]Ibid., p. 197.

[4]Ken Battle and Sherri Torjman, *How Finance Re-Formed Social Policy* (Ottawa: Caledon Institute of Social Policy, 1995).

[5]Human Resources Development Canada (HRDC), *Persons with Disabilities: A Supplementary Paper* (Ottawa: Minister of Supply and Services Canada, 1994).

[6]Sherri Torjman, "The Canada Pension Plan Disability Benefit and the Disability Income System," in *Proceedings of the Experts' Forum on Canada Pension Plan Reform* (Ottawa: Caledon Institute of Social Policy, 1966), pp. 97-122.

[7]HRDC, *Persons with Disabilities*, p. 4.

[8]Ibid.

[9]Ibid., p. 23.

[10]Sherri Torjman and Ken Battle, *Seniors Beware: This Review's for You Too* (Ottawa: Caledon Institute of Social Policy, 1994).

[11]C. Crawford, *Ensuring the Well-Being of Persons with Disabilities: An Overview of the Problematic* (Toronto: Roeher Institute, 1997), p. 5.

[12]National Council of Welfare, *Welfare Incomes 1996* (Ottawa: Minister of Public Works and Government Services Canada, 1997), p. 24.

[13]Ibid.

[14]Crawford, *Ensuring the Well-Being of Persons with Disabilities*, p. 6.

[15]See B. Perrin, "Disability and Labour Market Integration: Clarifying Federal Responsibilities in the Evolving Social Union," in *The Will to Act for Canadians with Disabilities: Research Papers* for the federal Task Force on Disability Issues (Ottawa: Minister of Public Works and Government Services Canada), p. 20; and J. Atkey, "The Future of the Vocational Rehabilitation of Disabled Persons," in *The Will to Act for Canadians with Disabilities*, p. 7.

[16]Torjman, "The Canada Pension Plan Disability Benefit and the Disability Income System."

[17]See H. Beatty, "Comprehensive Disability Compensation in Ontario," *Journal of Law and Social Policy* 7: 100-42, 125.

[18]HRDC, *Persons with Disabilities*, p. 4.

[19]See M. Biggs, *Building Blocks for Canada's New Social Union* (Ottawa: Canadian Policy Research Networks, 1996).

[20]Ibid.

[21]Ibid.

[22]Ibid.

[23]Battle and Torjman, *How Finance Re-Formed Social Policy*.

[24]Sherri Torjman, *CHST Spells COST for Disabled* (Ottawa: Caledon Institute of Social Policy, 1995).

[25]Sherri Torjman, *Dollars for Service: Aka Individualized Funding* (Ottawa: Caledon Institute of Social Policy, 1996).

5

THE GOVERNANCE OF DISABILITY
PROGRAMS IN THE GERMAN
INTERGOVERNMENTAL REGIME

Ursula Muench

CLASSIFYING GERMAN FEDERALISM IN THE TYPOLOGY OF INTERGOVERNMENTAL REGIMES

The kind of federalism being practised in Germany differs in many ways from the intergovernmental regime known in Canada. The outstanding feature of German federalism is the evolution of a so-called system of *interlocking federalism (politikverflechtung)*. Although this kind of intergovernmental policy-making has gained importance since the 1960s and 1970s it would be wrong to state that the German federal system has ever functioned as *classical* or *disentangled federalism*. The main features of the German system of interlocking federalism result from the formal constitutional distribution of powers, especially from the highly integrated structure of the tax system, the mechanisms of fiscal equalization (vertically as well as horizontally), the role the Bundesrat (the upper house of parliament) plays in federal legislation, and, last but not least, the political culture in which the German federal system works.

It is equally important to note that in Germany the question is not how to achieve and maintain a social union. With regard to the federal system the point of view seems to be just the other way around: contrary to Canada, the German division of powers does not have important social policy prerogatives which rest substantially with the Länder. Since 1949, German federalism was formed by the idea that intergovernmental relations and government-citizen relations should be practised in such a way that the uniformity of living conditions (*Einheitlichkeit der Lebensverhaeltnisse*) is achieved and maintained. Therefore, German citizens have the same social rights and obligations regardless of where they live.

Germany as a Multi-Tiered System

To understand intergovernmental relations in Germany it is important to note that there are not only two orders of government, but four: besides the federal government and the Länder there is the local level of government, which constitutionally forms part of the Länder and participates in the field of social policy — an important but not powerful role. On the other hand, there has developed a new system of governance: the European Union (EU). Although Germany, as a member of the EU, retains a powerful, often determinative role in policy formulation and reigns supreme in social policy, the EU shows a growing resemblance to traditional regimes of intergovernmental relations.[1] This development has an important impact on the field of social policy as policy-making now takes place in a complex interplay of social actors and decisionmakers; furthermore it puts the various national (i.e., federal) governments in a position to blame the European Community, especially the Commission in Brussels, for changes in the social policy field, which otherwise they would be afraid even to contemplate.[2]

The Main Features of German Interlocking Federalism

The Formal Constitutional Distribution of Powers

While the central state is responsible for nearly all important areas of (legislative) policy-making, the Länder are involved in all aspects of policy implementation. Only at first sight does the formal constitutional distribution of powers seem to provide significant powers to the Länder. There is a provision (article 30 of the constitution) that allows competences to devolve onto the federal government only if the Basic Law provides for them, and powers not assigned to the national government belong to the Länder. But since important areas of legislation are in fact stated by the Basic Law to be within the federal jurisdiction, the significance of this constitutional provision is correspondingly reduced to a minimum. In fact, the policy-making powers are distributed asymmetrically between the federal and the Länder governments. In addition, the legislative competences of the federal government are not restricted to those policy areas enumerated by the Basic Law as exclusive federal powers; the wide array of concurrent legislation has to all intents and purposes been absorbed by the federal level of government with the consequence of limiting the legislative powers of the Länder to a small number of exclusive powers. The dominance of the federal government in the field of concurrent powers is especially true in the field of social policy. Until 1994 the federal constitution stated that the federal government has the right to legislate in matters of concurrent legislation to the extent that a need for regulation by federal legislation exists, since, for example, the maintenance of uniformity of living conditions necessitates such regulation. Although this provision was weakened by the constitutional reform of 1994 the policy goal of attaining social equity is still dominant.

Legislation at the Länder level is therefore more or less restricted to the policy areas of culture and education, local government, law and order and the police, and the regulation of broadcasting. While the Länder have almost no legislative competences in the realm of social policy, their powers and functions in administration and implementation are much more important. The Länder have to execute nearly all federal laws because the federal government deals with specific matters based on federal authority. The normal situation is to have federal laws applied by the Länder. Although the federal government retains substantial powers of normative influence and supervision of administrative activities, the Länder are not mere administrative subdivisions of the federal government. They enjoy a large degree of autonomy in the administering of federal policies. In addition, municipalities have considerable discretionary jurisdiction, that is, the right to engage in activities that do not violate federal or Länder law, which are especially important in the field of social policy. Provided with sufficient economic resources, Länder and municipalities are able to use their administrative powers in order to offer additional social programs. By granting "voluntary subsidies" (*freiwillige Leistungen*) without creating legal claims both subnational levels of government are able to get involved in areas of social policy otherwise dominated by the federal laws. These voluntary subsidies are very important for the governance of disability programs in the German intergovernmental regime.

The Organization and Functioning of the German Upper House of Parliament

Although the important legislative competences as well as those for taxes stay with the federal government, the Basic Law ensures substantial Länder influence, especially through the Bundesrat, which includes members of the Länder governments. All federal laws have to pass the Bundesrat, many of them needing Bundesrat approval. In order to understand the system of German federalism, it is important to reflect on the provision of the Basic Law (article 77) which states that those laws that greatly affect the interests of the Länder, such as financial matters or administration, require the approval of the Bundesrat. While in the early years of the Federal Republic approximately 42 percent of all federal legislation required approval, the percentage has undergone a distinctive increase: nowadays more than 60 percent of all federal laws have to be approved by the Bundesrat. As a result of this development the role of the second chamber of the federal parliament and thereby of the Länder has gained even more importance. The regime of interlocking federalism has intensified.

Intergovernmental Mechanisms

The system of sharing competences laid down in the constitution enforces a number of intergovernmental mechanisms. The coordination between both orders of government takes place at every stage of policy preparation and implementation. There are institutionalized as well as informal meetings on the vertical level (representatives of the federal government and the Länder governments) and on the horizontal level (only representatives of the Länder without involvement of the federal government). Besides the setting up of hundreds of working parties on all political levels ranging from the heads of government and departmental ministers to the departmental officers on sectional levels, the Bundesrat also fulfills an important function with regard to the coordination between both orders of government. Through this independent institution, the Länder do not only participate in the federal legislation but also in the administrative procedures of the federal government. It enables the Länder to influence those federal laws whose implementation affects Länder authorities.

The other most important feature of German federalism is the intensive cooperation among the Länder (interstate cooperation). The concept of uniformity of living conditions determines not only relations between the federal and Länder governments. It is applied even in those policy fields that fall under

Länder jurisdiction. The self-coordination of the Länder involves varied mechanisms from treaties and administrative agreements to informal understandings which are shaped by the basic concept to reduce the differences between the Länder through jointly devised and financed solutions. By this interstate cooperation the Länder administration is strengthened at the expense of the state parliaments. This development of the German intergovernmental regime impairs the commitment to democratic government. While the rule of electoral majorities is expressed by the periodic (every four or five years) elections of representatives to national and state legislative bodies it is important to note that the representatives in a Länder parliament do not have any substantial and effective role in the decision-making processes.

The intergovernmental regime in Germany has proved rather inflexible. While this was true also before the unification of 1990, especially during periods of economic recession, the problem has very much intensified since, because of the growing discrepancies in the level of efficiency between the Länder. "The emergence of active, long-term and redistributive policies tends to be impeded, due to differences that exist among the states in terms of levels of economic wealth, economic structure, rates of growth, levels of unemployment, tax revenues ('poor states' versus 'rich states') and differences in interests between the Länder and the federal government."[3]

Financing

The tax structure presents another specific feature of the German system of interlocking federalism. The responsibility for financial legislation is separate from the power of allocation and from financial administration. Whereas the legislative sovereignty for taxes lies predominantly with the federal government, the income from taxation is allocated in accordance with independent principles.

Compared to other intergovernmental regimes, the freedom of both orders of government to raise revenues is relatively small. The competences of the Länder governments in the area of tax legislation are extremely small; and the freedom of the federal government to raise revenues is restricted, because the federal government depends on the consent of the majority in the Bundesrat in order to change any law that affects the tax system.

For particularly profitable taxes a compound system exists. This practice of apportionment of the most important tax revenues as "joint taxes" (income taxes, corporate taxes, or value-added tax) aims to achieve a substantial

measure of vertical balance; it should provide the basis for the Länder to insti-
tutionalize (social) programs on their own and to implement the federal laws
without interference from the federal government.

The distribution of the particularly profitable VAT not only presents an
instrument to reduce vertical imbalances in revenues, but it is also important
as the first step of horizontal financial equalization (article 107, Basic Law).

Because the primary distribution of tax revenues between the federal
and the Länder governments is not sufficient, a need for other financial provisions remains. First, there is the mechanism of horizontal fiscal equalization,
facilitating the redistribution among the financially weak or less efficient and
the financially stronger Länder. Second, there exists a constitutional provision
for the federal government to provide grants-in-aid to those Länder which are
less efficient and financially weak. Despite the constitutional and legislative
provisions, including elements of equalization, there are still relevant horizontal imbalances. Since German reunification in 1990, the problem of financing
German federalism has become a severe challenge to the intergovernmental
regime.

With regard to social policy, it is important to note that the German
federal system normally does not work on the basis of shared-cost programs.
In general, there are no federal transfers to state governments in order to fund
social assistance programs as is the case in Canada. Although there are a number
of exceptions, the basic assumption is that the federal government and the
Länder meet separately the costs resulting from the discharge of their respective tasks.

Only those federal laws executed by the Länder and involving the dis-
bursement of funds may provide that such funds shall be contributed wholly or
in part by the federal government (*Geldleistungsgesetze,* article 104 a, section
3, Basic Law). None of the policy sectors relevant to the case studies (health
care, labour market, or policies relating to persons with disabilities) are, however, directly touched by this provision.

The Role of Local Government in Social Policy

Since municipalities have to provide important services, such as social assistance (*Sozialhilfe*), but do not receive adequate funds from the share of public
revenue, there is a problem. Their share of the income tax and some negligible
local taxes are regularly supplemented by Länder grants which cause both

political and legal conflicts between the municipalities and the respective Länder governments. This financial problem has direct consequences on local government functions in the area of social policy On the one hand, they are obliged to fulfill those transferred responsibilities, which are to be carried out on behalf of the Länder or the federal government. Most importantly, local governments are not only obliged to implement general social assistance but they must also finance it, even though they are not able to influence federal provisions. Since the expenditures for general social assistance are rising because of growing unemployment, municipalities are, on the other hand, forced to reduce their so-called volunteer services which are also an important feature of social policy. These are services the local government is not obliged to provide, for example, vouchers for disabled persons to make use of a certain number of free taxi rides per month. Because there is no legal claim forcing local governments to pay for these services, they are reduced as soon as the government has trouble financing their responsibilities.

To understand the relationship between the structural problems and deficits of fiscal federalism, social policy and interlocking federalism, the political initiatives of two Länder are described. In 1988, the Land Lower Saxony (*Niedersachsen*) and in 1995, the Land Saarland tried to change the system of financing social assistance.[4] They shared the opinion of the financially weaker Länder that social assistance expenditures by municipalities in the respective Länder were too high and that the federal government should contribute by covering half of these expenditures. Because the suggested method of financing this proposal would have had significant effects on the apportionment of taxes as well as for the system of horizontal equalization it proved highly controversial.[5] Since social welfare expenditures are higher in northern and in eastern Germany than in the southern parts of the country, these Länder would have benefited more than Bavaria or Baden-Württemberg, for example. At the same time, the method of financing this switch from Länder to federal expenditure via a new distribution of tax revenues between both orders of government would have had profound consequences for all the Länder. The reason for the "rich" Länder to oppose this proposal in the Bundesrat is therefore obvious. It is also evident, that any other attempt to solve the problems of financing social assistance in the regime of interlocking federalism will fail because of its specific technique of consensus-building on the one hand and the differences in fiscal resources between the Länder and the impact of party competition on the other.

Corporatist Relationships in the Social Security System

While cooperation and coordination are significant features in the German regime of interlocking federalism, the system of intergovernmental relations is supplemented in important sectors of social policy by corporatist relationships. Those elements of German social policy which are based on the social security system are organized into a system of self-government by the "social partners" as a corporatist employer-employee relationship. For this reason the intergovernmental regime in the sector of health care is much more influenced by effects of the corporatist organization than by the federal regime (see the case study by Dietmar Wassener). This is also true for some aspects of policies relating to persons with disabilities. In order to understand the processes and outcomes of rehabilitation policies, it is, therefore, much more important to analyze the organizational structure of the system of social security than the intergovernmental regime.

Independence versus Interdependence and Hierarchical versus Non-Hierarchical Intergovernmental Relations

With regard to the interplay of two sets of factors relevant for the typology of intergovernmental regimes it was already argued that the degree of interdependence in German federalism is rather high. This interdependence goes along with a relationship that seems to be less hierarchical than non-hierarchical. While neither order of government is constitutionally subordinate to the other (with the exception of local governments which are regarded as subordinated parts of the Länder) this does not imply that the Länder are really equal either in terms of the powers they hold or the resources available to them. Nevertheless, this system is different from the regime of federal unilateralism: it is most important to remember that in German federalism the Länder governments are directly involved in the making of federal laws as well as in revenue-sharing — through the role the Bundesrat plays in federal legislation.

Because the main responsibility of the Länder rests in the administration of federal laws, they have the ability to influence the modalities of implementing and the kind of administration used.

The result of this process seems confusing: while the Länder are influential with regard to the politics at the federal level as at the European level their genuine competences and powers are quantitatively, as well as qualitatively, restricted. German federalism is therefore often described as an intergovernmental regime where the Länder participation in policy-making at the federal and European levels is much more important than at the Länder level. This type of intergovernmental regime is clearly distinguished from a disentangled interstate system of federalism where the federal and the state governments act independently of one another in their respective areas of legislative competence. The German system can be characterized by the following observation: while the Länder parliaments, such as Munich or Hannover, are powerless outside their areas of expertise, they are able to influence important decisions taken in Bonn or in Brussels.

The critique put forward about the process of federal-state joint decision-making in the interlocking system of federalism is certainly not new. Ever since those constitutional reforms which established the so-called joint task forces (*Gemeinschaftsaufgaben*) of both levels of government were institutionalized in the late 1960s, it was argued that the extended system of interlocking federalism causes anti-federal tendencies, a process by which the Länder may eventually loose their statehood (*Staatsqualitaet*).

New Tendencies in German Federalism since Reunification

One of the main features of German federalism is the fact that the practice of shared policy-making produces proclivities toward lowest common denominator and "packaged" policies. The functioning of the intergovernmental regime tends to obstruct all policy initiatives aimed at the solution to those complex problems which are most likely to be found in the welfare system. This structural problem already existed before German reunification. Now the situation has turned into a serious problem which dominates the current political debate in the Federal Republic. The main reason is that not only German society but economic and political structures have substantially changed since 1990. First, the far-reaching differences between the eastern and western parts of the now unified Federal Republic justified increases in intervention by the federal government in a broad array of Länder policy areas in order to build or modernize and maintain the necessary infrastructure and to ensure the existence of public services.[6] This was especially true in the field of social policy: after reunification, the federal government initiated different financial programs in order to enable the Länder in the East and their respective municipalities to build up institutions necessary for the maintenance of social services, etc.[7] The activities on the part of the federal government to help the financially weak Länder and to improve and harmonize the living conditions caused changes in the relationship between the federal and Länder governments. Formerly non-hierarchical relations turned into a more hierarchical structure of decision-making not only with regard to those Länder in the eastern part of the country, but for all of them. It challenged the established relationship between the two orders of government.

Because the capacity of a Land government to make policy in the German intergovernmental regime of interlocking federalism depends on the ability and the will of the majority of all Länder to assume responsibilities, the poorer Länder hinder the wealthier Länder. This feature of interlocking federalism is the main reason why some Länder governments reassert a federalism based on Länder autonomy. For the last years they have tried to promote a process of "refederalization" through a new system of distribution of powers and a broadening of the financial capacity. It is important to note that this attempt to reduce interdependence between the federal and Länder levels on the one hand and the cooperation between the Länder on the other is not only an issue of controversy between the Länder and the federal government but also among the Länder governments.

Intergovernmentalism, Effectiveness and Democratic Governance

As already mentioned, the German system of interlocking federalism means, above all, that the Länder parliaments cannot provide their representatives with a substantial and effective role in decision-making. While executive federalism does not meet the high normative standards of democracy, it is, however, equally obvious that in the German political system the protection of electoral minorities and the commitment to providing a variety of ongoing avenues for citizen consultation and participation are fostered by the intergovernmental regime. One of the main advantages of power-sharing between federal and state governments in a political system with political parties playing an important role seems to be the opportunity for the political opposition at the federal level to act as the governing party in several Länder governments. The main opposition party is thereby not only able to demonstrate its political ability but it can also — in the event that it forms a majority in the Bundesrat — influence federal policy extensively. This enlargement of the participation of citizens and expansion of the system of checks and balances must be seen as being in conflict with another democratic principle: the commitment to "public" or transparent decision-making. The right of both the public and the legislature to hold governments accountable for the decisions taken is greatly restricted in the regime of interlocking federalism under certain circumstances. Especially in periods when the Bundesrat is dominated by the federal political opposition, political responsibilities can no longer be clearly identified.

Whereas the regime of interlocking federalism once seemed able to satisfy political, economic, and social needs, in recent years, in particular, it has been criticized for having serious defects with respect to its effectiveness. The slow decision-making process caused by the "divided government" (different party majorities in both houses of parliament) and by the effects of the fiscal crisis brought on by the costs of reunification is bringing under attack the current regime of intergovernmental relations. For several decades, the assessment of the German system of intergovernmental relations was dominated by the criteria of the division of powers and its consistency with the political goal of achieving social equity despite the formal distribution of powers between the two levels of government. The political goal was therefore to achieve a federal regime not in conflict with the maxim of uniform living standards. With the growing horizontal imbalance resulting from post-reunification political and economic changes, the consensus on this policy goal seems to be diminishing: while politicians and voters in the poor Länder hope to achieve uniformity by strengthening the position of the federal government and preserving the system of horizontal equalization, the other Länder governments are attempting to go in for an alternative governance regime. But their hopes of changing the existing system in the direction of a more disentangled federalism will be very difficult to achieve. The functioning of interlocking federalism, with its decision-making process based on consensus, will prevent substantial changes.

THE GOVERNANCE OF DISABILITY PROGRAMS IN THE GERMAN INTERGOVERNMENTAL REGIME

Legal Basis, Definitions, Principles

The performance of the three sectors — health care, labour market, and policies relating to persons with disabilities — is to be seen in direct relation to those constitutional provisions in the Basic Law according to which the Federal Republic of Germany is a social federal state (*sozialer Bundesstaat*). The provision cannot be changed by any legislative majority (article 79, section 3, Basic Law).

Although a convincing material definition of this welfare state principle has not yet been formulated, general agreement exists that it should be oriented toward social justice, social security, and a fair and just social and economic system. The welfare state principle lays the constitutional foundation for the different programs for persons with disabilities. Because citizens will not be able to derive any legal claims from this general guideline it is necessary that all legislative bodies define the different services and supports more precisely.

The coordination and efficiency of disability programs is negatively affected, not only in Canada but also in the Federal Republic of Germany, by the lack of a clear definition of the term "person with disabilities" which is generally valid and recognized in legal and social terms. Among other reasons, this deficit is probably due to the fact that in German-speaking countries the term "Behinderung" (disability) is a relatively new one. Only after World War I did the term "Behinderter" (person with disabilities) replace the term "Krueppel" ("cripple"), which many veterans injured during the war considered to be discriminatory.[8] Another factor that impeded the development of a uniform legal definition is the large number of varied institutions and service providers.[9]

The *Federal Severely Disabled Persons Act* defines a disability as the "consequences of an impairment of functions that is not just of a temporary nature and which is based on an irregular physical, mental or psychological state. An irregular state is a state that is different from the state typical for a certain age."[10] This definition is guided by the three-category definition applied by the World Health Organization which refers to impairment, disability (functional), and handicap (social). A German particularity exists in that the Act defines different levels and lays down a differentiation according to the level of disability.[11] A person is considered "severely disabled" if he or she is more than 49 percent disabled.

A relatively new principle of the German disability programs states that persons with disabilities are entitled to aid regardless of the cause leading to the disability. Until 1963 the Act contained a principle of causality. Accordingly, only those people whose disabilities were due to a provable cause qualified for assistance.[12] thus, for a long period a differentiation was made as to whether the disability was a result of disease, or an accident, or there at birth.[13]

Whereas federal laws legally define the term disability and do not differentiate based on the effects of the disability on an individual's life, the Länder's definition does differentiate. These definitions, which are used to provide assistance and services to disabled persons, are frequently more appropriate when it comes to doing justice to the situation in which disabled persons live. A description is the one found in the *Bavarian Plan for Persons with Disabilities.* According to this plan, persons with disabilities are "persons who, due to physical, mental or psychological disabilities, are severely and permantly impaired in a social relational field of vital importance, above all in the areas of education, vocational training, employment, communication, housing and spare time activities and who therefore require special assistance on the part of society."[14] This shows that the Länder, with their closer proximity to the affected persons and since one of the functions of the Länder along with the municipalities is the provision of services, might be better suited to bring about the results of policies than federal laws which define entitlement to insurance benefits or the protections against discrimination at work.

The guidelines defining the overall rehabilitation policy and the governance of disability programs in the Federal Republic of Germany as well as the general policy goal in this respect are based on the "social right" of persons with disabilities to assistance and their right to integration into society.[15] This principle is valid for all levels of government. But the question of how disabled persons are to be integrated into society is a very controversial matter among those who actualize the policies for disabled persons (charitable institutions, organizations representing and defending the rights of disabled persons, social security authorities and organizations, and politicians at the various levels). Another principle of German governance of disability programs is to take action at the earliest stage possible and provide required assistance. The severity of the disability is to be limited as far as possible and the unavoidable consequences of a disability are to be fought in an optimum way. In order to meet this goal, it is necessary to offer assistance that is geared to the needs of the disabled person. In this regard, the nature of Germany's intergovernmental regime becomes clearly visible. Whereas on the one hand the principles established by the federal government are general in nature, the guidelines adopted at the Länder level are mainly based on a much more detailed differentiation and are therefore more appropriately adjusted to the needs of disabled persons.

In November 1994, in the framework of the constitutional reform the non-discrimination clause of the Basic Law was amended in article 3, with the adding of the sentence "No one may be discriminated against on the account of their disability."[16] Even though this wording allows for positive discrimination for the first time ever, the prohibition of discrimination on the basis of disability being enshrined in the constitution is an appeal only.[17] This does not mean, however, that because of that amendment disabled persons have the right to form legal claims over housing, employment, and mobility. An anti-discrimination act comparable to the legislation in Canada or the United States, pursuant to which the principle of equal treatment is a right enforceable by law, is rejected by the federal government while referring to the fact that the German legal system is completely different from that in the US or Canada.

Basic Principles of Allocation of Responsibility in the Field of German Governance of Disability Programs

Germany's governing of disability programs is highly complex and inconsistent: neither legally speaking nor in terms of allocation of responsibility. In order to give an overview of the organizations playing a role in this field, one needs to take into account that there are different levels of action:

* the allocation of responsibility between the federal government, the Länder, and the municipalities (different orders of government),
* the allocation of responsibility between the different social security organizations: their abilities do exist regardless of the distribution of tasks in the federal system, and[18]
* allocation of responsibility between governmental and non-governmental organizations (associations of private welfare work).

Vertical Allocation of Responsibility

The benefits offered to disabled persons by the authorities (the governance of disability programs) correspond with the allocation of responsibilities in the federal welfare state.[19] The relevant laws are federal, they have to be passed by both houses of parliament — e.g., the Social Code, *Rehabilitation Adjustment Act, Employment Promotion Act, Federal War Victims Relief Act, Severely Disabled Persons Act*, and *Federal Social Welfare Act*.

The tasks of the Länder consist mainly in the enforcement of different types of federal laws. For this purpose, they pass provisions for implementation. When it comes to federal laws that provide for the creation and maintenance of certain institutions/facilities for disabled persons, it is the federal government that is responsible for setting the rules, but the Länder are responsible for implementing the regulations. However, services are generally offered by charitable organizations and not by governmental institutions. In this case the authorities act in a supervisory capacity and grant financial aid. There are some federal laws that contain detailed provisions as to their implementation. The *Severely Disabled Persons Act* provides for the statutory setting up of so-called central welfare offices, and each of the Länder needs to have at least one such office plus a corresponding number of branch offices. The costs incurred in establishing these and in implementing federal laws are to be borne by the Länder. The allocation of responsibility regarding federal legislation and its enforcement at the Länder level — which is one of the most typical character-istics of the German system of interlocking federalism — is rendered even more difficult by the fact that it is not absolutely necessary that the implemen-tation be executed by governmental institutions only. This is due to the so-called principle of subsidiarity which plays a very important role in the area of German social policy and according to which governmental authorities are only to take action if non-governmental organizations are not capable of doing so. An ap-plication of that principle to the field of governance of disability programs means that whenever possible social security organizations, charitable organi-zations, and self-help organizations are to provide the required services.[20] Only in those cases in which these non-governmental institutions are not in a posi-tion to provide the services guaranteed by law, will governmental organizations take over.

One thing that is true for many different types of social benefits is also particularly applicable to the governance of disability programs: in addition to the grants under federal law, there are complementary programs, but the af-fected persons do not have any legal claim to these benefits. These are not essential for the maintenance of the social-security system in Germany. The existing social-security programs that are legally guaranteed would also com-ply with the welfare state requirements even if the Länder and the municipalities did not grant such indemnity. Nevertheless, they are very important for the relevant individuals and they contribute in an essential way to the overall gov-ernance of disability programs (as well as to overall social policy). Many measures taken in the framework of the governance of disability programs rep-resent a so-called "administration of benefits."[21] These measures refer to voluntary benefits to which the persons affected do not have any legal claim and which were not passed as laws but as administrative regulations or guide-lines. The Länder frequently resort to this instrument, the advantage of which is that it can be handled and applied more flexibly than laws. Due to the fact that measures based on guidelines and administrative regulations do not grant citizens any legal entitlement and they receive financing only in line with the funds available in the Länder budget, the Länder are less tightly bound by them than by legal claims.[22]

This possibility to grant voluntary subsidies to disabled individuals or to non-governmental organizations assisting persons with disabilities is the major reason why in the Federal Republic of Germany the governance of disability programs varies significantly from Land to Land even though the most essential legal provisions are of a federal nature.

Horizontal Allocation of Responsibility

In order to integrate disabled persons into society and to do justice to the principal goal of governance of disability programs, both financial assistance (economic security) and rehabilitation measures are necessary. But Germany has no uniform system of benefits. Financial services and rehabilitation measures are granted by the most diverse organizations. Of particular importance in this respect are the social-security organizations. These are among the six rehabilitation agencies, in addition to the institutions responsible for paying compensation for disabilities suffered by victims of war or by individuals during the course of military service, along with social assistance agencies and youth welfare agencies.[23]

In addition to their other duties, each fund in Germany's social system is also responsible for a particular aspect of rehabilitation. Contrary to the Canadian system, a high proportion of the supports provided for persons with disabilities are delivered and financed under the aegis of the different funds in Germany's social system.

Social Security Organizations. The social-security system is based on legally independent institutions that act in line with the principles of subsidiarity and self-government. Representatives of employers and employees are included in the decision-making bodies.[24] These institutions are not governmental organizations, but they are so-called corporations under public law which, on the one hand, are subject to governmental supervision but, on the other, manage their affairs themselves. The organizations of health, accident, and old-age pension insurances run rehabilitation facilities in which the persons insured obtain medical and rehabilitative services pursuant to federal law prescriptions. At the same time, these organizations provide financial assistance while individuals are receiving medical rehabilitation services, so that costs of living for disabled persons and/or their families are covered. The entitlement to both types of benefits is based on the insurance principle. This means that the social-security organizations are only obliged to provide benefits if an insured event occurs.

The criteria that need to be complied with in order to qualify for benefits depend on contribution periods and are different for the four insurances. If a disability is caused by an accident suffered at the workplace or on the way to work and/or if it is the result of an occupational disease, the employers' liability insurance association will assume responsibility. The organizations of the social-security pension insurance (statutory old-age pension insurance for non-self-employed people) are responsible if the working/earning capacity of a person insured with them is reduced substantially or endangered and if no other carrier has prior ranking.

Pursuant to the provisions of the *Employment Promotion Act*, under certain circumstances, the Federal Employment Services, in their capacity as a carrier of the social-security unemployment insurance, are assigned the role of the institution responsible for financing the rehabilitation measures. The persons insured are entitled to file a claim if disabilities impede or impair occupational integration. Also in this respect, the prerequisite is the non-existance of a prior-ranking carrier.

An additional vertical differentiation between federal and Länder level is possible when it comes to statutory pension insurance and health insurance funds. Whereas salaried employees are insured by the *Bundesversicherungsanstalt fuer Angestellte* (the Federal Insurance Fund for Salaried Employees), wage earners are insured regionally, at the Länder level. This means that the matter of responsibility of insurance organizations within a federal system is determined according to whether the person insured is a wage earner or salaried employee. This allocation of functions in turn means that changes in the socio-economic structure of the German society will have far-reaching consequences for the allocation of state responsibilities. If the employment structure changes such that in the end there will be more salaried employees than wage earners, this will have a consequence on the insurance system.[25] Due to these socio-economic structural changes, the social-security organizations who act at the Länder level — e.g., the *Landesversicherungsanstalten* (Regional Insurance Institutions/Pension Insurance for Wage Earners) and the *Ortskrankenkassen* (Local Health Insurance Funds) — face a permanent loss of income to the federal central organizations like the *Bundesversicherungsanstalt fuer Angestellte* (Federal Insurance Office for Salaried Employees) and the *Ersatzkassen* (Substitute Private Health Insurance Companies under German Public Law). Without any doubt, these changes are of importance for the different levels of government. This determines whether a federal or regional ministry will be in charge of governmental supervision. On the other hand, the pension insurance organizations (pension insurance schemes) are very important for a region since they usually invest their funds locally. In addition to the health insurance and pension insurance organizations, it is also the employers' liability insurance funds, in their capacity as organizations of occupational accident insurance funds, that are responsible for the governing of disability programs.

Charitable Organizations. Whereas self-help organizations are based on the activities of the disabled persons themselves as well as on the work of their families, charitable organizations are interest groups which enjoy constitutional privileges and which are sometimes idealistically motivated: they work with staff members from the most diverse professional backgrounds ranging from social workers to nurses, but they also rely on volunteers. This way, thanks to the important role played by the charitable organizations in administering disability programs, a relatively strong voluntary commitment on the part of the public (citizen involvement) is guaranteed. Based on the principle of subsidiarity, charitable organizations also act in their capacity as institutions of social policy and fill the gaps left by governmental social policy.[26] This position is "semi-official." They form a bridge between the public administration and the private sector. There are five leading associations of private welfare work — three of which have an ecclesiastical or religious orientation.

Self-help. Another characteristic of the German administration of disability programs is through "self-help." This is based on the principle that persons with disabilities should be granted more responsibility of their own. The growing importance of self-help groups is viewed against the background in which both individuals with disabilities and their families feel that services provided by governmental and welfare institutions have certain elements of patronage and restriction. Thus, in recent decades many new associations for the disabled and self-help groups have been organized. It has become their job to deal with the concerns and defend the interests of persons with disabilities, in order to enable them to lead their lives in the most independent and self-determined fashion possible along with giving them some control over their own situations. Even though the concept of self-help is to complement and to be an alternative to professional assistance, it cannot exist without governmental and/ or public financial support. Financial assistance is mainly granted by the Länder and municipalities. The decision as to which self-help organizations qualify for financial support is also frequently a result of party politics and priorities of the different parties: Länder and municipalities governed by the Social

Democrats and the Green Party frequently give priority to the promotion of other societal minorities while those governed by the Christian Democrats tend to give priority to the promotion of disabled persons. Since subsidies given to self-help groups are of a voluntary nature, they frequently lack security/continuity in terms of planning, which they so urgently need.[27] But it is not only governmental agencies that financially support these self-help groups. Health insurance companies also have the possibility of granting financial support to these groups and agencies involved in rehabilitation.

Coordination of Support and Services in the Governing of Disability Programs

In order to integrate the German governance of disability programs into a framework that complies with the basic principle of "uniformity of living conditions" — despite the fact that there are so many different organizations and ideas, both at the federal and Länder level — coordination mechanisms had to be created. This is an attempt to offset the deficits in terms of efficiency and transparency concerning the different programs, which might be said to be a natural result of the horizontal diversity of the organizations on the one hand, and the vertical distribution of functions and responsibility on the other. It means that the coordinating agencies also serve the purpose of meeting the social needs of the disabled in a more appropriate way. At the federal level, coordination rests with the federal Ministry of Labour and Social Affairs which uses the consulting services of the Council for Rehabilitation of Persons with Disabilities consisting of representatives of the organizations involved in the governance of disability programs.

The Länder, because of their position in the federal system, are obliged to enforce and implement federal laws regarding the concerns of the disabled and they are also entitled to be involved in social planning. Within the framework of this social planning, most Länder draw up regional plans centred around the needs of persons with disabilities. The objective of these plans is two-fold: (i) they are to describe the current situation in terms of assistance granted to the disabled and its individual elements and (ii) they are to formulate programs as to how the support for persons with disabilities can be further extended in the future. These regional plans mainly comprise the voluntary services provided by the Länder. The purposes of these social plans are manifold: they help the organizations orientate their measures toward governmental objectives and they inform those affected about the services and assistance available. In this way, the regional plans also fulfil a coordinating function.

The coordinators administering the disability programs at the municipal level play an important role in the provision and the harmonization of services and support for disabled persons. In the areas where there are no local coordinators, this function is partially fulfilled by independent organizations. These coordination offices/coordinators are contacts for persons with disabilities as well as contacts for social-security organizations.

Supports and Services for Persons with Disabilities

Rehabilitation

Rehabilitation, considered a social right, is provided for in the first volume of the Code of Social Law. It is defined first as the supports and services necessary to prevent disabilities: to eliminate, improve, and prevent their aggravation or to alleviate their consequences, and second as the supports and services necessary to guarantee a person with disabilities, or threatened with disabilities, a place in the community and above all in the labour market in accordance with his/her preferences and skills. Pursuant to the *Rehabilitation Adjustment Act*, the rehabilitation process has to pursue the objective of integrating those with disabilities into the labour market, a profession, and society and, if possible, on a permanent basis. Since different measures of rehabilitation are assigned to the different branches of the social-security system, the Federal Republic does not have a uniform law governing rehabilitation. Instead, there are federal laws in the different books of the Social Code as well as in the *Severely Disabled Persons Act*, the *Employment Promotion Act* and the *Federal Social Welfare Act*. Rehabilitation is defined in the regulations adopted by the rehabilitation organizations, but not yet part of legislation. Due to the way the German social-security system is structured, it is complicated to decide which carrier is in charge of providing which type of rehabilitation services.

Medical Rehabilitation for the Restoration of Health

In the area of medical treatment, rehabilitation[28] is equal to prevention and cure.[29] Since rehabilitation measures always have priority over the supports and services/benefits granted by a pension insurance or the nursing care insurance, insurance companies apply the same order. According to the insurance principle, medical rehabilitation support and services are mainly paid for by the individual social-security organizations. They are also the ones who are in charge of the provision of the services required. As long as measures of medical rehabilitation are granted, the provider of benefits is also obliged to pay the living expenses of the persons with disabilities and their families. The large number of laws and regulations and the scope of responsibility of different agencies renders coordination of the different rehabilitation offers extremely difficult. As there are so many different organizations, it is frequently very difficult to do justice to the principle of providing comprehensive and optimum support and services. In order to tackle that problem, the rehabilitation agencies, as early as 1969, joined forces and set up the federal Association for Rehabilitation. Its objective is an improved cooperation among the different rehabilitation agencies by means of coordination and communication. In addition to that, the federal parliament passed a rehabilitation law in 1974 which is to contribute to a harmonization of the support granted in the field of medicine and employment promotion as well as involving complementary services. As soon as there is more than one carrier in charge of rehabilitation, for the purpose of an improved coordination of the subsequent measures of support, an overall plan is drawn up that defines conditions, the role of a leading carrier, problems related to changes in organizations, participation of the disabled, and the time frame for services. But on many occasions not even this coordination attempt has been sufficient to define clearly who is responsible. In order to avoid anyone suffering from delayed support and services for medical rehabilitation, the organizations of the statutory pension insurance must provide advance benefits.[30] Since politicians are aware of the fact that problems in terms of jurisdiction nevertheless frequently result in unfavourable consequences for those with disabilities, the federal government has been trying to unify and harmonize the different laws in a new Code of Social Law. In the meantime, the different social security agencies will probably continue to attempt to define their competence or non-competence in the already overburdened German Social Courts. Thus, it is clear that with the current structure of the social-security system, it is often difficult to access services without a great deal of bureaucracy.

Rehabilitation at Pre-School and School Level (Measures for Educational Integration)

Measures to integrate individuals with disabilities into educational situations include care in remedial pre-school centres, remedial schools, and day-care centres as well as special education for pre-school children.

Since under the intergovernmental structure, pre-school and school matters are within the jurisdiction of the Länder, rehabilitation measures at the
pre-school and school levels have to be handled by the Länder. Therefore, the
governments of the Länder decide whether children with disabilities are to be
integrated into regular schools or whether a particular Land is to offer special
schools for disabled children. Both decisions must be taken, both for rehabilitation at the pre-school and the school level. Whereas these school-related
decisions can be taken without prior consultation with the federal government,
cultural matters — including rehabilitation in schools — are to a large extent a
matter to be handled in accordance with the ideals of cooperative federalism.
In this area, the Länder coordinate themselves. As early as in 1948 (a year
before the founding of the Federal Republic of Germany), the existing Länder
created the Permanent Conference of Ministers of Education. Its task was to
handle the areas requiring joint action, such as schools and education policy,
as these are supra-regional and relate to the ideal of uniform living conditions
throughout Germany. In 1972, the Permanent Conference of the Ministers of
Education issued a "Recommendation on the System of Special Schools." Although decisions taken by the ministers theoretically do not bind the individual
Länder and only become valid if and when they become part of Länder legislation, the self-coordination of the Länder has substantially limited their flexibility
and that of their parliaments. Despite this self-coordination, particularly with
regard to rehabilitation at the school level, there are considerable differences
between the Länder. In the past two years, the political goal of integration has
meant that the majority of the Länder have integrated children with disabilities
into regular classrooms. These efforts, aimed at overcoming the treatment of
children with disabilities in institutions — increasingly seen to be
marginalization — were intensified even further with the Basic Law prohibiting discrimination against persons with disabilities. Whereas, in the new Länder
— who, with German reunification, were required to reorganize rehabilitation
in schools — now offer integrated institutions. In Bavaria, for example, there
is a comprehensive system of Special Schools for children with disabilities, as
well as a trend toward more integration in terms of education.

Among the problems encountered in the attempt to overcome the disad-
vantages and marginalization of disabled persons in the German school system,
is the question of responsibility for funding of kindergartens. As opposed to
the financing of regular and special kindergartens, where responsibility is clearly
defined, the question of who finances integrated kindergartens has not been
resolved. There is some agreement on the principle that allows financing of

integrated forms of schooling from social welfare funds and youth funds and/ or under the respective Länder laws on kindergartens. This type of mixed financing does result in controversy over the question of which carrier is to assume costs and to what extent.

Vocational Rehabilitation

Elements of vocational rehabilitation include: assistance to disabled persons to keep or obtain a job. This includes encouragement to employment such as integration grants paid to employers who employ disabled persons, as well as training measures or refresher courses. Vocational rehabilitation benefits cover the cost of food and accommodation when the severity of the disability is such that a disabled person cannot live at home.

These measures are used in order to maintain, improve, establish or re-establish the earning capacity of disabled persons in line with their capacity and to integrate these persons on a permanent basis. The overall purpose of the disability programs — namely the integration of people into society — is served in a sustained manner by the concept of vocational rehabilitation. The major problem when it comes to the concrete realization of this objective does lie in the fact that, given the situation in the German labour market, a disabled person runs a higher risk than the rest of the population of being unemployed on a long-term basis. Although, pursuant to the legal and regulatory situation in Germany, theoretically all benefit providers apart from the health insurance funds could act as agencies of vocational rehabilitation and in practice most rehabilitation measures are financed by the Federal Employment Agency. This agency, in its capacity as carrier of the statutory unemployment insurance fund is — like the other social-security institutions — organized according to the principle of self-government and has a solid base of regional employment agencies and local offices. It is true that the Länder are represented on the administrative committees of the regional employment agencies, but the enforcement of the *Employment Promotion Law* as well as the fulfillment of other functions rests exclusively with the federal administration.[31] Regardless of the governance of disability programs, a few Länder have criticized the "strongly centralized organizational structure" of the Federal Employment Agency. With decentralization, the Länder will have chances to design regional labour market policies. Above all, with a view to European integration, the Länder are demanding more control in the area of labour market policy.[32] Due to the structure of the Federal Employment Agency, this kind of decentralization (which is presently an unrealistic idea) would also have consequences for administering the disability programs. In addition to the Federal Employment Agency, the statutory pension insurance also plays a role when it comes to vocational rehabilitation.

There are different facilities for vocational rehabilitation: vocational training centres *(Berufsbildungswerke)* work in conjunction with firms in their respective region to provide initial vocational training for young disabled persons who require medical, psychological, and educational assistance as a result of their disability and are therefore unable to receive in-plant training. Vocational retraining centres *(Berufsfoerderungswerke)* provide retraining and further training for disabled adults, also in cooperation with firms in the region. One aspect of vocational rehabilitation are the workshops for disabled persons.

The legal supervision of these facilities rests with the Länder because of the administrative jurisdiction. Funds are provided based on the principle of mixed financing: the costs of operating these vocational training and retraining centres are financed by the Land, the federal government, and the Federal Employment Agency. Each pays one-third of the costs.

Workshops for Disabled Persons

These workshops offer suitable jobs for persons who are permanently or temporarily unable to find employment in the open job market due to the nature or severity of their disability. Workshops should provide disabled persons an opportunity to develop, increase or regain ability to work productively.

The workshops are financed from social welfare funds: their structure is determined by the Länder and financing is a direct function of their organization. Training a person with disabilities serves the purpose of providing basic skills for his or her job in the workshop and is considered to be a training measure and therefore is paid for by the Federal Employment Agency. The other activities of the workshops, which enable a disabled person to function at work are partially financed by the "compensatory levy."

Workshops for disabled persons are not governmental facilities but are financed mainly by the associations of the disabled and those of private welfare work. Frequently they are organized in the form of societies and foundations. It is also possible for municipalities to run workshops such as these, but this is seldom the case. A workshop can only be officially recognized if it complies with the legal prerequisites of the *Severely Disabled Persons*

Act. Funding for these workshops comes from many sources: the compensatory levy (contribution on the part of the federal and the Länder governments) provides the major portion; and the Federal Employment Agency and the respective Lands dedicate part of their own funds to pay some of the costs, while operating costs are usually paid for by social welfare agencies (supralocal organizations); and some income comes from the products made and sold by the workshop.

Welfare Benefits/Social Assistance (Economic Security for Persons with Disabilities)

Measures of rehabilitation are not financed only by the social-security organizations pursuant to the insurance principle. Social assistance as well as youth welfare agencies come into play in all areas of rehabilitation, though only when no other body is responsible. If social welfare agencies are responsible for the payment of benefits, public funds from the municipalities and the Länder are used. Regarding the provision of institutional facilities, responsibility does not exclusively rest with the social-security organizations but also with the supralocal social assistance agencies.

The task of the social welfare agencies, and the social network, is to supply medical, educational, and vocational measures to the affected persons aimed at facilitating that individual's integration into society. Social welfare is subdivided into supra-local and local agencies and associations of private welfare enterprises.[33] Whereas the supra-local organizations[34] are in charge of institutional facilities, the local agencies[35] are responsible for the individual needs of the affected persons.[36] Social welfare benefits are classified into two categories: "assistance towards living expenses" which enables the welfare recipient to live a decent life and "assistance for special circumstances"[37] which provides financial support in special situations of distress and in particularly difficult situations.[38]

These benefits cover preventive health care as well as assistance during illness. Most importantly for those who are disabled is that these benefits also cover assistance for people with significant physical, mental or psychological disabilities who want to become integrated into society and the working world.

Social welfare is of particular importance for persons who were born with a disability. Because the social-security organizations are not responsible for paying assistance in this situation, welfare is the only fund that provides financial support to the parents. Frequently, periods spent in homes, institutions or facilities that offer a combination of in- and outpatient care is paid for by the "assistance for special circumstances" program. Nevertheless, social welfare benefits are granted only if the disabled person (or his/her parents) do not have funds of their own. Since a major share of the services and support for those who are disabled is financed from the "assistance for special circumstances," program the Länder and the municipalities — in terms of financing and organization — are strongly involved in the German administration of disability programs.

It is true that the Länder do have the possibility of participating in the elaboration of this law, but their possibilities in terms of designing their legislation/policies is limited due to the fact that the federal government — by means of the *Federal Social Welfare Act* — sets the general framework and minimum standards for benefits that must be complied with by the Länder and the municipalities. Regardless of this legislative jurisdiction on the part of the federal government, social welfare is financed and implemented by the Länder and the municipalities. The Länder, however, are mainly responsible for financing the institutional facilities. Participation at the federal level is outlined in the framework of financial compensation provided within the social welfare system. In regards to the relationship between social welfare design and responsibility in terms of financing, the municipalities face an even worse situation than the Länder: in their capacity as the local agency of social welfare they have to pay for individual assistance given to persons with disabilities — part of the financing is done through the funds transferred to them by the Länder under municipal equalization,[39] but the possibilities of designing their own disability programs are insignificant.[40]

Coverage of Benefits Granted to Disabled Persons (Universality of Coverage)

It can be said that the scope of services and support for disabled persons in Germany is very broad. The protection provided by the various insurance benefits and the principle that allows services not covered by social security to be financed by welfare produce a system of comprehensive care. In practice, however, this is not really borne out in reality. On the one hand, many of the individuals affected are not informed of which services and supports they are entitled to, and on the other, there frequently are conflicts with regards to the scope of responsibility, which means that the different organizations do not agree as to who is to pay which costs. In addition, welfare — assistance along the lines of the principle of subsidiarity — is still stigmatized. Psychologically, for persons with disabilities and their families, there is an important difference between receiving welfare or social-security benefits, since having paid contributions one is entitled to social-security benefits. It is different when applying for welfare benefits. Even though individuals requiring assistance are legally entitled to these benefits, there is still the traditional notion of asking for alms. Therefore, many individuals do not at all, or only at a very late stage, apply for these benefits.

Financing of the Governance of Disability Programs

The benefits and rehabilitation measures paid for by the social-security institutions make up a major proportion of the services and support under the disability programs in Germany. They are financed by compulsory contributions of insured persons. The support and services granted by the federal government, the Länder, and the municipalities are financed partly by means of the earmarked funds raised by the compulsory levy, but a major share (such as welfare) is financed by means of the general budget. In the fiscal relationship between the federal and the Länder governments, the Länder finance their services and support of the disabled by means of their general share in tax revenues and of the funds that they receive within the framework of the horizontal and vertical fiscal equalization. In Germany, earmarked funds allocated by the federal government to the Länder are rather an exception. Since these funds, pursuant to the German constitution, are purpose-oriented, they have to, for example, avert a disturbance of the overall economic equilibrium (*gesamtwirtschaftliches Gleichgewicht*); and this in turn means that, generally speaking, in terms of social policy, they are not relevant.

Part of the governmental services and support for the disabled is financed via a compensatory levy which is to be paid by employers who do not have a sufficient number of severely disabled persons on their payroll. Any government or private employer with more than 15 jobs to fill is required to reserve 6 percent of them for those who are severely disabled. Otherwise they are required to pay a compensatory levy of DM200 per job-month. Among the problems faced by German governance of disability programs, most employers, public and private, prefer to pay the relatively low compensatory levy. At the moment, in only one of the 16 Länder is the employment ratio (6 percent of all employees being severely disabled persons) complied with. This is one of the reasons why an increase of the compensatory levy is being reviewed.

The compensatory levy, however, is not only of importance as an instrument of integration of persons with disabilities into the labour market. It is also intriguing since it is an obligatory levy that is earmarked and therefore must be spent on those designated by this area of social policy and it involves a form of mixed financing which is currently being rejected by the Länder.

The compensatory levy is charged by the central welfare offices. These central welfare offices need to be established at the level of the Länder, as stated by the *Federal Severely Disabled Persons Act* and they are subject to Länder supervision. The funds raised by means of the compensatory levy are distributed vertically (between the federal government and the Länder). The federal share (45 percent) goes into an equalization fund and serves the purpose of financing supra-regional measures aimed at the integration of severely disabled persons into employment, professions, and society. Half of the federal share is used by the Federal Employment Agency in order to promote the employment of severely disabled persons. The Länder share of the compensatory levy (55 percent) is used by the central welfare offices in order to promote job and training offers for severely disabled persons. In this respect, there is a horizontal equalization between the Länder. The compensation levy is of utmost importance when it comes to the financing of governmental benefits and services and in particular those provided by the Länder. The revenues obtained from that levy are to be used in a purposeful way: they must only be used to subsidize job and training promotion for severely disabled persons and for complementary accompanying assistance on the job. Administrative costs are not paid for by using the compensatory levy. In 1994, the Land of Bavaria received approximately DM180 million from the compensatory levy; DM50 million of which were used for voluntary supports and services. The remaining money was spent on statutory measures (e.g., workshops for persons with disabilities), that is, services and supports provided for by federal and Länder laws.

As can be seen from a draft bill dated spring 1996 and drawn up by the Bundesrat, the German Länder are equally dissatisfied with the distribution of funds raised by means of the compensation levy and with the allocation of tasks, the latter mainly being the promotion of workshops and homes for persons with disabilities. Their criticism is focused on the fact that federal funds are used in order to finance measures of a regional or local character. The federal government is interfering in Länder responsibility and in doing so violates the principles of federalism and of subsidiarity. Consequently, the Länder are demanding a redistribution of the compensatory levy (reduction of the

federal share to 25 percent) and a clear-cut definition and separation of jurisdiction: measures at both regional and Länder levels are no longer to be financed
from the federal share but from the increased Länder share; whereby the corresponding funds would be directly managed by the Länder. The Länder want a
decentralization of measures and the use of funds concerning workshops for
disabled persons and want to be involved in making labour market policy for
severely disabled persons. By means of this reform of the compensatory levy
system, the principle of mixed financing of the workshops would be abandoned in favour of exclusive financing on the part of the Länder. According to
the Länder, this type of facility has only local or possibly regional importance.
The Länder consider the current method of financing to be a violation of the
principle of subsidiarity. According to their evaluation of the situation, workshops and homes are the exclusive responsibility of the Länder. The federal
government, however, rejects this assessment and initiative on the part of the
Länder, claiming that the facilities subsidized by the federal government are
supra-regional facilities which are part of the cross-Länder planning system.
An essential argument put forward by the federal government is the point regarding the services and support provided in the framework of the governance of
disability programs where there is a need for uniform standards throughout
Germany. The federal government — when stating that the changes proposed
would not do justice to the problems in the new Länder — refers unmistakenly
to the fact that the governance of disability programs has to comply with the
mandate of the creation of equal living standards. This means that the Länder's
demand for decentralization of the governance of disability programs is rejected based on a reference made to the uniform all-German validity of the
welfare-state principle.

Problems of the Current Governance of Disability Programs

The fact that the German governance of disability programs only partially meets
the target of integration of persons with disabilities into society and in more
concrete terms into the labour market is considered to be one essential problem.
The allocation of responsibility between the social-security organizations, on
the one hand, and the welfare agencies at the level of the Länder and the municipalities on the other, along with the federal level — which not only takes
action within the framework of legislation but also with (co-)financing of services and support — is thought to be a major problem of the German governance
of disability programs.

Unlike Canada, the complexity of governance of disability programs in Germany not only results from the vertical cooperation of the federal government, the Länder, and the municipalities (the intergovernmental regime), but from the point of view of persons with disabilities and their families, one of the major problems is that the provision of support and services is also allocated horizontally between the different sectors. Since the jurisdiction of the social-security organizations is, among other factors, determined by the insurance-related situation of the disabled persons and because many of the people with disabilities also rely on social welfare benefits, it is made very difficult to tackle the problems holistically.

The associations for disabled persons are among the most vocal critics of the fact that the system is extremely difficult to understand, and this in turn substantially impairs the efficiency of the governance of disability programs and makes it difficult for the disabled to access the services. Therefore, the principle of a comprehensive insurance coverage (universality of coverage) is clearly limited in its scope since the services and support provided are frequently very difficult to access as the system is extremely difficult to understand. Seen from the point of view of a person with a disability, a system that is centred around the individual with all the required services organized would be very helpful. However, the German reality is different. In line with the basic concept of a mature and emancipated citizen, individuals with disabilities and their families have to select from the large range of services and support available and then arrange for the assistance they are entitled to and which they require. However, the plurality of supply contributes to the fact that it is very likely that some of the offers are not utilized. This could be due to the disabled person not knowing about the offer or to the organizations not being able to agree on jurisdiction and financing. A large number of counselling institutions exist, but the individual is required to take the initiative. In this aspect, the differences between this concept and the governance of disability programs in the former GDR becomes clear. In the former GDR, persons with disabilities were under governmental custody.

Due to these organizational problems, there are repeated demands in Germany for a disentanglement of the current system. However, this is not realistic. It would mean new organizational structures and the exclusion of a governance system that has worked and is based on social-security institutions. Since such a step toward a uniform governance of disability programs on the horizontal level is rather unlikely, those responsible wish for improved coordination. One example of an attempt to achieve this reorganization is for all interested institutions to have "commissioners representing disabled persons' interests." In order to make the system (the provision of services and the area of jurisdiction) more transparent, these commissioners play the role of intermediaries between persons with disabilities, the authorities, and the agencies of rehabilitation facilities. Despite the fact that these coordination bodies have already begun their work, even the federal government agrees that the major problem is coordination of services and the guarantee of smooth and uninterrupted handling processes. These problems of efficiency are a burden for the individuals and their families, but they also represent a financial burden for the organizations. The fact that the majority of all social-security institutions — above all health insurance and pension funds — are facing enormous financial difficulties anyway, aggravates the problems even further. In addition, the Federal Employment Agency and the organizations of social welfare who assume important responsibilities in the field of governance of disability programs are very stressed, financially speaking, due to the high unemployment rate in the Federal Republic of Germany.

NOTES

[1]Paul Pierson and Stephan Leibfried, "Multitiered Institutions and the Making of Social Policy," in *European Social Policy: Between Fragmentation and Integration*, ed. Paul Pierson and Stephan Liebfried (Washington: The Brookings Institution, 1995), pp. 1-40.

[2]In May 1998, the European Commission blamed Germany for offering a system of general social welfare, thus making it less attractive for jobless persons to seriously look for a job.

[3]Manfred G. Schmidt, "Learning from Catastophes. West Germany's Public Policy," in *The Comparative History of Public Policy*, ed. Francis G. Castles (Oxford: Polity Press 1989), pp. 56-99.

[4]Ulrich Exler, "Financing German Federalism: Problems of Financial Equalisation in the Unification Process," in *Federalism, Unification and European Integration*, ed. Charlie Jeffery and Roland Sturm (London: Cass, 1993), pp. 22-37.

[5]The federal government was to finance 50 percent of the social assistance costs and should have received part compensation via the distribution system for sales tax revenues.

[6]Rainer-Olaf Schultz, "Foederalismus," *Die Westlichen Länder: Lexikon der Politik*, ed. M.G. Schmidt. Book 3, ed. Dieter Nohlen (Muenchen: Beck, 1992), pp. 95-110.

[7]Ursula Muench, *Sozialpolitik und Foederalismus. Zur Dynamik der Aufgabenverteilung im sozialen Bundesstaat* (Opladen: Leske und Budrich, 1997), pp. 172-74.

[8]Andreas Kammerbauer, *Behindertenpolitik: Eine Chance fuer Hoergeschaedigte* (Hamburg: Signum, 1993), p. 11.

[9]Bundesarbeitsgemeinschaft Hilfe für Behinderte e.V.: Die Rechte behinderter Menschen und ihrer Angehoerigen (Duesseldorf, 1997), p. 33.

[10]*Federal Severely Disabled Persons Act*, Article 3, Section 1.

[11]The level of disability is generally determined by the war pensions office *(Versorgungsamt)*.

[12]Kammerbauer, *Behindertenpolitik*, p. 12.

[13]Bundesministerium fuer Arbeit und Sozialordnung (ed.), *Ratgeber fuer Behinderte* (Bonn, 1997), p. 9.

[14]*Dritter Bayerischer Landesplan fuer Menschen mit Behinderung* (Muenchen, 1994), p. 34.

[15]Bundesministerium fuer Arbeit und Sozialordnung (ed.), *Uebersicht ueber das Sozialrecht* (Bonn, 1995), p. 335.

[16]Regarding European integration we can see that the Treaty of Amsterdam also lays special emphasis on disabled people and sets the European Union the task of taking action to combat discrimination against persons with disabilities.

[17]Printed matter of the German Bundestag (Bundestags-Drs.) 13/9514, p. 3.

[18]Compare to the study by Dr. Dietmar Wassener.

[19]Compare with the earlier part of the chapter, "Classifying German Federalism Within in the Typology of Intergovernmental Regimes."

[20]Kammerbauer, *Behindertenpolitik*, p. 37.

[21]Arthur Benz, *Anpassungsprozesse in der foederativen Staatsorganisation der Bundesrepublik Deutschland* (Frankfurt/Main: Speyer Hochschulschiriften, 1987), p. 111.

[22]Bertram Schulin, "Rechtliche Grundprobleme der Medizinischen, Beruflichen und Sozialen Rehabilitation," in *Behinderte und Rehabilitation: Beitraege zum Vierten Sozialpolitischen Symposium*, ed. Eckhard Krappe (Frankfurt/Main: Campus, 1991), p. 21.

[23]Social-security authories are health insurance funds (including long-term care insurance), pension insurance funds, occupational accident insurance funds, and federal employment services.

[24]Bertram Schulin, *Ein Sozialrecht* (Duesseldorf:Werner-Verlag, 1991), p. 62.

[25]Muench, *Sozialpolitik und Foederalismus*, p. 198.

[26]Josef Schmid, *Wohlfahrtsverbaende in Modernen Wohlfahrtsstaaten. Soziale Dienste in Historisch-Vergleichender Perspektive* (Opladen: Leske and Budrich, 1996).

[27]Schulin, "Rechtliche Grundprobleme der Medizinischen, Beruflichen und Sozialen Rehabilitation," p. 21.

[28]Medical rehabilitation benefits can be provided for medical and dental treatment, pharmaceutical and dressing materials, remedies including physiotherapy, speech therapy and occupational therapy, the provision of artificial limbs, orthopaedic and other aids, work therapy. They also cover inpatient treatment in hospitals, sanatoriums, and special treatment facilities (and any charges for food and accommodation).

[29]Anita B. Pfaff, "Rehabilitation aus Aekonomischer Sicht," in *Behinderte und Rehabilitation*, ed. Knappe, p. 93.

[30]Sozialverband Reichsverbund e.V., *Leitfaden fuer Behinderte. Haubuch zur Rehabilitation in der Bundesrepublik Deutschland* (Bonn, 1997), p. 39.

[31]Markus Heintzen and Christoph Kannengiesser, "Die Regionalisierung der Sozialversicherung aus Verfassungsrechtlicher und Verfassungspolitischer Sicht," *Die Angestelltenversicherung* 2(1993):59.

[32]Compare the case study by Steffen Schneider.

[33]Heinz Lampert, *Lehrbuch der Sozialpolitik* (Berlin: Springer, 1991), p. 365.

[34]Supra-local organizations (*Ueberoertliche Sozialhilfetraeger*), which are responsible for different social services, are to be found in the Länder on a regional level, the terminology differs.

[35]Local organizations of social welfare (*oertliche Traeger der Sozialhilfe*) are those towns that do not belong to a county (*kreisfreie Staedte*) and the counties (*Landkreise*).

[36]See the earlier section on "The Role of Local Government in German Social Policy."

[37]Approximately one-fifth of all recipients of welfare are disabled persons. Their share of welfare expenditures is one-third.

[38]Bundesarbeitsgemeinschaft Hilfe fuer Behinderte, p. 20.

[39]George H. Milbradt, "Die kommunalen Sozialhilfeausgaben: Das Fuer und Wider verschiedener Finanzausgleichskonzepte aus kommunaler Sicht," in *Sozialhilfe und Finanzausgleich*, ed. Wolfgang Kitterer (Heidelberg: Campus, 1990), p. 154.

[40]Lampert, *Lehrbuch der Sozialpolitik*, p. 365.

6

DISABILITY POLICY IN THE UNITED STATES: POLICY EVOLUTION IN AN INTERGOVERNMENTAL SYSTEM

Stephen L. Percy

Throughout the twentieth century, public policy in the United States has been formulated to address the needs and aspirations of people with disabilities, beginning with income replacement and medical support services and culminating, in the last decade, with comprehensive legislation to protect the rights of and advance opportunities for disabled Americans. This chapter examines the evolution of disability policy in America. Particular attention is given to the formation of these policies and the governmental, and often intergovernmental, mechanisms by which disability policy has been formulated, implemented, and enforced. This intergovernmental perspective is an appropriate viewpoint from which to study disability policy given that today's policies are the result of political movements, debates, and decisions that have taken place both within state capitals and the US Congress and sometimes *between* state and national policymakers.

This chapter outlines several key features of disability policy as it has emerged in the United States. First, contemporary disability policy shows a pattern of protections, coverage, and services that has grown from minimal and restricted to broad-based. Second, like many other forms of social policy in the United States, policies aimed at people with disabilities have evolved through a federal system of governance whereby the national and state governments have taken both independent and integrated action, sometimes concurring about, and other times battling over, policy creation, implementation, and enforcement. Third, like other US civil rights policies, protections and services for people with disabilities represent central questions concerning public sector responsibilities to protect groups within American society and ensure justice. And, fourth, contemporary policies are not stagnant but, instead, continue their evolution as society and political actors debate the level of assistance and protections to be afforded to persons with disabilities as well as the most effective strategies to achieve these objectives.

A MINORITY GROUP OFTEN UNSEEN

In order to understand the field of disability policy studies,[1] it is helpful to consider the status of people with disabilities historically and in more recent times. Disability in America has often been viewed as a form of social stigma, generating reactions of pity, helplessness, distrust, uneasiness, and even fear.[2] Non-handicapped people have historically not understood the problems and realities in the lives of persons with mental and physical disabilities. Certain classes of disability, including drug abuse, alcoholism, and mental retardation, have particularly been misunderstood and viewed in a negative light. This is nowhere more true than in the context of psychological illness where, until recent decades, institutionalization was the primary strategy of treatment, often coupled with heavy medications that suppressed not only the symptoms of illness but also awareness and cognitive functions. Sterilization, shocking as it may seem was practised against people with disabilities into the twentieth century.[3] Only recently have non-institutional, community-based forms of treatment, such as halfway houses and sheltered workshops, been made available to those with serious mental disabilities.

Researchers have examined the origins of social attitudes about disability and handicapped persons and have found that negative and inaccurate perceptions arise from many sources. One source has been the literary and media depictions of disabled people. Thurer describes how literary characters with disabilities, from Captain Hook to the Hunchback of Notre Dame to Captain Ahab, have been depicted as evil, vengeful, and freakish.[4] In a review of other research studies, Elliot and Byrd reach a similar conclusion about the negative images of disabled persons as portrayed in literature and on television.[5]

The development of negative and unrealistic attitudes toward persons with handicaps is attributed to other sources besides literature and the media.

Livneh examined the formation of attitudes toward handicapped people and concluded that these attitudes are "learned and conditioned over many years," and that attempts to change them require substantial effort.

Researchers have considered the extent as well as the source of public attitudes toward handicapped people. Analyst William English, in reviewing empirical research on this question, argues that "the attitudes of the general public toward physically disabled persons in general suggest that nearly half of the non-disabled public have primarily negative attitudes that extend to many aspects of the lives of disabled persons.[6] Public attitudes about and perceptions of disabled individuals arise from many sources, ranging from personal fears and anxieties to inaccurate media and literary portrayals. These attitudes appear to be deeply based and difficult to change. Their impact cannot be overstated, for it is clear that these attitudes have generated behaviours and decisions that have limited the opportunities and life-styles of disabled persons.

Because of these perceptions and attitudes, society as a whole, until quite recently, has not been open to the idea that disabled individuals can meaningfully participate in most life activities. As has been argued, "Society invariably perceives the disabled in terms of their disabilities, for what they cannot do, not for what they can do. This almost universal view is far more handicapping than any particular disability."[7] Because of its blindness to these potentialities, society has erected many barriers — tangible and intangible and with motives that range from neglect to prejudice — that impede the ability of disabled persons to participate in many facets of contemporary life. It is against this background that disabled citizens have struggled to change society so as to increase their opportunities and end their segregated status.

THE IMPACT OF DISABILITY AND DISCRIMINATION

A survey of disabled individuals conducted by Louis Harris and Associates for the International Center for the Disabled in late 1985 profiles the status and perceptions of persons with physical and mental handicaps.[8] The portrait provided by the study shows that 44 percent of those interviewed experienced some form of physical disability; 13 percent suffered sensory impairment (e.g., blindness, deafness); 6 percent reported mental disability; 5 percent had respiratory ailments; and 16 percent suffered from other disabling diseases (e.g., heart and blood diseases). Compared to non-disabled persons, handicapped individuals received much less education, were far more likely to be unemployed, and earned less income when employed.

The impact of disability on the lives of handicapped persons is clear from survey questions about social interactions and ability to reach personal potential. Over half of the respondents reported that their disabilities prevented them from achieving full potential in life, and 56 percent said that their handicaps prevented movement within the community, such as attending cultural and sports events, and socializing with friends outside the home.

Respondents were asked about barriers that prevented them from entering the mainstream of society. The most frequently cited impediment was fear that their disabilities might cause them to get hurt, sick, or victimized by crime if they left home more frequently. In addition to health and safety concerns, respondents also pointed to physical obstacles to their mobility. Of those interviewed, 49 percent said that they were not able to use public transportation or gain access to specialized transportation services; 40 percent said mobility was limited by buildings that were inaccessible or unequipped with restrooms they could use; and 47 percent of working-age respondents stated that employers would not recognize that they were capable of performing full-time work. While those interviewed indicated that significant progress had been made since the 1960s to improve the position of disabled persons, persistent and still operative barriers were identified by survey respondents.

EVOLVING FEDERALISM IN AMERICA'S INTERGOVERNMENTAL SYSTEM

To understand the development of policy to mitigate the negative impacts of disability and promote the opportunities of people with disabilities in the United States, it is useful to present an overview of the evolution of intergovernmental relations, with particular attention to changing power relationships among the key players in the American federal system: the national (or federal government) and state governments. It is in this governance context that disability policy has been debated, formulated, implemented, and reconsidered. A noted scholar on American federalism, Daniel J. Elazar, has described the US federal system as a matrix or network of arenas within arenas, where individual arenas are distinguished by being larger or smaller rather than higher or lower in a hierarchical sense.[9] Elazar sees federalism in the United States as an expression of non-centralization where constitutional power is diffused among many centres and yet the power centres are interconnected within the overall system of governance.

Debates about and resolution of disputes between the national and state governments about governing power have been key to the evolution of American democratic government. Policy disputes among the federal players, or "cells" within the intergovernmental matrix, have resulted in evolving definitions, or understandings, of the appropriate policy and governing responsibilities of the national and state governments. Federalism in the United States, therefore, "is a system of rules for the division of public policy responsibilities among a number of autonomous governmental agencies. These rules define the scope of authority available to the autonomous agencies — which do what — and they provide a framework to govern relationships between and among agencies. The agencies remain autonomous in that they levy their own taxes and select their own officials, but they are also linked together by rules that govern common actions."[10]

Intergovernmental relations between the states and the national government were characterized by a general separation of governing functions throughout much of the first century of American history. The national government tended to defence, regulation of commerce, and foreign relations, while the states (and local governments operating under their strictures) handled more "local" governance issues such as law enforcement, public infrastructure development, and, moving into the twentieth century, human and social services delivery. This pattern of governance has been termed "dual" federalism to denote the relative separateness of governing responsibilities. During this period of American history, neither the national nor the state governments were particularly active in disability policy.

Relative separateness of governing action gave way in the second century of America's existence, causing the complex federal governing system to become even "messier." Dual federalism has given way to new forms of state-national government relations that have been characterized by such terms as "cooperative federalism," "creative federalism," and "competitive federalism."[11] All of these conceptions recognize that governing responsibilities by state and national governments have become more intermixed, with both parties sharing governing action in the same policy areas and arenas.

The fundamental structure of American federalism rests with the US Constitution enacted in 1789. The literal wording of the Constitution grants the national government a series of specific governing functions that were deemed critical to the operation of the new confederation of American states: national defence, conduct of foreign affairs, creation of a national currency, and regulation of commerce among the states. Responding to a long-time distrust of central authority and seeking to protect their own governing authority, the American states, while granting some authority to the national government, retained substantial governing rights for themselves. The concerns of the states are reflected in the tenth Amendment to the Constitution, known as the reserve clause, which holds that all powers not specifically delegated to the national government were reserved to the states.

Within this constitutional framework, the relative power position of the national government increased as constitutional interpretations and understandings evolved, especially during the twentieth century. This occurred for several reasons. The fourteenth amendment and its equal protection clause is one factor that has extended constitutional rights and responsibilities originally applied to the national government to the actions of state governments. The equal protection clause (enacted following the end of America's Civil War in 1868) was added to the US Constitution as a means to instruct southern states to treat all citizens, including former slaves, equally under the law. Through a process known as "selective incorporation," the rights and liberties outlined in the Constitution and Bill of Rights have been coupled to the equal protection clause, thereby extending coverage to the actions of state and local governments. In this way, most of the rights and liberties articulated in the Bill of Rights have been "nationalized," meaning that the civil liberties and protections, originally designed to protect citizens from the actions of the *national* government, now work to provide citizens with protections from *state and local governments* as well.

The reach of national government power also expanded as the result of interpretations of the Constitution that see this important rule book as elastic. Actions beyond those expressly listed in the Constitution have been judged permissible. For example, the US Constitution's necessary and proper clause empowers the national government to enact laws necessary to perform its responsibilities. The *commerce clause* of the Constitution, which permits the national government to regulate interstate commerce, has increased national power. Given the nature of the modern economy, most goods and services produced in the country are transported across state boundaries. Using the commerce clause power, Congress has enacted laws to regulate monopolies, clean the environment, and protect consumers.

Another source of expanding national government power is known as the spending power. Where the national government is not constitutionally empowered to take action it can instead offer funds to support programs that the national government deems of value in the country. States are not required to create federal programs, but instead are given financial incentives to devise and operate programs that follow guidelines and stipulations set by the national government. Federal financial transfers, the spending power of the national government, have been used to create a large number of other social welfare programs, such as Aid to Families with Dependent Children (AFDC) and Medicare (subsidized health care for senior citizens). Because state participation is legally optional, the Supreme Court has ruled that the federal spending power does not violate the reserve clause of the Constitution. While recognizing the constitutionality of the federal spending power, some critics see "fiscal federalism" as tantamount to fiscal intimidation and power play.[12]

Beyond affecting state policy and spending priorities, the spending power increases the power of the national government in another way. Most federal grants include stipulations — or *mandates* — that must be followed if the state wishes to participate in the program and receive federal funds.[13] This form of mandate attached to the spending power — termed *condition-of-aid mandates* — has been utilized in many policy contexts to expand national government policy visions and structures into the actions and responsibilities of states and local governments.

PUBLIC POLICY AND DISABILITY

With the exception of schools for handicapped children, particularly those serving hearing- and sight-impaired students, and the creation of public institutions providing custodial care, public policy efforts on behalf of persons with disabilities have largely taken place during this century. Policy initiatives have been categorized into at least three types: rehabilitative services, income supports, and civil rights protections.[14] One set of policies focuses on services to help disabled persons deal with and overcome their disabling conditions. Vocational rehabilitation programs originated in the United States following the First World War, in response to the number of veterans who returned home with combat injuries. Programs were expanded to all physically disabled persons, with the expectation that vocational rehabilitation would return them to the workforce and remove them from public assistance programs. Later, mental disabilities came to be included within the set of conditions that made individuals eligible for rehabilitative services.

Other public programs were established to provide income supports to persons whose disabilities prevent gainful employment. Relevant here are Social

Security Disability Insurance and Supplemental Security Income. These programs were designed to ensure that disabled citizens and their families receive
financial support. A related program — workers' compensation — was created
in individual states to aid those experiencing on-the-job injury or workplace-
related illness developed at the same time.

The third policy initiative has centred on efforts to legislate and enforce
legal protections for those who experience mental or physical handicaps. The
wave of disability rights is more recent and, building upon lessons learned
from earlier policies and the expanded political capacity of groups representing persons with disability, represents a new policy type. Unlike programs
created earlier in the century that focused on corrective services and income
maintenance, disability rights policy sought to expand the full range of modern life's opportunities to a group of people who had long suffered
discrimination — intentional and unintentional. As we shall see, disability rights
legislation includes provisions of the *Rehabilitation Act* of 1973, the *Education for All Handicapped Children Act* (1975), and the *Architectural Barriers
Act* (1968). These laws, following a half-century of federal programs to provide rehabilitation services and income supports to citizens with handicaps,
represented a new and bold direction in public policy for disabled citizens.
Policy advocates were not satisfied, however, with the achievements of this
first barrage of disability rights programs. They sought a more comprehensive
set of protections that would emanate across the entire nation to end discrimination based on handicap. Within two decades, their efforts bore fruition in
passage of the *Americans with Disabilities Act* of 1990.

The remaining sections of this chapter will explore specific policies that
operate within the overall rubric of "disability policy," including workers' compensation, income maintenance, vocational rehabilitation, and disability rights.
The final section will explore the cumulative policy "lessons" of these individual policy studies, with a focus on the important political dynamics that
surround disability and the impact of federal governing systems on the dynamic evolution of disability policy.

Workers' Compensation

Workers' compensation policy in the United States evolved as a direct result of
the industrial revolution in America which, over time, resulted in growing numbers of incapacitating industrial-based injuries. Prior to workers' compensation
laws, individuals injured on the job were forced to seek redress for their injuries

by suing employing companies in court. Here, compensation could be delivered by judges and juries who weighed the competing claims of workers and employers to decide if the employer was responsible and, if so, the amount of compensation to be awarded to the injured worker.[15]

In court deliberations, the claims of workers for redress from industrial employers were based on common law duties imposed upon the employer, including the provision of a safe place to work, safe tools and equipment, warnings of danger, sufficient able workers to perform assigned tasks, and rules (and their enforcement) to ensure a safe work place.[16] Using this judicial mechanism to provide workers' compensation proved costly and uncertain to both parties. For employers, claims for compensation could lead to hefty settlements, thereby generating an ongoing risk that harmed the ability of the company to grow. Injured workers worried about whether judges or juries would recognize their injury, employment loss, and need for adequate compensation. Recognizing the potential for serious, even life-threatening, injury faced by industrial workers as well as understanding the negative impact of the risk associated with potential compensation claims, led to the search for public policy to handle workers' compensation issues.

Policy changes came in the states. As early as 1855, the State of Georgia responded to growing accidents in the construction of new railway systems by enacting a statute that made railroad companies liable to employees and others for workplace negligence leading to worker injury. Other states followed suit and by 1908 practically all states had created similar laws regarding the railroad industry. But, with the continuing industrial expansion in the nation, similar protections were sought for other industries.

In the early years of the twentieth century, political pressure grew for public policy to deal broadly with the issue of workers' compensation. Pressure again broke at the state level, where a broad range of players — including business leaders, labour officials, and progressive individuals — were successful in convincing legislators to enact laws protecting workers injured on the job. Maryland was the first state to enact workers' compensation legislation in 1902, with the number of states with such legislation growing to 21 in 1913 and to 43 by 1919. While these programs initially covered hazardous occupations, they have since been expanded to include most forms of employment. In designing these policies, many states drew upon workers' compensation laws of Great Britain, including the *Workmen's Compensation Act* of 1897. As with the activation of other social policy initiatives in the US, policy entrepreneurs and legislation drafters turned to policy precedents in Western Europe as guides for policy development.

The workers' compensation model adopted in the United States, similar to programs in nations like Germany, represents a compromise approach between employees and employers. Williams describes this social compromise:

> Employers became responsible for all industrial injuries and diseases, regardless of who was at fault. Workers' compensation became the exclusive remedy of the employee against the employer for industrial injuries and diseases, i.e., employees lost the right to sue the employer for these injuries and diseases even if the employer was at fault. Workers are compensated for their medical expenses and income lost because of disability or death. No compensation was provided for the pain and suffering the worker might endure because of an industrial accident or sickness.[17]

This "exclusive remedy" approach, despite some shortcomings, represented an improvement over relying on the courts where decisions were much less predicable for both sides. Some states have modified the exclusive remedy provisions to allow employees to sue their employers in certain limited situations.

Throughout the first century of workers' compensation program operation, many workers received benefits and certification replaced adjudication as the means of awarding benefits. Yet despite the reduction in litigious disputes, questions were raised about the overall program. Concerns were voiced about individuals who "fell between the cracks," experiencing workplace-related injury but being excluded from benefits on technicalities. Other concerns focused on the adequacy of benefits received and the inadequacy of response to job-related illness as opposed to injury. By the 1950s, major tensions between employees (and the unions representing them) and employers arose, complicated by interrelated concerns of insurance companies. This situation resulted in a stalemate: "Workers' compensation laws were inadequate, but reform appeared out of reach. Efforts to expand federal disability rights laws at the expense of the state workers' compensation programs laws met with sanctimonious resistance."[18]

In the 1970s, Congress created a national commission to study state workers' compensation laws, largely in response to the growing concerns about the program. Some critics of the status quo called for the creation of national standards to guide and regulate state programs; other critics suggested whole-scale takeovers of state programs by the national government. After substantial study and consideration of alternatives, the National Commission on State Workmen's Compensation Laws issued a report that reaffirmed a vital role for the state programs.[19] At the same time, the commission identified problems, made recommendations for changes, and gave the states three years to reform their programs in response to commission findings. In particular, the commission stated firmly that cash benefits should be substantially increased. Many states in turn reformulated their programs and increased benefits, resulting in an increase of workers' compensation premiums from $6.8 billion in 1973 to almost $23 billion a decade later.[20]

Contemporary workers' compensation programs provide a variety of benefits generally without regard to the amount of time the individual has had on the job. Assistance includes medical benefits to support treatment and possibly provision of replacement limbs and income support during time off work due to injury. Disabled workers in the United States are also eligible for vocational rehabilitation services provided through a separate national government program.

In current state workers' compensation laws, employers may provide coverage to workers in one of three ways. They can purchase a workers' compensation and employer liability policy from a private insurance vendor, they can purchase coverage through a state workers' compensation fund, or they can set aside sufficient reserves to cover compensation risks. Given the uncertainties involved, most companies rely on one of the first two methods. Payment schedules for individuals eligible for workmen's compensation vary across the 50 US states. One method is to base payments on fixed tables that relate well-defined impairments to specific payments. Another method is to base payments on some fraction of estimated wage or income loss. Some states use variants of both methods.[21] Payments may be made periodically over time or through lump-sum awards.

Vocational Rehabilitation

The vocational rehabilitation program — one of the earliest national government initiatives to aid persons with disabilities — dates from the period immediately following World War I. The *Smith-Sears Veterans' Rehabilitation Act* of 1918 established a program to vocationally rehabilitate returning veterans injured during the war. Two years later, the Smith-Fess Act of 1920 (*The Civilian Vocational Rehabilitation Act*) created an extensive national government program to provide vocational assistance to individuals with handicaps who were unable to adequately perform in the workplace.[22] The program was launched as a partnership with the states whereby the national government provided funding — on a 50/50 match with state governments — to support state rehabilitation agencies in providing counselling, vocational training, and job-placement services for physically handicapped individuals. Thus, while workers' compensation arose as a state-based program, vocational rehabilitation was created to operate as an intergovernmental collaboration where program funding and governance would be shared between the players of the federal system of governance in the US.

As with many of the social programs in the US, the breadth of individuals covered by the vocational rehabilitation program has expanded significantly from program beginnings. In 1943, with the passage of the *Barden-La Follette Act*, the rehabilitation program was expanded to include mentally-ill and mentally-retarded individuals. Beginning in 1954, the program was revised so as to include research and demonstration projects in addition to traditional service delivery programs.

The original supporters of vocational rehabilitation programs expected a close connection between their new program and the workers' compensation programs operated in the states. In fact, it was anticipated that the rehabilitation program would receive its participants from the compensation programs for injured workers. This partnership between programs did not occur, however. Instead, workers' compensation programs became more affiliated with the labour establishment while the rehabilitation programs became affiliated with educational models and institutions.[23]

From its genesis in 1920, the vocational rehabilitation program has grown extensively in the realm of persons served and the breadth of services offered. The *Social Security Act* of 1935 provided permanent status to the program, while subsequent legislative changes expanded the program in many directions, including the provision of medical services and prosthetic devices; creation of programs to serve people with mental disability, migratory workers, and disadvantaged youth; and the provision of assistance to families of disabled persons. The program today remains service-oriented, with its central mission of assisting disabled persons to enter or re-enter the workforce. These programs are seen as cost-effective in that spending on vocational rehabilitation is viewed as an investment in human capital, an investment intended to pay off through reduced social support spending and enhanced payroll tax collections, as disabled individuals move into productive employment and move off social support programs.

Individuals qualify for the vocational rehabilitation program based upon the following criteria established by the national government. To be eligible,

individuals must experience (i) the presence of a physical or mental disability
and the resulting functional limitations or limitations in activities; (ii) the existence of a substantial handicap to employment caused by the limitations
present; and (iii) a reasonable expectation that vocational rehabilitation may
render the individual fit to engage in a remunerative occupation. Once judged
eligible, individuals have access to the array of training and support services
offered by the vocational rehabilitation program in their state.

The intergovernmental arrangement for operating the vocational rehabilitation program has proved lasting, with the national government providing
half of the funding and setting basic program outlines, and with the states operating the programs and providing services. Significant policy issues
surrounding the vocational rehabilitation program have focused on areas such
as insufficient funding to serve all eligible participants, cost-effectiveness of
the overall program and of different rehabilitation strategies,[24] and level of
professionalization of program staff.

Income Support

One of the most profound social innovations of American domestic policy in
the twentieth century was the creation of the social-security program. Among
the features of the *Social Security Act* of 1935, enacted during the most severe
economic depression in the US, was a program whereby the national government provided states with funds to assist indigent children, elderly adults, and
blind citizens. Some of these specialized programs were lumped together into
the Supplemental Security Income (SSI) program in 1972.[25] While the 1935
social-security legislation also initiated unemployment and old age insurance
programs, it did not establish a program of disability insurance — a program
of income assistance for people with disabilities — although it was considered
at the time. Sponsors of the *Social Security Act* were concerned and unsure
about the costs of a disability insurance program and feared that including this
provision in the Act would reduce support for the legislation. A key concern
focused on defining disability. It was feared that a floodgate of participants
would be unleashed — threatening the fiscal solvency of any disability insurance program — unless a specific and generally restrictive eligibility of
disability was established. Creating a definition that would be satisfactory to
all interested parties proved elusive.

Recognizing the severe income support needs of people with disabilities, some states created disability insurance programs as part of their

unemployment insurance programs. This state action stimulated renewed national government attention to the issue. After administrative study and legislative debate, a system of disability payments, known as Social Security Disability Insurance (SSDI), for workers between the ages of 50 and 64 was created in 1956 through amendments to the *Social Security Act*. Payments were set at the same amount the individual would receive if he or she were 65 years of age, and initially, recipients had to be at least 50 years of age. No needs test was applied, but disabled workers were required to have had coverage for a minimum number of quarters.

SSDI was created as yet another form of intergovernmental partnership. While initial plans called for an exclusively national government operation, the program, as enacted, gave the states the role of determining eligibility and assigned the national government responsibility for funding this income maintenance program. This intergovernmental model was key to legislative passage of SSDI, since it modified the concerns of many about exclusive operating control by the national government.

Still further changes to the *Social Security Act* expanded the breadth of the SSDI program by removing the age 50 limitation for eligibility and changing the definition of disability from one of "long, continued, and indefinite duration," to one where disabilities have lasted, or are expected to last, not less than 12 months. Congressional action in 1972 hinged benefit payments to the cost of living and provided that persons who had been receiving disability benefits for two years or more could become eligible for Medicare (health-care) assistance.

Significant tensions have surrounded SSDI and raised questions about the intergovernmental partnership that underlies program operation. National government officials were dissatisfied with the speed with which state agencies certified eligibility and with the fact that vocational rehabilitation programs were not moving disabled persons off the income maintenance rolls. At the state level, the process of determining eligibility proved difficult, especially as individuals who were denied eligibility were allowed access to administrative and judicial review of eligibility decisions. And, despite these operational problems and delays in eligibility determination, the magnitude of the program grew substantially in terms of both participants served and fiscal resources needed to support the program.

By the mid-1970s, the national government recognized the never-ending fiscal drag created by its entitlement programs, particularly those routed in major social programs. Through entitlements, those individuals who are judged eligible for participation automatically receive benefits. There are no spending caps on entitlement programs like SSDI; government spending is determined by program participation and not annual legislative decisions on budgets. The fiscal difficulties associated with entitlement programs were aggravated by the cost-of-living adjustments (COLAs) that were added to the programs in the previous decade. COLAs provided for automatic adjustments (i.e., increases) in benefit payment levels to compensate for the impact of economic changes. While protecting beneficiaries, COLAs expanded the spending requirements for the public sector.

Financial pressures came to a head in the early 1980s as the Reagan administration pressed for a more thorough re-evaluation of SSDI recipients — an action allowed by earlier legislation that called for re-evaluation of disability status every three years. The subsequent evaluations were tough, leading to almost one of three recipients being no longer eligible for the program. This action generated an uproar, horror stories portrayed in the media about the plight of individuals unexpectedly losing their benefits, and, ultimately, a political response. While many appealed their change in program status, and won reinstatement, the negative stories about people suffering as a result of benefit cut-offs were persistent in the media. Ultimately, Congress enacted revisions to SSDI in 1984 that significantly restricted the ability of the government to conduct systematic reviews to remove individuals from the SSDI rolls. In this way, the political juggernaut to reduce participation in SSDI as one means to combat the costs of entitlements gave way to political pressures for protecting the rights and benefits of people with disabilities.[26]

DISABILITY RIGHTS

The *Americans with Disabilities Act* (ADA) of 1990 ushered in a new era of public policy innovation targeted at individuals who experience mental or physical disability. The ADA creates a comprehensive mandate for eliminating discrimination against, and providing new opportunities for, people with disabilities. In signing this historic legislation, President George Bush declared that the law "will provide our disabled community with a powerful expansion of protections and then basic civil rights. It will guarantee fair and just access to the fruits of American life which we all must be able to enjoy."[27] This law was the culmination of what has been termed the "last civil rights movement."[28]

Origins

The *Americans with Disabilities Act* did not emerge spontaneously or without policy precedent. Instead, it was formulated as a reflection of previous national and state government laws and policies.[29] At the level of the national government, ADA draws upon several pieces of important legislation as precursors. The push for federally-based legal protections for persons with disabilities began over two decades before the ADA with the passage of laws like the *Architectural Barriers Act* of 1968, legislation that required new national government buildings to be physically accessible to persons with disabilities. The law also required that when modifications are made to buildings owned or leased by the national government these changes must provide for accessibility. Through this legislation, the national government enacted a mandate on itself for the purpose of expanding access to the offices and services of the national government, offices and services intended to be available to all citizens.

The *Education for All Handicapped Children Act,* enacted by the US Congress in 1975, was a major step forward in the provision of education to children with mental or physical disability. This law — resulting from a hard fought struggle by parents whose children experienced disability as well as neglect, even discrimination, in public education — required that public schools provide a *free and appropriate* education to all disabled children. Schools are required to determine the unique educational needs of disabled children, to devise an individualized instructional plan for each child, and to provide services that will satisfy the educational goals outlined in each child's plan.[30] In creating this educational mandate, the national government relied largely upon its spending power: school districts refusing to produce free and appropriate education for disabled children faced a cut-off of all federal funding to the district. Even though the state and local sector's shares of public education funding far outweigh the funds provided by the national government, federal funds are substantial enough that school districts are unwilling to lose these funds and thus accept this national government mandate.

Undoubtedly the most significant disability rights legislation pre-dating the ADA was the *Rehabilitation Act* of 1973, legislation that provided reauthorization of the national government's vocational rehabilitation program.[31] This legislation included some provisions that were enacted with little fanfare and debate but which, nonetheless, generated substantial action, controversy, and backlash. Included in this legislation were:

Section 501: Requires that the agencies of the federal government take affirmative action to employ qualified people with disabilities: thus a Congressional mandate placed upon the employment practices of national government agencies.

Section 503: Requires persons and organizations that have contracts with the national government in excess of $2,500 to take affirmative action to employ, and advance in employment, qualified people with disabilities. Contractors violating this mandate were subject to contract revocation and loss of federal dollars.

Section 504: Prohibits recipients of federal financial assistance (grants) to discriminate on the basis of handicap. Using its spending power, the national government exerted a nondiscrimination mandate upon state and local governments receiving federal funding.

No legislator, nor any of the parties to be regulated by these provisions, anticipated the substantial impact that these disability rights provisions, especially section 504, would ultimately exert on American society.

Without question, and seldom with sufficient recognition, state laws and policies also provided useful input into the creation of the ADA. As of the end of the 1980s, state laws were sometimes more encompassing than national government policies in providing assistance to people with disabilities, while in other policy areas the national government provided greater protections for this group of Americans. The status of state laws for people with disabilities immediately prior to the passage of the ADA has been described as follows:

The 50 states and the District of Columbia have laws that provide employment protections for persons with disabilities and require architectural accessibility for them. The related federal mandates are stronger than many of their state counterparts in requiring program accessibility and reasonable accommodation in employment. In general, the federal law also provides employment rights to a wider set of persons with disabilities than do state laws, although 15 states have added coverage for mental disabilities in the past decade to help close this gap. State requirements for both architectural accessibility and nondiscrimination in employment generally apply more broadly than federal requirements in that they are placed on the private as well as public sectors.[32]

The policy dimension in which the states were the greatest distance ahead of the national government in providing for disability rights was their regulation of private, as well as public, sector organizations: something the national government would emulate in the ADA.

The Perspective of Advocates

Despite the symbolic importance of disability rights laws predating the ADA, and the positive impacts associated with their implementation, there remained a substantial consensus in the 1980s, especially among civil rights advocates and groups representing persons with disabilities, that national government protections were insufficient. Existing laws, both at the national and state levels, were a start, but were not considered adequate to ensuring access for disabled individuals to the full range of opportunities and services available in contemporary society.

One criticism of disability rights policies prior to the ADA was that they were based almost exclusively on the federal spending power, functioning as condition-of-aid mandates.[33] This regulatory approach had three consequences which, in the eyes of advocates, substantially limited the scope of federal protections offered to people with disabilities. First, the condition-of-aid approach was seen as a less powerful weapon than the more potent mandates in other civil rights laws protecting women and minorities. Regulatory mandates concerning discrimination on the basis of race, for example, did not rely on the federal spending power, which can be avoided by entities that refuse federal funding. Instead, mandates intended to overturn racial discrimination have been strongly grounded in such constitutional principles as the equal protection clause of the fourteenth amendment and the commerce clause.

Second, reliance on the federal spending power as the key to activating disability rights mandates was identified as causing confusion and inequity in the implementation of disability rights policies by state and local governments. As the House Committee on Education and Labor noted in its report on the ADA:

> Many agencies of State and local governments receive Federal aid and thus are currently prohibited from engaging in discrimination on the basis of disability. However, where there is no state law prohibiting discriminatory practices, two programs that are exactly alike, except for funding sources, can treat people with disabilities completely differently than others who don't have disabilities. The resulting inconsistent treatment of people with disabilities by different State and local governments is both inequitable and illogical for a society committed to full access for people with disabilities.[34]

A third consequence of the condition-of-aid approach was that unlike other federal civil rights policies designed to protect women and minorities, those for disability rights were confined almost exclusively to the *public* sector. The National Council on the Handicapped, a body charged with reviewing federal laws and policies affecting disabled citizens and responsible for creating the first version of the ADA, cited this limitation in the scope of non-discrimination mandates: "an examination of the major Federal disability programs reveals little effort to encourage, expand, or strengthen Federal/private sector partnerships that address disability problems."[35] Advocates believed that without regulation of disability rights in the private sector, substantial and invidious discrimination against persons with disabilities would continue even if the condition-of-aid approach evoked substantial changes in the public sector.

Another criticism of pre-ADA laws and regulations was that their language was insufficient to clarify congressional intent with regard to the form and scope of disability rights protections. Section 504 of the *Rehabilitation Act* of 1973, the centrepiece of pre-ADA disability rights, contained only a few words stipulating that recipients of federal financial assistance shall not discriminate on the basis of handicap. These few words were laden with symbolic commitment but lacking in directions or strategies for enforcement. The National Council on the Handicapped identified statutory ambiguity as a substantial impediment to achieving non-discrimination: "Confusion and inconsistency have resulted, not so much about the goal [ensuring the rights of persons with disabilities], but from the historical and continuing failure to structure and administer some Federal laws and programs in such a way as to reflect and further the national goal."[36]

Those regulated by early disability rights policies — including states and localities, public transit providers, and public schools — also worried about ambiguity in statutes. While groups representing disabled persons saw ambiguity as a means for regulated parties to challenge policies and avoid compliance, those being regulated saw ambiguity as allowing advocacy groups to press for stringent regulatory mandates. Much of the complaint of state and local governments and other regulated parties, therefore, focused on a desire for greater clarity in regulatory policy so that compliance requirements could be interpreted more clearly.

The Perspectives of Regulated Parties

Parties regulated by pre-ADA laws expressed their own concerns about regulatory mandates. State and local officials did not routinely voice objections to the general concept of federal mandates to protect persons with disabilities, although Edward Koch, as Mayor of New York City, identified handicapped rights requirements as among the federal mandates operating "as millstones" around the necks of local governments.[37] These entities did, however, object to the extent of accommodations and accessibility modifications stipulated by section 504 and other federal laws and the costs required to achieve compliance. Probably the loudest cries of cost burden were raised about accessibility in public transit systems (discussed in more detail below).[38] The entities regulated by section 504 and other federal laws regularly testified at congressional hearings about the difficulties encountered in complying with federal requirements. State and local officials argued that federal funding to achieve regulatory compliance was insufficient and lobbied diligently for more federal financial assistance to relieve the compliance burden.[39]

Civil Rights Replaces Condition-of-Aid Approach

The *Americans with Disabilities Act* abandoned the condition-of-aid approach and set forth a variety of statutory mandates prohibiting some actions and prescribing others for state and local governments and the private sector. This shift in policy approach was congruent with the view of ADA advocates that strong federal requirements bearing upon both the public and private sectors were required to break down persistent discrimination based on disability. Through the ADA, national standards concerning non-discrimination and those providing reasonable accommodations were established across the nation through a single statute — *pre-empting the governing authority of states and localities.*[40]

Adopting a national rather than subnational, or centralized versus decentralized, policy model for disability rights protections responded to a concern that not all states could be counted on to enact serious non-discrimination statutes. The Senate Committee on Labor and Human Resources (of the US Congress), in its report on the ADA, cited the testimony of one disability rights activist who claimed that "Enough time has, in my opinion, been given to the States to legislate what is right. Too many States, for whatever reason, still perpetuate confusion. It is time for Federal action."[41]

The ADA's federal pre-emption of state and local authority was also propelled by the general agreement in Congress that the ADA represented another in a series of civil rights policies for which the federal government had accepted primary responsibility for enacting and enforcing. Despite the fact that Republicans during the presidential administrations of Ronald Reagan and

George Bush regularly railed against the creation of new federal mandates, there was widespread support for the ADA in both houses of Congress and in the White House — unusual bipartisan support for major civil rights legislation. While some Republicans, taking a conservative stance, voiced displeasure about ADA provisions concerning coverage, enforcement, and penalties, they were generally comfortable with the plan for a national civil rights bill for people with disabilities which would strengthen and expand the mandates included in earlier federal laws. Attorney-General Richard Thornburgh, for example, testifying on behalf of President Bush at congressional hearings on the ADA, claimed that "Over the last 20 years, civil rights laws protecting disabled persons have been enacted in a piecemeal fashion. Thus, existing Federal laws are like a patchwork quilt in need of repair. There are holes in the fabric, serious gaps in coverage that leave persons with disabilities without adequate civil rights protections."[42]

The move to "nationalize" disability rights policy also reflected the willingness of Congress to enact pre-emption statutes in the area of civil rights[43] and a shift in federalism away from aiding places and toward directly aiding persons.[44] By the late 1980s, the disability movement had reached full political force, joining interest groups that had proliferated in other policy areas and who were having a growing impact on policy issues related to federalism.[45] Scores of national, state, and local organizations representing persons with disabilities had, by this time, organized politically, adopted effective political tactics, and learned to cooperate in pursuit of national civil rights legislation to end discrimination based on disability. These groups demanded that people with disabilities be recognized as full citizens of the United States and that the federal government take action to ensure that they receive the full benefits of that citizenship. They were joined by civil rights organizations representing women and minorities who helped sustain the push for enactment of comprehensive national civil rights legislation.

Constitutional and Political Foundations of the ADA

The language of the ADA carefully specifies the constitutional basis for the mandates it creates. The statute invokes "the sweep of congressional authority, including the power to enforce the Fourteenth Amendment and to regulate commerce, in order to address the major areas of discrimination faced day-to-day by people with disabilities."[46] Through this statement, Congress moved disability rights laws into a parallel position with other civil rights laws where the fourteenth amendment and commerce clause have been "the two principal founts of congressional power that have been used to enact previous federal nondiscrimination laws."

The ADA language goes to unusual lengths to specify coverage of state and local governments. Under Title II, the public services section, the Act prohibits discrimination by any "public entity" including "any State or local government" or "any department, agency, special purpose district, or other instrumentality of a State or States or local government."[47] This relatively extensive definitional language was intended to clarify that all forms of state and local government are covered by the ADA. Where state or local law sets equal or stronger non-discrimination requirements, the ADA does not pre-empt state and local authority. [48]

The ADA stipulates that the enforcement powers, remedies, and procedures set forth in the *Civil Rights Act* of 1964 are extended to embrace discrimination based on disability. Such remedies include injunctive relief, back pay, and award of attorney's fees. In the ADA the Congress empowered the courts to assess civil penalties (not exceeding $50,000 for a first violation and $100,000 for subsequent violations) in civil cases brought by the US attorney general concerning discriminatory actions, including those that raise an issue of "general public importance."[49] While some members of Congress objected to the inclusion of civil penalties in the public accommodation section that applies to private enterprises — Senator Orrin Hatch argued that "Our purpose here should not be punitive. Providing for monetary damages and huge civil penalties ... is excessive"[50] — majorities in both houses upheld the civil penalties provision, which put real "teeth" into the regulatory mandate.

The ADA and Stronger Regulatory Mandates

Employment: The Great Equalizer

For people with disabilities, employment can be the "great equalizer,"[51] providing them with the ability to forsake dependence and achieve self-sufficiency. Unfortunately, substantial and persistent obstacles have made it difficult for disabled persons to find work and to achieve promotion once hired; often employers "appear more inclined to judge handicapped persons on the basis of disability rather than on what they are capable of performing."[52] Negative attitudes and misperceptions by employers and co-workers about the capabilities of persons who experience mental and physical impairments have been documented in a variety of studies.[53] These attitudes have persisted despite substantial evidence documenting the productivity and reliability of disabled workers[54] and the relative low cost associated with making the workplace accessible to individuals with disabilities.[55]

The ADA's non-discrimination mandates borrowed concepts developed in earlier national laws and the administrative rules used to implement them. The ADA's definition of disability is based on those specified in the *Rehabilitation Act* amendments of 1974[56] and stipulated in section 504's administrative rules:[57] protections are extended to any individual who has a physical or mental impairment that substantially limits one or more of the individual's major life activities, has a record of such impairment, or is regarded as having such an impairment. And again, borrowing from section 504 regulations,[58] the ADA requires that employers make reasonable accommodations to the physical or mental limitations so as to hire otherwise qualified employees (i.e., a person with a disability who, with or without reasonable accommodation, can perform the "essential functions of the job"). Accommodations in employment, which might include restructuring job duties, eliminating physical barriers in the workplace, or providing specialized devices, are required only so long as they do not impose *an undue economic hardship* on the employer. The ADA does not define this hardship but notes that its determination should be based on such factors as the nature and cost of accommodation, overall financial resources of the operation, size of the business, and type of operations performed by the enterprise. The principle of reasonable accommodation represents a creative balancing by first stipulating a potent mandate (e.g., requisite changes in workplace features or operations) and then stipulating circumstances which temper compliance with the mandate (e.g., undue economic hardship). This approach symbolizes a regulatory compromise and reduces impressions of regulatory intransigence.

The ADA substantially expands the scope of employers covered by disability rights mandates, spreading protections into the *private* sector by defining an employer subject to the Act as a person or entity engaged in industry affecting commerce who has 15 or more employees. Private sector employers covered by federal requirements, previously limited to federal contractors, were expanded to include all but small firms. By exempting small firms and specifying the undue economic hardship caveat to compliance, Congress felt assured that the private sector would be protected from overly burdensome financial requirements as the result of the ADA's employment mandates.

The ADA moved the federal government in the regulatory direction taken earlier by most state governments: mandating protections for people with disabilities in both the private and public spheres. As of the late 1980s, 46 states had enacted laws providing employment protections to persons with disabilities in at least some private sector operations. Like the ADA, many state laws provided exemptions to small businesses. State laws vary in the scope of disabilities covered in employment protection mandates. As of the late 1980s, 39 states provided protections to individuals with either physical or mental impairments, while the remaining state laws gave protection only to those who experience physical disability.[59]

Access to Transportation and Public Services

Title II of the ADA expands the mandated responsibilities of state and local governments in the realm of public service delivery by requiring all such units to (i) comply with the accessibility requirements promulgated for section 504; (ii) make reasonable accommodations to rules, policies, and procedures concerning public services to make them accessible to persons with disabilities; (iii) achieve removal of architectural barriers; and (iv) ensure the provision of auxiliary aids and services.

Title II also contains specific regulatory mandates relevant to public transit. Advocates for disabled individuals have continually stressed the importance of access to public transportation for people with disabilities; such access is critical to employment, service consumption, and even exercising the democratic right to vote.[60] The ADA specifies several regulatory mandates designed to ensure that individuals with disabilities have access to public transportation systems both within and between cities.[61] The ADA's provisions concerning public transportation mark the culmination of previous disability rights policies concerning transportation of disabled persons: policies that vacillated in many directions as federal agencies created and revised administrative regulations under strong political pressure.[62]

The regulatory mandates specified in the ADA for public transportation are tough and reflect a strong commitment to making transit systems accessible. The law stipulates that it is discriminatory and illegal for public transit operators to purchase or lease vehicles or operate key stations in rapid and light-rail systems that are not readily accessible to and usable by individuals with disabilities. For inter-city rail operations, the ADA requires that within a specified time period, purveyors must provide at least one passenger car per train accessible to persons with disabilities.

The concept of paratransit services is explicitly addressed in the ADA which, borrowing heavily from earlier Department of Transport regulations implementing section 504, requires that public entities which operate fixed route transit systems provide paratransit and other specialized services to individuals with disabilities that are sufficient to provide such individuals a level of service comparable to the service provided to non-disabled passengers. The paratransit mandate holds only to such a point that it does not create an undue financial burden on the public transit entity. The last provision was seen as key by public transit purveyors who recognized the costliness of paratransit operations and feared an unlimited responsibility to provide demand-responsive transportation to disabled riders.

Access to Accommodations

One of the most significant changes in federal disability rights policy achieved through the ADA is the extension of regulatory requirements to the services and accommodations offered by the private sector. While many business organizations and trade associations applauded the ADA generally, some of them raised broader questions about the regulatory approach being pursued in the Act. At a House of Representatives hearing on the ADA, for example, a representative of the National Federation of Independent Businesses gave support for an incentive rather than regulatory mandate approach to accessibility goals.

> The approach taken by the ADA bill to mandate significant and expensive equipment, services, and structural changes in nearly every business in America is simply wrong-headed. Instead of providing incentives, education, and opportunities to encourage greater access, the ADA bill takes a negative approach of imposing vague requirements followed by significant penalties if businesses fail to comply.[63]

Unpersuaded by the argument that incentives were better than mandates, Congress, through Title III of the ADA, created a new federal mandate regarding the access of persons with disabilities to a wide array of services, facilities, and accommodations offered by the private sector. The ADA states that "No individual shall be discriminated against on the basis of disability in the full and equal enjoyment of the goods, services, facilities, privileges, advantages, or accommodations of any place of accommodation by any person who owns, leases, or operates a place of public accommodation." The definition of "public accommodation" is broadly conceptualized and encompasses most private sector establishments, including hotels and motels, banks, business locations, restaurants, bars, theatres, concert halls, service facilities (e.g., laundromats, banks, travel agencies, and health-care providers), parks, places of education, and recreation centres.

Operators of public accommodations are (i) prohibited from denying access or participation to disabled persons, (ii) required to made reasonable modifications in policies, practices, and procedures to afford goods, services, privileges, and opportunities to persons with disabilities, and (iii) mandated to make "readily achievable" modifications (i.e., "easily accomplished and able to be carried out without much difficulty or expense") to architectural and communications barriers that impede the access of disabled individuals. The public accommodations title of the ADA strengthens substantially the federal accessibility mandate, which now surpasses the strongest mandates specified in state laws concerning the access of disabled individuals to public and private operations. Thirty-two states, as of the late 1980s, had laws requiring barrier removal or accessibility modifications in at least some privately owned and operated buildings, but none had such extensive coverage of private sector enterprises as the ADA.[64]

The ADA as National Policy

There is no question but that the *Americans with Disabilities Act* represents application of significant governing authority by the national government, power activated by constitutional authority in place of a condition-of-aid mandate. Americans as citizens, and the state governments that represent them, generally accepted this assertion of power aimed at protecting the rights and opportunities of people with disabilities. While such national assertions of power have generated controversy, even rebellion, in the past, the ADA did not raise the hackles of the states; instead the states accepted the ADA with the primary worries focusing on the costs of compliance rather than the need to challenge national government authority.

The overall acquiescence of the states to nationally defined and implemented protections for people with disabilities can be explained by multiple factors. First, the national government's assertion of policy-making authority in the area of civil rights dates back to the 1950s as the United States contemplated laws to protect the rights first of people of colour and then rights of women. By the late 1980s as the ADA was drafted and debated, civil rights controversies pitting the state governments against the national government had abated with overall acceptance of national government prominence in civil rights policy. From this perspective, the ADA became one of a long developing set of civil rights policies with the national government operating at the helm.

Another explanation of state government acceptance of national government authority as articulated in the ADA is that states had themselves already moved by the 1980s to create disability rights policies. Some states had laws that surpassed the national government's pre-ADA laws and policies in terms of coverage and scope. The policy provisions of the ADA were often consistent with elements of laws in most states allowing states to see the ADA not so much as a rival but as a companion to state laws.

A final explanation of state acquiescence to national government power in the context of the ADA concerns the depth of public recognition of discrimination and growing public sentiments for strong protections. During the two decades preceding the ADA, Americans not only witnessed greatly expanded civil rights protections for many groupings of Americans but also began to learn about the plight of people with disabilities, the limiting impact of policies and design features, and the potential contributions that people with disabilities can make to American life. These recognitions generated political support for the ADA, support that was nationally, not regionally or state, based. Civil rights protections designed and enforced by the national government were therefore consistent with popular conceptions of how civil rights are to be defined and enforced within the overall federal system of the US.

CONCLUSION

As the United States faces a new millennium, the disability policy front is relatively quiet. While significant issues about program implementation continue, there are no major initiatives in the legislative hopper. The prominent social issues of the time are related to health-care reform, something that will impact people with disabilities but is not identified as a disability rights issue. The end of this century, then, is an appropriate juncture at which to reassess disability policy, identify achievements and challenges that remain, and reconsider the effectiveness of intergovernmental strategies for implementing disability programs.

All analysts would agree that the policy world in the United States has significantly changed in the past half-century, with a number of important programs created at the state and national government levels to aid people with disabilities and expand their opportunities in society. Income maintenance programs, including workers' compensation and Social Security Disability Insurance, have been created and expanded. These entitlement programs have survived onslaughts against entitlements and today face no significant challenge. The vocational rehabilitation program operating as a nation-state partnership also continues. Undoubtedly the most significant development of this period is the passage of the *Americans with Disabilities Act* of 1990, legislation that extended civil rights mandates for disabled individuals to both the public and private sectors of American life.

Looking Forward: Concerns and Challenges

Despite these achievements, many challenges remain, and disability policy will re-emerge on the forefront of policy-making within the next decade or two. What are the lingering issues? There are many, but a few are prominent. One concern, to no surprise, focuses on operating costs. Concerns about the costs of these myriad of programs fits within the broader context in which the national government has sought to cut both spending and taxes. Issues of costs and financing are not limited to disability policy, but these pressures, at both the state and national government levels represent significant and ongoing challenges for disability policy

A second concern focuses on effectiveness, that is, to what extent are the programs designed to aid people with disabilities actually achieving their objective. Critics of the vocational rehabilitation program, for example, continue to challenge the overall cost-effectiveness of the program in general, and the evidence furnished by governmental agencies to document positive performance.

Third, as the US overhauls its welfare system — largely as the consequence of widespread beliefs that traditional welfare policy created permanent dependence rather than providing assistance for short-term need — entitlement programs of income maintenance like SSDI have come under scrutiny.

A fourth and critical issue relates to the overall coordination of the set of disability policies now in place in the United States. To be effective, the range of disability policies now in place need adequate interface because, after all, they serve the same population of people. For example, a person receiving SSDI or workers' compensation should be able to receive vocational rehabilitation, when appropriate, to restore his or her labour capacity and return to the workforce (thereby eliminating the need for public assistance). If the rehabilitation system functions poorly, not only do disabled individuals receive inadequate service, but the income support systems are also affected.

For the last two decades analysts and critics have worried aloud about the effectiveness of system coordination. The National Council on Disability, an independent federal agency responsible for monitoring disability policy and making recommendations for change, sees coordination issues as critical at the present time.

> People with disabilities receive conflicting messages from national disability policy ... There are multiple federal programs for people with disabilities, administered by different federal agencies. The programs differ in their eligibility criteria and foci, depending on their purposes and target populations.[65]

The council, in its 1996 report, provided a set of recommended policy changes, many of which seek to increase disability policy coordination. It also recommended that the principles and goals of the *Americans with Disabilities Act* be used to guide policy coordination efforts.[66]

Questions about policy coordination invariably raise issues about implementing disability policies from an intergovernmental, rather than centralized national, arrangement. Unlike Western European nations, the US system utilizes a more decentralized, yet interdependent, policy system to serve people with disabilities.[67] This system, while generally consistent with American principles of governance through a federal system where powers are shared between the national government and the states, does not guarantee effective policy at every turn. Decentralization provides the potential for more locally, rather than centrally, designed policy efforts that can be more responsive to locally-defined problems and more appropriately tailored to local conditions. The American states, therefore, can serve as laboratories for policy "experiments" through which effective policy implementation strategies can be identified and then shared back with the other states. Conversely, greater centralization is more likely to provide consistent services and benefits across the states, at least with regard to establishing minimal levels. These tensions have been rife since the formation of the United States and will remain so long as the democratic system remains based upon a federal, power-sharing model of governance. The persistent questions in the context of disability policy is determining which programs and services are best provided at which level of governance and how state and national programs can be more effectively coordinated and mutually reinforcing. These questions are ongoing in disability policy and will continue to be the focus of policy debates and plans for system reform.

One final issue focuses on the fundamental conception of the human beings for which disability policy is intended to serve. Initial concepts, as noted at the start of this chapter, were rooted in fear, pity, and preferences for separation from mainstream society. This model changed, beginning in the 1960s, toward a perspective of people with disabilities first as individuals deserving of public assistance (with some element of pity still prominent) and then to a minority group model where a disadvantaged group pressed for elimination of discrimination. This latter model was effective in pushing forward disability rights policies, particularly. There is evidence that this model is yet again changing, this time toward a perspective of people with disabilities as individual human beings with variations rather than deficits. Advocates contend that this "new" model should emphasize the variability inherent in disability and that disability thus may be seen as an extension of the natural physical, social, and cultural variability of human species.[68]

One extension of this model has been the move toward "universal design" and away from "handicapped accessibility" among engineers concerned with designing guidelines and regulations to ensure that people with disabilities have access to public buildings and accommodations. This universal model recognizes that (i) most individuals are physically disabled at some point in their lives, (ii) the limitations experienced by people with disabilities can be shared with others in society such as elderly persons, and pregnant women, and (iii) designs initially created for people with disabilities (e.g., larger restroom stalls, ramps into buildings) can benefit (and may even be preferred by) people who do not experience permanently disabling conditions.

The human variability model offers potential to remove stereotypes about disability and positively influence the formulation and reformulation of disability policy. It remains to be seen whether the disability community as a whole, and the broader American political system, will forsake the civil rights approach and move toward acceptance of the human variability model.

Assessing Accomplishments

So where are we? Accomplishments have been made, current and future challenges have been identified. What is the bottom-line today (recognizing that the status of disability programs and their implementation remain dynamic)? One analyst concludes that there is more to do, that the policy work remains unfinished:

So what is the situation? First, people are already concerned about the size of beneficiary populations of the disability programs. After examining the changes contemplated in other income support programs, the declining demand in the labor market for low-skilled and disadvantaged workers, and the growing gaps in health care protection for workers, thinking that demands on the disability systems are going to decline through a strategy of benign neglect is not plausible. So, there remains a great deal of unfinished business.[69]

Proposals have been, and will continue to be, offered to improve the disability policy system, to make policies more effective in aiding people with disabilities. The National Council on Disability, an independent agency of the national government, suggested a variety of action proposals that, cumulatively, were expected to enhance the employability and life situations of disabled persons. The council urged the US Congress "to tap into the potential provided by people who have disabilities. America's citizens with disabilities want very much to contribute to their country's continued preeminence in the world of nations. They have the talents and the capabilities to do so."[70]

If the ADA represents the important linchpin of contemporary disability policy, we can also inquire as to its current status. The full answer to this question is not yet in. On the one hand, the administrative work to implement the program is in place, on the time line established in the ADA: "Collectively considered, preliminary indications suggest that the ADA is on track in terms of accomplishing its goals. Congress clearly stated its intent, regulatory agencies developed compliance standards and enforcement mechanisms, and potential beneficiaries are engaged in the process. On this basis, the prospects for successful implementation and vigorous enforcement of the ADA appear promising."[71] One the other hand, less is known about the outcomes of the ADA. The sheer magnitude of the ADA mandate — covering multiple policy dimensions (i.e., employment, transportation, public accommodations) and both the public and private sectors — makes it difficult to know just what has been accomplished.

The issue of ADA costs will remain at the forefront of the political whirlwinds that surround the implementation of this law to protect people with disabilities. Given the scope of the Act and insufficient information on such things as the number and type of employment accommodations and the extent of architectural barrier-removal projects that will be needed, it is extremely difficult to estimate the total costs of achieving nation-wide compliance with the ADA. While many types of accommodation can be made with little cost, substantial costs will be incurred in such areas as providing paratransit services, making key transit stations accessible, and making physical changes in services and facilities used by the public.

One partial yet plausible set of estimates on ADA compliance was prepared by the Congressional Budget Office (CBO), which estimated that the cost to the federal government in implementing the ADA would range from about $5 million in the first year to $31 million by 1995.[72] But the real cost of compliance is with the content of the ADA — unlike other disability rights policies borne by state and local governments and private sector establishments, of course — will be substantially higher. With regard to the compliance costs to state and local governments, CBO estimated that it would cost $20–30 million per year over several years to purchase additional lift-equipped buses, $15 million annually to provide maintenance to these buses, and several hundreds of millions of dollars over 30 years to make key rail and transit stations accessible. Still other dollars will be required to achieve compliance with other ADA mandates, including reasonable accommodation in employment and housing.

Cost issues and the elevated opportunities for people with disabilities has the potential to generate a backlash against the ADA and its strong regulatory mandates. While significant political revolts against the ADA have not yet materialized, complaints have arisen in some quarters about expansivenss of ADA mandates and the fiscal requirements needed to achieve compliance. Communities, large and small, have complained about compliance costs for such things as major building renovations and interpreter services. Complaints range in scope from mandated actions that represent little more than anger about the "nuisance" of compliance to accommodations that represent substantial fiscal outlays (e.g., provision of paratransit services). Academics have entered the fray, challenging whether disability policies which advance the opportunities of people with disabilities are fair and just or whether they can enable undeserving claims to "jump the queue" while other more deserving public needs are left unmet.[73] And while these critiques from practitioners and academics remain, these seem unlikely to derail the ADA. One analyst warns state and local governments that: "Given the militancy of the disabled, the activism of the [US Justice Department and the sympathies of most of the judiciary, ignoring the 'little things' [adherence to ADA mandates] can turn out to be the riskiest strategy of all."[74]

Finally, there is substantial agreement that we have more to learn about disability policies, their effects, individual and cumulative, and whether or not policy modifications are needed to ensure that public programs achieve their intended consequences. As one disability policy analyst contends, it is now a critical time for policy analysts to join the fray to answer these important policy questions: "Disability policy engages the attention of decision makers in a way it did not in the past. It is the responsibility of the policy analysis community, especially those analysts who identify with the disability community, to focus on disability policy and its implications."[75] There is much wisdom here, since we are now past the point of policy formulation and preliminary implementation. It is time now to learn from policy experiences in the United States, at both the state and national levels, to inform the next generation of disability policies — most of which will be revisions of current policy rather than bold new initiatives.[76]

NOTES

[1]This field of policy studies is moving toward disciplinary status as evidenced by the creation in 1993 of a new interdisciplinary journal, *The Journal of Disability Policy Studies*, published at the University of Arkansas.

[2]For a comprehensive review of research studies through the late 1970s on attitudes toward persons with disabilities, see John G. Schroedel, *Attitudes toward Persons with Disabilities: A Compendium of Related Research* (Albertson, NY: Human Resource Center, 1979).

[3]Robert L. Burgdorf, Jr. and Marcia Pearce Burgdorf, "The Wicked Witch is almost Dead: *Buck v. Bell* and the Sterilization of Handicapped Persons," *Temple Law Review* 50 (1977):995-1033.

[4]Shari Thurer, "Disability and Monstrosity: A Look at Literary Distortion of Handicapping Conditions," in *Rehabilitating People with Disabilities into the Mainstream of Society*, ed. Allen D. Spiegel and Simon Podair (Park Ridge: Noyes Medical Publications, 1981).

[5]Timothy R. Elliott and Keith Bryd, "Media and Disability," *Rehabilitation Literature* 43 (1982):348-55. It should be noted that some literary depictions are not only accurate but also provide useful insights into the life experiences of persons with disabilities. Bower has edited an interesting text with literary extracts intended for use by students and others wishing to learn about and emotionally experience the handicap situation. See Eli M. Bower, *The Handicapped in Literature: A Psychological Perspective* (Denver: Love Publishing, 1980).

[6]William R. English, "Correlates of Stigma Toward Physically Disabled People," *Rehabilitation Research and Practice Review* 2 (1971):1-17. See also Jerome Siller *et al.*, *Attitudes of the Nondisabled toward the Physically Disabled* (New York: School of Education, New York University, 1967); and Robert B. Nathanson, "Campus

Interactions: Attitudes and Behavior," in *The College's Challenge* (New York: Teacher's College, Columbia University, 1980).

[7]Florence Isbell, "How the Handicapped Won their Rights," *Civil Liberties Review* (November/December, 1977): 62.

[8]The International Center for the Disabled and the National Council on the Handicapped, *Bringing Disabled Americans into the Mainstream* (Washington, DC: International Center for the Disabled, 1986).

[9]Daniel J. Elazar, *American Federalism: A View from the States* (New York: Harper & Row, 1984), p. 3.

[10]Thomas J. Anton, *American Federalism and Public Policy: How the System Works* (Philadelphia: Temple University Press, 1989), p. 3.

[11]A detailed examination of different patterns and periods of American federalism is presented in Deil S. Wright, *Understanding Intergovernmental Relations*, 3d ed. (Pacific Grove, CA: Brooks/Cole Publishing Company, 1988), pp. 65-112.

[12]For more on fiscal federalism, see Thomas R. Swartz and John E. Peck, *The Changing Face of Fiscal Federalism* (Armonk, NY: M.E. Sharpe, 1990).

[13]The US Advisory Commission on Intergovernmental Relations (ACIR) has documented the forms and magnitude of regulatory mandates placed by the federal government upon states and localities. By the mid-1980s, ACIR counted over 35 *major* federal laws regulating state and local governments; this number increased through the early 1990s. The breadth of regulatory power is evident in the number of different areas being regulated by the federal government, including environmental protection, civil rights, consumer protection, labour issues and workplace safety, and energy conservation. Advisory Commission on Intergovernmental Relations, *Regulatory Federalism: Policy, Process, Impact and Reform* (Washington, DC: ACIR, 1984).

[14]For a thorough examination of the development of federal disability policies, see Edward D. Berkowitz, *Disability Policy and Government Programs* (New York: Praeger Publishers, 1987).

[15]Edward D. Berkowitz, *Disabled Policy: America's Programs for the Handicapped* (Cambridge, MA: Cambridge University Press, 1987), p. 15.

[16]Jack B. Hood, Benjamin A. Hardy, Jr. and Harold S. Lewis, Jr., *Workers' Compensation and Employee Protection Laws* (St. Paul, MN: West Publishing Company, 1990), pp. 1-2.

[17]C. Arthur Williams, Jr., *An International Comparison of Workers' Compensation* (Boston: Kluwer Academic Publishers, 1991), p. 187.

[18]Berkowitz, *Disabled Policy*, p. 34.

[19]National Commission on State Workmen's Compensation Laws, *The Report of the National Commission on State Workmen's Compensation Laws* (Washington, DC: Government Printing Office, 1972).

[20]Philip S. Borba and David Appel, *Benefits, Costs, and Cycles in Workers' Compensation* (Boston: Kluwer Academic Publishers, 1990), p. 2.

[21]Robert H. Haveman, Victor Halberstadt and Richard V. Burkhauser, *Public Policy toward Disabled Workers: Cross-National Analyses of Economic Impacts* (Ithaca, NY: Cornell University Press, 1985), p. 55.

[22]For a discussion of the origins of the vocational rehabilitation program in the US, see C. Esco Obermann, *A History of Vocational Rehabilitation in America* (Minneapolis, MN: T. S. Denison & Company, 1967).

[23]Berkowitz, *Disabled Policy*, p. 155.

[24]See, for example, Monroe Berkowitz, ed., *Measuring the Efficiency of Public Programs: Costs and Benefits in Vocational Rehabilitation* (Philadelphia: Temple University Press, 1988).

[25]For an early assessment of SSI, see Paul L. Grimaldi, *Supplemental Security Income: The New Federal Program for the Aged, Blind, and Disabled* (Washington, DC: American Enterprise Institute, 1980).

[26]Berkowitz, *Disabled Policy*, pp. 150-51.

[27]Statement by President George Bush in signing the *Americans with Disabilities Act* of 1990 at White House Ceremony, 26 July 1990, reprinted in *Worklife 3 (Fall 1990):9-11.*

[28]Diane Driedger, *The Last Civil Rights Movement: Disabled People's International* (New York: St. Martin's Press, 1989).

[29]Stephen L. Percy, "Challenges and Dilemmas in Implementing Disability Rights Policies," *Journal of Disability Policy Studies* 4 (1993); "The ADA: Expanding Mandates for Disability Rights," *Intergovernmental Perspective* 19 (Winter 1993):11-14.

[30]Erwin L. Levine and Elizabeth Wexler, *P.L. 94-142, An Act of Congress* (New York: Macmillan, 1981).

[31]For a detailed discussion of federal efforts to clarify and refine disability policy, see Stephen L. Percy, *Disability, Civil Rights and Public Policy: The Politics of Implementation* (Tuscaloosa, AL: University of Alabama Press, 1989); and Richard Scotch, *From Goodwill to Civil Rights: Transforming Disability Policy* (Philadelphia: Temple University Press, 1984). For a broader view of the evolution of disability policies, see Berkowitz, *Disabled Policy*; and Deborah Stone, *The Disabled State* (Philadelphia: Temple University Press, 1984).

[32]Stephen L. Percy, *Disability Rights Mandates: Federal and State Compliance with Employment Protections and Architectural Barrier Removal* (Washington, DC: Advisory Commission on Intergovernmental Relations, 1989), p. 2; see also Thomas Holbrook and Stephen L. Percy, "Exploring Variations in State Laws Providing Protections for Persons with Disabilities," *Western Political Quarterly* 45,1 (1992):201-20.

[33]Percy, *Disability, Civil Rights, and Public Policy.*

[34]US House of Representatives, Committee on Education and Labor, *Report on the Americans with Disabilities Act of 1990*, 101st Congress, 2d Session (Washington, DC: US Government Printing Office, 1990), p. 310.

[35]National Council on the Handicapped, *Toward Independence: An Assessment of Federal Laws and Programs Affecting Persons with Disabilities* (Washington, DC: US Government Printing Office, 1986), p. 14.

[36]Ibid., p. 7.

[37]Edward I. Koch, "The Mandate Millstone," *The Public Interest* (Fall 1980): 42-57

[38]For example, see Timothy B. Clark, "Regulation Gone Amok: How Many Billions for Wheelchair Transit?" *Regulation* (March/April 1980): 47-52.

[39]With regard to assessment of federal funding of regulatory mandates, see Stephen L. Percy, *Disability Rights Mandates*, pp. 71, 85.

[40]Stephen L. Percy, "ADA, Disability Rights, and Evolving Regulatory Federalism," *Publius: The Journal of Federalism* 23 (Fall 1993):87-105.

[41]US Senate, Committee on Labor and Human Resources, *Report on the Americans with Disabilities Act of 1989*, 101st Congress, 1st Session (Washington, DC: US Government Printing Office, 1989), p. 116.

[42]Ibid., p. 117.

[43]Advisory Commission on Intergovernmental Relations, *Federal Statutory Preemption of State and Local Authority*; Timothy J. Conlan and David R. Beam, "Federal Mandates: The Record of Reform and Future Prospects," *Intergovernmental Perspective* (Fall 1992): 7-15; Daniel J. Elazar, "Opening the Third Century of American Federalism: Issues and Prospects," *The Annals* 509 (May 1990):11-21.

[44]John Kincaid, "Constitutional Federalism: Labor's Role in Displacing Places to Benefit People," *PS: Political Science and Politics* 26 (June 1993):172-77.

[45]Timothy J. Conlan, "Politics and Governance: Conflicting Trends in the 1990s?" *The Annals* 509 (May 1990):128-38.

[46]104 Stat. 329, 42 U.S.C. _ 12101 (Supp. III 1991).

[47]104 Stat. 337; 42 U.S.C. _ 12131 (Supp. III 1991).

[48]104 Stat. 369, 42 U.S.C. _ 12201 (Supp. III 1991).

[49]104 Stat. 364, 42 U.S.C. _ 12188 (Supp. III 1991).

[50]Additional views of Senator Hatch included with US Senate, Committee on Labor and Human Resources, *Report on the Americans with Disabilities Act of 1989*, p. 100.

[51]Ronald Mace, "Physical Facilities and the Handicapped," *Civil Rights Issues of Handicapped Americans: Public Policy Implications* (Washington, DC: US Commission on Civil Rights, 1980), pp. 264-76.

[52]Peter M. Jamero, "Handicapped Individuals in the Changing Workforce," *Journal of Contemporary Business* 8 (1979):38.

[53]See, for example, John G. Schroedel and Richard J. Jacobsen, *Employer Attitudes toward Hiring Persons with Disabilities* (Albertson, NY: Human Resource Center, 1978); and Gopal C. Pati, John I. Adkins, Jr. and Glenn Morrison, *Managing and Employing the Handicapped: The Untapped Potential* (Lake Forest, IL: Brace-Park/Human Resources Press, 1981). For discussion of co-worker attitudes, see Karl

H. Seifert, "The Attitudes of Working People towards Disabled Persons," in *Rehabilitating People with Disabilities into the Mainstream of Society*, ed. Spiegel and Podair.

[54]See E.I. DuPont de Nemours and Company, *Equal to the Task* (Wilmington, DL: E.I. DuPont de Nemours and Company, 1982); and Arno B. Zimmer, *Employing the Handicapped: A Practical Compliance Guide* (New York: Amacom, 1981).

[55]See, for example, Berkeley Planning Associates, *A Study of Accommodations Provided to Handicapped Employees by Federal Contractors: Final Report*, Vol. 1, Study Findings (Washington, DC: US Department of Labor, Employment Standards Administration, 1982); and Jack R. Ellner and Henry E. Bender, *Hiring the Handicapped* (New York: Amacom, 1980).

[56]88 Stat. 1617, 29 U.S.C. 706(8)(B) (1988).

[57]28 *Code of Federal Regulation* 42.540 (k).

[58]28 *Code of Federal Regulations* 42.511. These regulations are described and analyzed in Percy, *Disability, Civil Rights and Public Policy* and Advisory Commission on Intergovernmental Relations, *Disability Rights Mandates*.

[59]Advisory Commission on Intergovernmental Relations, *Disability Rights Mandates*; see also Ann M. Wolfe, *Disabled Persons: State Laws Concerning Accessibility and Discrimination* (Washington, DC: Congressional Research Service, 1989); and Charles D. Goldman, *Disability Rights Guide: Practical Solutions to Problems Affecting People with Disabilities* (Lincoln, NE: Media Publishing, 1987).

[60]Dennis Cannon, "A Funny Thing Happened on the Way to the Bus Stop: Transportation and the Handicapped," in *Civil Rights Issues of Handicapped Americans: Public Policy Implementation* (Washington, DC: US Commission on Civil Rights, 1980), pp. 307-28; Christopher G. Bell and Robert L. Burgdorf, Jr., *Accommodating the Spectrum of Individuals' Abilities* (Washington, DC: US Civil Rights Commission, 1983).

[61]Robert A. Katzmann, "Transportation Policy," *The Americans with Disabilities Act: From Policy to Practice*, ed. Jane West (New York: Milbank Memorial Fund, 1991), pp. 214-37.

[62]Michael Fix, Carol Everett and Ronald Kirby, *Providing Public Transportation to the Disabled: Local Responses to Evolving Federal Policies* (Washington, DC: The Urban Institute, 1985); Robert A. Katzmann, *Institutional Disability: The Saga of Transportation Policy for the Disabled* (Washington, DC: The Brookings Institution, 1986); and Percy, *Disability, Civil Rights and Public Policy*.

[63]US House of Representatives, Committee on the Judiciary, Subcommittee on Civil and Constitutional Rights, *Hearings on H.R. 2273 Americans with Disabilities Act of 1989*. 101st Congress, 1st Session, 7 August, 11, 12 October (Washington, DC: US Government Printing Office, 1989), p. 85.

[64]Advisory Commission on Intergovernmental Relations, *Disability Rights Mandates*, p. 46.

[65]National Council on Disability, *Achieving Independence: The Challenge for the 21st Century* (Washington, DC: National Council on Disability, 1996), pp. 23-24.

[66]Ibid., p. 27.

[67]Edward D. Berkowitz and Richard V. Burkhauser, "A United States Perspective on Disability Policies," in *Curing the Dutch Disease*, ed. Leo J.M. Aarts, Richard V. Burkhauser and Philip R. DeJong (Brookfield, VT: Ashgate Publishing Company, 1996), pp. 71-92.

[68]Richard K. Scotch and Kay Schriner, "Disability as Human Variation: Implications for Policy," *Annals of the American Academy of Political and Social Science (The Americans with Disabilities Act: Social Contract or Special Privilege?)* (January 1997):148-59.

[69]Jerry L. Mashaw, "The Unfinished Business of Disability Policy," in *Disability: Challenges for Social Insurance, Health Care Financing and Labor Market Policy*, ed. Virginia P. Reno, Jerry L. Mashaw and Bill Gradison (Washington, DC: National Academy of Social Insurance, 1997), p. 191.

[70]National Council on Disability, *Removing Barriers to Work: Action Proposals for the 105th Congress and Beyond* (Washington, DC: National Council on Disability, 1997), p. 48.

[71]Peter C. Bishop and Augustus J. Jones, Jr., "Implementing the Americans with Disabilities Act of 1990: Assessing the Variables of Success," *Public Administration Review* 53 (March/April 1993):127.

[72]The CBO estimates were included in the following report: US House of Representatives, Committee on Public Works and Transportation, *Report on the Americans with Disabilities Act of 1990*, 101st Congress, 2nd Session, May 14 (Washington, DC: US Government Printing Office, 1990), pp. 255-59.

[73]Mark Kelman and Gillian Lester, *Jumping the Queue: An Inquiry in the Legal Treatment of Students with Disabilities* (Cambridge, MA: Harvard University Press, 1997).

[74]Ellen Perlman, "Disability Dilemmas," *Governing* (April 1998):33.

[75]David Pfeiffer, "Overview of the Disability Movement: History, Legislative Record, and Political Implications," *Policy Studies Journal* 21, 4 (1993):732. See also S. Litvak, "Financing Personal Assistance Services," *Journal of Disability Policy Studies* 3,1 (1992):83-105.

[76]For suggestions on how the ADA can be studied and assessed, see Frederick C. Collignon, "Is the ADA Successful?: Indicators for Tracking Gains," *Annals of the American Academy of Political and Social Science* 549 (Fall 1997):129-47.

Queen's Policy Studies
Recent Publications

The Queen's Policy Studies Series is dedicated to the exploration of major policy issues that confront governments in Canada and other western nations. McGill-Queen's University Press is the exclusive world representative and distributor of books in the series.

School of Policy Studies

The Nonprofit Sector and Government in a New Century, Kathy L. Brock and Keith G. Banting (ed.), 2001 Paper ISBN 0-88911-901-5 Cloth ISBN 0-88911-905-8

The Dynamics of Decentralization: Canadian Federalism and British Devolution, Trevor C. Salmon and Michael Keating (eds.), 2001   ISBN 0-88911-895-7

Innovation, Institutions and Territory: Regional Innovation Systems in Canada, J. Adam Holbrook and David A. Wolfe (eds.), 2000   Paper ISBN 0-88911-891-4 Cloth ISBN 0-88911-893-0

Backbone of the Army: Non-Commissioned Officers in the Future Army, Douglas L. Bland (ed.), 2000 ISBN 0-88911-889-2

Precarious Values: Organizations, Politics and Labour Market Policy in Ontario, Thomas R. Klassen, 2000 Paper ISBN 0-88911-883-3 Cloth ISBN 0-88911-885-X

The Nonprofit Sector in Canada: Roles and Relationships, Keith G. Banting (ed.), 2000 Paper ISBN 0-88911-813-2 Cloth ISBN 0-88911-815-9

Security, Strategy and the Global Economics of Defence Production, David G. Haglund and S. Neil MacFarlane (eds.), 1999   Paper ISBN 0-88911-875-2 Cloth ISBN 0-88911-877-9

The Communications Revolution at Work: The Social, Economic and Political Impacts of Technological Change, Robert Boyce (ed.), 1999   Paper ISBN 0-88911-805-1 Cloth ISBN 0-88911-807-8

Institute of Intergovernmental Relations

Federalism, Democracy and Health Policy in Canada, Duane Adams (ed.), 2001 Paper ISBN 0-88911-853-1 Cloth ISBN 0-88911-865-5, ISBN 0-88911-845-0 (set)

Federalism, Democracy and Labour Market Policy in Canada, Tom McIntosh (ed.), 2000 ISBN 0-88911-849-3, ISBN 0-88911-845-0 (set)

Canada: The State of the Federation 1999/2000, vol. 14, *Toward a New Mission Statement for Canadian Fiscal Federalism,* Harvey Lazar (ed.), 2000   Paper ISBN 0-88911-843-4 Cloth ISBN 0-88911-839-6

Canada: The State of the Federation 1998/99, vol. 13, *How Canadians Connect,* Harvey Lazar and Tom McIntosh (eds.), 1999   Paper ISBN 0-88911-781-0 Cloth ISBN 0-88911-779-9

Managing the Environmental Union: Intergovernmental Relations and Environmental Policy in Canada, Patrick C. Fafard and Kathryn Harrison (eds.), 2000   ISBN 0-88911-837-X

Stretching the Federation: The Art of the State in Canada, Robert Young (ed.), 1999   ISBN 0-88911-777-2

Comparing Federal Systems, 2d ed., Ronald L. Watts, 1999   ISBN 0-88911-835-3

John Deutsch Institute for the Study of Economic Policy

The 2000 Federal Budget, Paul A.R. Hobson (ed.), Policy Forum Series no. 37, 2001 Paper ISBN 0-88911-816-7 Cloth ISBN 0-88911-814-0

Room to Manoeuvre? Globalization and Policy Convergence, Thomas J. Courchene (ed.), Bell Canada Papers no. 6, 1999   Paper ISBN 0-88911-812-4 Cloth ISBN 0-88911-812-4

Women and Work, Richard P. Chaykowski and Lisa M. Powell (eds.), 1999 Paper ISBN 0-88911-808-6 Cloth ISBN 0-88911-806-X

Equalization: Its Contribution to Canada's Economic and Fiscal Progress, Robin W. Boadway and Paul A.R. Hobson (eds.), Policy Forum Series no. 36, 1998 Paper ISBN 0-88911-780-2 Cloth ISBN 0-88911-804-3

Available from:
McGill-Queen's University Press
Tel: 1-800-387-0141 (ON and QC excluding Northwestern ON)
        1-800-387-0172 (all other provinces and Northwestern ON)

E-mail: customer.service@ccmailgw.genpub.com

Institute of Intergovernmental Relations
Recent Publications

The Spending Power in Federal Systems: A Comparative Study by Ronald L. Watts, 1999
ISBN 0-88911-829-9

Étude comparative du pouvoir de dépenser dans d'autres régimes fédéraux par Ronald L. Watts, 1999
ISBN 0-88911-831-0

Constitutional Patriation: The Lougheed-Lévesque Correspondence/Le rapatriement de la Constitution: La correspondance de Lougheed et Lévesque, with an Introduction by J. Peter Meekison/avec une introduction de J. Peter Meekison, 1999   ISBN 0-88911-833-7

Securing the Social Union: A Commentary on the Decentralized Approach, Steven A. Kennett, 1998
ISBN 0-88911-767-5

Working Paper Series

2001

1. *Tax Competition and the Fiscal Union: Balancing Competition and Harmonization in Canada.* Proceedings of a Symposium held 9-10 June 2000, edited by Douglas Brown, Queen's University

2. *Federal Occupational Training Policy: A Neo-Institutionalist Analysis* by Gordon DiGiacomo, Consultant in Workplace Relations, Greely, Ontario

3. *Federalism and Labour Market Policy in Germany and Canada: Exploring the Path Dependency of Reforms in the 1990s* by Thomas R. Klassen, Trent University and Steffen Schneider, University of Augsburg, Germany

4. *Bifurcated and Integrated Parties in Parliamentary Federations: The Canadian and German Cases* by Wolfgang Renzsch, Otto-von-Guericke Universität Magdeburg, Germany

2000

1. *The Agreement on Internal Trade: An Institutional Response to Changing Conceptions, Roles and Functions in Canadian Federalism* by Howard Leeson, University of Regina

2. *Tax Competition and the Fiscal Union.* Selected proceedings of a Symposium held at Queen's University 9-10 June 2000, edited by Doug Brown

1999

1. *Processes of Constitutional Restructuring: The Canadian Experience in Comparative Context* by Ronald L. Watts, Queen's University

2. *Parliament, Intergovernmental Relations and National Unity* by C.E.S. Franks, Queen's University

3. *The United Kingdom as a Quasi-Federal State* by Gerard Hogan, Queen's University

4. *The Federal Spending Power in Canada: Nation-Building or Nation-Destroying?* by Hamish Telford, Queen's University

1998

1. *The Meaning of Provincial Equality in Canadian Federalism* by Jennifer Smith, Dalhousie University

2. *Considerations on the Design of Federations: The South African Constitution in Comparative Context* by Richard Simeon, University of Toronto

3. *Federal Systems and Accommodation of Distinct Groups: A Comparative Survey of Institutional Arrangements* by Ronald L. Watts, Queen's University

For a complete list of working papers see: www.iigr.ca

These publications are available from:
Institute of Intergovernmental Relations, Queen's University, Kingston, Ontario K7L 3N6
Tel: (613) 533-2080 / Fax: (613) 533-6868; E-mail: iigr@qsilver.queensu.ca